PERSPECTIVES IN SOCIOLOGY

Perspectives in Sociology

Edited by

E. C. Cuff and G. C. F. Payne

Contributors

E. C. CUFF
Head of Department of Educational Studies,
Didsbury School of Education, Manchester Polytechnic

D. W. FRANCIS
Senior Lecturer in Sociology,
Department of Social Science, Manchester Polytechnic

D. E. HUSTLER
Senior Lecturer in Sociology, Department of Educational Studies,
Didsbury School of Education, Manchester Polytechnic

G. C. F. PAYNE
Head of Sociology, Department of Educational Studies,
Didsbury School of Education, Manchester Polytechnic

W. W. SHARROCK
Senior Lecturer in Sociology, University of Manchester

London
GEORGE ALLEN & UNWIN
Boston   Sydney

George Allen & Unwin (Publishers) Ltd,
40 Museum Street, London WC1A 1LU, UK

George Allen & Unwin (Publishers) Ltd,
Park Lane, Hemel Hempstead, Herts HP2 4TE, UK

Allen & Unwin, Inc.,
9 Winchester Terrace, Winchester, Mass 01890, USA

George Allen & Unwin Australia Pty Ltd,
8 Napier Street, North Sydney, NSW 2060, Australia

First published in 1979
Fourth impression 1981
Second edition 1984
Second impression 1985

British Library Cataloguing in Publication Data
    Perspectives in sociology—2nd ed.
1. Sociology
I. Cuff, E. C.   II. Payne, G. C. F.
301   HM66
ISBN 0-04-301157-8

Library of Congress Cataloging in Publication Data
Main entry under title.
    Perspectives in sociology.
Bibliography: p.
Includes index.
1. Sociology. I. Cuff, E. C.   II. Payne, G. C. F.
HM66.P37 1984   301   83-8732
ISBN 0-04-301157-8 (pbk.)

Set in 10 on 12 point Bembo by Alan Sutton Publishing Ltd

Printed and bound in Great Britain by
Anchor Brendon Ltd, Tiptree, Essex

Preface to the First Edition

In recent years an awareness has been developing, at all levels of education, that successful learning requires an explicit focus on the nature of knowledge, on how knowledge is acquired and on the fact that there are different kinds of knowledge. Within this framework we believe that sociology can best be understood as a variety of perspectives, all of which collectively comprise our ways of understanding the social world.

The original impetus for writing this book was prompted by the first-hand experience of some of us in teaching and examining GCE Advanced Sociology courses, and the book is primarily written for 'A' level students and their teachers. Sociology at this level can degenerate into a collection of memorisable sociological findings to be regurgitated in examinations – the examination scripts of most students at 'A' level generally show insufficient awareness of the various methodologies employed to produce those findings. In subscribing to the view that sociology is better understood as being a variety of ways of thinking about the world, we hope to encourage more active learning situations, in which students can develop a deeper understanding of the nature of sociological work. We recognise that rote learning of facts might well be replaced by rote learning of perspectives, and have attempted to organise our book in a manner designed to meet this danger.

We appreciate that practising sociologists do not operate with all of these perspectives. By and large, they tend to opt for one or another in pursuing their empirical studies. We feel, however, that it would be improper in an introductory textbook to advocate our personal preferences. Instead, we have endeavoured to outline the nature of each of the various perspectives and to emphasise the strengths rather than the weaknesses of each approach. The book should therefore not be read 'developmentally', with the implication that later chapters represent more advanced sociological work. Rather, the order of chapters is organised chronologically, in so far as different perspectives often emerge as reactions to existing ones.

We have been encouraged in our approach by recent changes in the AEB syllabus, which now requires students to adopt a more critical approach. Furthermore, the recently introduced JMB syllabus for 'A' level sociology is specifically created around the notion of sociological perspectives.

Our experience as teachers of sociology in polytechnic, university and college of education settings suggests that this book will also be of value to first-year degree students. Its emphasis on the theoretical and methodological characteristics of sociology could usefully complement other introductory textbooks, many of which tend to be topic-based.

We have included some suggestions for further reading and a number of questions at the end of each chapter. The further reading highlights excerpts from some of the original work discussed in the chapter and has been generally selected for its easy availability. The questions at the end of each chapter are designed to help the reader to think about key issues and to enable him to reinforce his understanding of the text. A more extensive and demanding list of sources and references for each chapter is provided at the end of the book.

We wish to acknowledge the help we have received in producing this book. Our primary debt is to the many students in our respective institutions and pupils in local schools for their comments and views on several drafts over a number of years. We are also grateful to M. A. Atkinson for his advice; to R. Anderson for his active encouragement and help at a crucial period; and to D. I. Shelton, a former colleague. Last – but far from least – we are indebted to Mrs D. Morris and her team – Mrs P. Curvis, Mrs J. Davies, Mrs J. French, Mrs E. Jones, Miss L. Mellor, Mrs J. Naylor and Mrs D. Ovington – for their excellent typing from some almost indecipherable drafts.

Preface to the Second Edition

Although several other introductory books in sociology have appeared since the publication of the first edition of *Perspectives in Sociology*, none of them directly explore what is involved in using sociological perspectives. Thus the distinctive characteristic of this book still remains its declared intention to examine methodological features of the perspectives themselves and to use studies in order to illustrate particular methodological concerns.

In response to suggestions by our readers, to whom we extend many thanks, we have taken the opportunity in this new edition to clarify some difficult sections, to expand others and to include some new materials. As our concern is to clarify the perspectives, not to 'cover' the topics and the most recent materials, we have not sought to 'update' for its own sake. We have, however, tried to include new materials where they help in this concern.

The methodological issues in sociology largely remain the same and for that reason we have not altered the basic structure of the book. We have, however, taken the opportunity to include some reference to current debates about the direction sociology might take in the future.

Finally, we wish to thank Jean Davies for doing all the typing in the second edition. We do not know what we would have done without her excellent work.

Contents

Chapter 3 STRUCTURALISM AS A PERSPECTIVE
(II) CONFLICT   71

Chapter 4 SYMBOLIC INTERACTIONISM AS A PERSPECTIVE   113

Chapter 5 ETHNOMETHODOLOGY AS A PERSPECTIVE 151

Chapter 1

The Nature of Sociological Perspectives

INTRODUCTION

In introductory textbooks on sociology the first chapter often begins
by posing the question: 'What is sociology?' The authors proceed
then tentatively to answer it by definitions such as 'Sociology is the
study of man in society' or 'Sociology is a scientific study of social
phenomena' and then go on to show the merits and, especially, the
weaknesses of whichever particular definition is used. Starting by
means of a definition may not be such a good idea, for one definition
may simply lead to yet more definitions, without noticeably
increasing understanding. For example, to define sociology as the
study of man in society necessitates some further definitions (of
'society' – and then of the terms used to define 'society') and does
nothing to help us to distinguish the kinds of study of man in society
of, for example, the novelist, the biologist and the sociologist.
Similarly, sociology may be a scientific study of social phenomena
but so may be economics, law, history and some branches of
psychology.

Even if we take a longer definition of sociology, the nature of the
subject remains unclear. For example, one author says that 'we can
state fairly simply what sociology is about. It is an effort to
illuminate as much of human behaviour as can be illuminated within
two kinds of limits: the limits imposed by a scientific frame of
reference and the limits imposed by focusing attention only on two
aspects – culture and "groupness"' (Bredemeier and Stephenson, p.
1.)

The original question 'What is sociology?' is, in effect, answered
by a series of further questions: 'What is culture?', 'What is
'groupness?', 'What is a scientific frame of reference?' Then, in

defining and describing 'groupness', terms like 'social structure', 'role', 'role-set', 'status', 'reference group', 'social system', and so on, are used. We need to ask the question 'What is . . .' of each of these terms. And we still have to deal with 'culture' and 'a scientific frame of reference'.

Clearly, in order to answer our original question 'What is sociology?' we need to know the answers to all the other questions which it generates. This is tantamount to saying that we have to know about sociology if we wish to know what sociology is about! Though to some extent this statement is obviously correct – we cannot know much about sociology until we have spent a fair amount of time studying the subject – it does little to help the newcomer to gain useful initial insights into the nature of sociology. We suggest that such insights, which will be developed but not superseded by later studies, can be achieved from a discussion of the nature of *sociological perspectives*.

Sociological perspectives are simply different ways of trying to understand the social world. As the title of this book implies, we take the view that sociology as a discipline or subject is basically best understood by stressing that it is made up of a *number* of separate though more or less interlinked approaches. If students are introduced to sociology in terms of its being a single, monolithic approach, with a single set of terms or concepts, a uniform set of theories and a standard collection of unified findings, we feel that they are either being misled or talked down to – albeit possibly for the best reasons. Instead, we prefer to credit students with both the intelligence and the desire to encounter the subject as it currently appears – not rounded off and smoothed for the purpose of easy digestion. Such a single presentation leads to worse evils than over-simplifications which can misrepresent and distort; it may lead to the wrong sort of learning which emphasises memorising and regurgitating information. We prefer a more worthwhile learning based upon the thinking which can derive from studying something about the social world.

Further, we wish to emphasise that no sociological perspective – or even all of them in combination – can give us 'the truth' about the world. Sociological perspectives merely provide us with *ways* of trying to understand the world; none of them has a built-in assurance that eternal and unshakable 'truth' will or can be provided. The danger of presenting sociology as a monolithic, uniform and standardised body of concepts, theories and findings is that students might presume that, in absorbing 'the facts' about sociology, they might also be absorbing bodies of 'truth', bodies of certain knowledge, which, once acquired, might be retained for all time.

In offering this approach to sociology not in terms of final truths, but rather in terms of ways of understanding, we are taking up a certain standpoint not only with respect to sociology, but also with respect to the nature of knowledge in general. It is with this view of the nature of knowledge in general that we wish to commence our more detailed exposition of sociology as comprised of various ways of understanding the social world.

FORMS OF KNOWLEDGE

It is the task of philosophers to ask questions about the nature of knowledge in general. Knowledge in general may be viewed, categorised and argued about in a number of ways. One way is to regard man's attempts to think about himself and his world by means of posing a number of key questions. These questions are:

In any way of thinking about and studying the world,

(1) What assumptions are being made, that is, what are the intellectual starting-points for such thinking?
(2) What sort of questions are being asked?
(3) In asking these questions, what sorts of concepts are being used?
(4) What sorts of methods are being used to find out about the world?
(5) What sorts of answers or solutions or explanations are given to the questions asked?

From these questions, it is possible to locate various forms of knowledge which appear to differ more or less in terms of answers to these questions. These forms of knowledge represent different ways of knowing about the world. One such list of the different forms of knowledge – other lists can be compiled because such lists are a matter of argument and debate, not of certainty – might include: literary and aesthetic understanding; religious understanding; natural scientific understanding; human scientific understanding; mathematical understanding; and, finally, philosophical understanding.

This list of possible forms of knowledge is based on differences between various approaches in terms of these questions about assumptions, methods, answers, and so on. It does *not* imply that there are no similarities between these forms of knowledge or that they are totally different. It does, however, provide us with a useful way of seeing how knowledge can be organised and ties in very well with how we tend to encounter knowledge as organised in the school curriculum.

For our purposes, we wish to focus on differences in forms of knowledge, and on one difference in particular, as it would take a book in itself to develop these philosophical views in any detail. This difference concerns the basic or 'bedrock' assumptions on which a particular form of knowledge rests; assumptions which, in the last resort, serve to justify or to underpin that particular way of understanding, thinking and studying.

We suggest that scientific approaches to understanding the world can be distinguished from other approaches in two fundamental and interrelated ways. First, an approach that claims to be scientific – irrespective of whether or not it originates in the field of natural or human science – must demonstrably have empirical relevance to the world. An empirical relevance involves showing that any statements, descriptions and explanations which are used or derived from this approach can be verified or checked out in the world. Thus, second, a scientific approach necessitates the deliberate use of clear procedures which not only show how 'results' were achieved, but are also clear enough for other workers in the field to attempt to repeat them, that is, to check them out with the same or other materials and thereby test the results. A scientific approach necessarily involves standards and procedures for demonstrating the 'empirical warrant' of its findings, showing the match or fit between its statements and what is happening or has happened in the world. These two criteria – empirical relevance and clear procedures – are bedrock assumptions built into any scientific approach. Further distinctions like types of methods (for example, experimental, historical, survey, interviewing), or distinctions like types of 'results' (for example, description or explanation, quantitative or qualitative), are merely embellishments – albeit important and often controversial embellishments – of these basic criteria which serve to distinguish scientific approaches or perspectives from other approaches to understanding the world.

It is not that other approaches have nothing to say about the world or even that none of their statements can be empirically tested and verified. Rather, the point being made is that their justification, their *raison d'être*, as ways of understanding the world is not solely or even largely dependent on these scientific criteria or basic assumptions. For example, no one would deny that we can learn much about ourselves and the world in which we find ourselves through reading and studying literature. We suggest, however, that novelists, poets and dramatists do not create their work in such a manner that it is consciously constructed in terms of the conventions of scientific procedures in order that its 'results' can be empirically warranted and verified by others in the field. Although novelists/writers often wish to portray human beings and their world in penetrating ways, they would wish their work to be judged not simply in terms of its 'accuracy' or 'truthfulness', but, more importantly, in terms of, for example, its structure, the feelings induced in the reader/watcher and the relationship of these induced feelings and emotions with the intentions of the writer. In short, literary and artistic approaches to the world are underpinned by their own bedrock assumptions which concern the aesthetic nature of the work. Agreement on the success or otherwise of such work is determined in terms of argument and discussion underpinned by these assumptions, rather than by an appeal to its 'scientific warrant'.

Similarly, the work of mathematicians can be usefully applied in the world in many ways. Such applications, however, do not provide the justifications and standards for good work in the field of mathematics. Instead, mathematical reasoning is evaluated in terms of rules of deductive logic which can be used both to construct and to check out the systematic and coherent character of a mathematical proof or argument. Thus Pythagoras's theorem (that in a right-angled triangle, the sum of the squares on the two shorter sides is equal to the square on the hypotenuse) can be created and verified by someone sitting down with pen and paper. There is no need to go out into the world measuring off fields; or to check and recheck in a number of different test situations. Given the acceptance of some fundamental axioms (self-evident truisms) such as one plus one equals two, and given the knowledge and willingness to use rules of logic, then the proof can there and then be stated to be true or false, barring calculational errors. No further endeavours can make it 'truer' or 'falser'. In this way, then, mathematics, like art and literature, may be seen as different approaches to knowing, producing different forms of knowledge. In like manner, religious and philosophical approaches to knowledge can be characterised in terms of their respective bedrock assumptions, which can be contrasted with those of scientific approaches.

These two illustrations, however, should be sufficient to illustrate this point. Needless to say, forms of knowledge do not differ only in these respects. The nature of the bedrock assumptions clearly greatly affects the kind of work done, that is, the kinds of concepts used, the sort of questions asked, the type of methods employed and the sort of 'results' obtained. In this way, we can recognise these different forms of knowledge. We might equally recognise that as they do represent different approaches to understanding, they are in no way competitive; they cannot be ranked in some sort of a heirarchy of importance. In that they are all doing different jobs, they are all equal in status as forms of knowledge. Of course, individuals may and do exercise their preferences, in terms of their interests and aptitudes, in choosing which forms of knowledge to study and they may, for their particular purposes, even rank them in importance. But there is no way of demonstrating that any form of knowledge is better than any other. In their different ways, they all contribute to man's knowledge.

THE SOCIAL SCIENCES

We have already suggested that the natural and human/social sciences are similar in respect of the underlying, bedrock assumptions which differentiate a scientific way of knowing about the world from other ways of knowing. They are similar in that both enterprises attempt to make statements about the world which can be warranted, that is, verified by empirical testing in the world. We can, however, crudely distinguish the two approaches in terms of their subject matter: the natural sciences largely deal with non-human phenomena; the social sciences deal with human action and behaviour. The distinction is crude for at least two reasons. First, some approaches in natural science do have things to say about human behaviour, for example, biology. Second, some approaches in the social sciences treat human action as an object of study in the same manner as natural scientists treat plants, rocks, or atoms. This point will provide a major focus of interest throughout this book, especially in Chapter 6.

Given this rough and ready distinction between the natural and social sciences, we now concentrate on the latter. Included in the social sciences are approaches or 'subjects' such as economics, psychology, anthropology, demography, politics and, of course, sociology.

Although these approaches have in common their basic scientific justification or rationale, they differ to varying degrees in terms of the concepts they use, the questions about the world they pose, the methods they use to deal with these questions and the sort of 'results' or explanations or solutions they consider to be satisfactory. Also, in addition to their bedrock assumptions, they differ in respect of other important assumptions which tend to characterise and distinguish each of these differing approaches within the general area of social science. It is often the case that the basic assumptions, the starting-points, of one social science constitute the basic problems or questions to which another social science devotes itself. For example, sociologists usually assume that human action is culturally and not genetically shaped. Sociologists recognise that the genetic make-up of parents and forebears does result in individual differences between people and they may take them into account in a particular empirical study of the world. But they will not specifically and methodically examine and explore individual differences from the standpoint of genetics. Instead, they tend to be more interested in how individual differences may be patterned and shaped by the way a society is organised: and in examining how these differences may be differently patterned and shaped in different societies which have contrasting cultures (ways of living). On the other hand, psychologists may assume the existence and even importance of what sociologists are studying, but for their part may study human behaviour from other angles, using different concepts, asking different questions and, in turn, allowing knowledge of cultural differences to be an unexplored, taken-for-granted assumption in their approach. In short, sociologists may start off by assuming that cultural factors are the key determinants of human behaviour: psychologists may start off by emphasising, say, the personality structure of individuals. Each of these approaches gives us a different basis for developing a perspective on human behaviour and action and each of them can be equally valuable.

CONCEPTS

The various social sciences offer us different, although interrelated, ways of trying to understand the social world. They give us par-ticular perceptions of, ways of looking at, the social world and enable us to develop a systematic and disciplined way of trying to understand aspects of it. Here, the *concepts* which the respective social sciences utilise are of great significance. Our perceptions of the world, what we make of it, how and what questions we ask of it, what sort of answers we obtain, are shaped by the concepts we employ.

Concepts provide us with tags or labels for a thing or an idea, for example, 'boy', 'rat', 'stratification', 'ego', 'justice', 'balance of power', 'desk'. Obviously, as users of language we are all users of concepts. Clearly, concepts allow us to organise and relate our perceptions of the world, whether as sociologist, psychologist, theologian, or simply as the man in the street. They do more than this, however, for in a very real sense our perceptions of the world, the world itself, consists of our concepts. By this, we do not mean to suggest the extreme philosophical position which states that the world exists only in our thoughts and that if we shut our eyes, the world vanishes. We have only to kick the table hard when our eyes are shut to receive a painful reminder of the fallacy of this view. Rather, we suggest that though there is a world 'out there', what we make of it is highly dependent on the conceptual equipment we have developed to perceive the world. Thus we might come across a 'sharp, pointed stick' in the Bolivian jungle; and might later discover that the 'stick' is 'really' a primitive 'plough' used by the largely nomadic tribes in that area.

Let us take up a more extended example of how the world is shaped by our perceptions of it. Let us examine the phenomenon of a lady who is buying a new fur coat. An economist might see this social event in terms of, say, consumer spending patterns, supply and demand, indifference curves, savings and income and purchasing power. A psychologist might see it in terms of drives to nurturance-succourance, emotional gratification or even, if he is a follower of Freud, as repressed infantile sexuality and a 'return to the womb'! A sociologist might see the event in terms of the normative patterns of a social class or category, or in terms of ostentatious consumption and its relation to claims for social honour and prestige. And even as a layman, merely to see someone buying a new fur coat, we must have the cultural knowledge, which necessitates the appropriate concepts, to be able to describe it in such terms. A Trobriand islander, if suddenly transplanted to a large department store, might be as confused as to what is happening as we might possibly be to find that a sharp pointed stick is after all a plough.

In all of these instances, the phenomenon in the world, the event being described, is in a sense 'the same'. But what is made of it is greatly determined by the conceptual apparatus we employ. It is thus that concepts can be said to shape our perceptions of the world.

Clearly, the kinds of questions we ask about the world are dependent on the concepts we employ. In any social science, a range of concepts is generally employed, permitting a range of types of question to be asked. In so far as these questions and concepts are related and thereby systematised, a distinctive approach to understanding the social world can emerge. Such an approach tends to develop its own distinctive methods for answering these questions; and, in keeping with the distinctive assumptions, concepts, questions and methods of a particular social science, the answers or solutions or explanations also tend to be distinctive.

SOCIOLOGY

It should, then, be clear to anyone who has followed the discussion so far that sociology, as an approach to understanding the world, can be differentiated from other approaches in that it attempts to be scientific, that is, to produce empirically warranted and verifiable statements about the social world. As such, it is but one of a number of other social sciences and is basically distinguished only by its distinctive assumptions, concepts, questions, methods and answers. It has no special ability to provide the 'truth' about social life or to provide solutions for social problems. All it can provide is a number of viewpoints or perspectives on the social world which might help us to develop greater understanding. Occasionally, such understanding might provide a clearer basis for practical action in the world. But it will never provide the 'truth' as an end-product. No scientific approach can do this because, quite simply, a scientific approach necessitates open-ended inquiry. Once the 'truth' is known, then inquiry can stop and, eventually, what is known becomes a matter of belief, rather than an empirical and testable/verifiable matter. Clearly, from the above arguments, there are many kinds of 'truth' – economic, psychological, theological, philosophical, mathematical, and so on – many of which are subject to revision or modification or, in the case of the sciences, to falsification over time. Thus sociology can claim no superiority over other forms of systematic knowledge in giving understanding. The only valid reason for studying it is in terms of interest in the questions posed about the social world, and not, decidedly not, in terms of wishing to acquire *the* definitive version of the world. For students who want 'the truth', some variant of theological studies is suggested; for in such studies, basic belief or faith is a legitimate aspect of that approach to knowledge.

Students who have grasped these arguments may not be too surprised to discover that sociology itself as a field of study can be seen to comprise a number of distinct though interrelated perspectives, or ways of understanding the social world. Each of these ways can be characteristically distinguished by the basic assumptions made, the concepts used, the questions raised, the methods employed and the 'solutions' obtained. We should not, however, be alarmed at the picture of sociology which is emerging. For we have argued that knowledge is complex and multi-sided. It can be viewed as having a number of different forms which offer us different ways of seeing things. Each of these forms can be subdivided into large areas like physics, chemistry, economics and sociology. And sociology itself can be seen to be made up of a number of linked but distinctive perspectives, each of which gives us a different way of viewing the social world. To add to this complexity, we have suggested that;

(1) there is no ultimate of determining the superiority of any of these forms, any of these areas, or any of these sociological perspectives;

(2) there is no ultimate way of determining the 'truth' of any of these forms, areas or perspectives.

Thus within the complex total field of knowledge, we derive a picture of sociology which is 'not even' a single unified approach to knowledge and which does not guarantee the truth of its findings. Given such information, students would surely be justified in giving up forthwith their study of sociology!

We suggest, however, that such an abandonment of sociology would be premature. This picture of sociology does not highlight several important features which ought to be considered before making such a decision.

First, full account should be taken of the fact that sociology is not the only subject to be made up of a variety of approaches. In fact most, if not all, living subjects are like this. In history, for example, we have proponents of the statistical approach as opposed to the proponents of more literary studies. And cross-cutting this division we find that social historians vie with political and economic historians. And if history is not a monolithic subject, neither is the 'queen of the sciences', physics. Since the Einsteinian revolution in physics, the subject has met with severe difficulties in reconciling the traditional macroscopic approach with the apparently different behaviour of small particles studied in molecular physics. Similar difficulties and divisions can be found in all other subject areas. What usually happens, however, is that such difficulties do not become apparent to students until they have done several years of study. Here, we take

the view that the nature of knowledge should be accurately por-
trayed to students at the outset. Then they may not be misled into
thinking that they have captured the 'truth' only to find that this
truth disintegrates into later difficulties and contradictions.

This point about 'truth' brings us to the second feature students
should take into account when assessing the merits of sociology. We
have argued that no subject which claims to be scientific can ever
reveal ultimate truths. The acceptance of ultimate truths would mean
that the scientific enterprise had come to an end because scientific
inquiry requires, in principle, the scrutiny and questioning of any
fact. Science must be open-ended. Open-endedness does *not* mean,
however, that solutions and explanations are no good at all because
they do not represent the ultimate truth. Instead, 'knowing better',
where 'better' is displayed in the standards, criteria and spelled-out
methodology of a subject, is not the same as knowing nothing, or
knowing no more after the study of a subject than before it. Thus
sociologists, from whatever perspective, would claim to produce a
better understanding of aspects of the social world. Understanding is
better in the sense of providing systematic and coherent and testable
ways of studying the social world; ways which enable us to enhance
and to develop our knowledge. Though such knowledge does not
represent final truths, it may at least help us to understand better the
social world.

At this stage, we can do no more than to state such claims in these
rather general and abstract ways. The only way students can evaluate
such claims is to examine the nature of the work done in sociology.
In the succeeding chapters, we will fill out in some detail this picture
of sociology as a number of different though linked perspectives. In
so doing, we will give plenty of examples of the substance or content
of sociological endeavours. Then, in the final chapter, we will return
to these questions about the nature of sociology, asking again 'Is it
worth studying?', 'Should we take seriously a subject which is made
up of a number of perspectives?'

Thus, in the remainder of this book we will describe in some detail
the basic perspectives which can be seen to comprise sociology.
While the emphasis will be on ways of thinking about the social
world, and not on 'results' or on 'findings', sufficient of the variety
and range of the 'content' of the subject will be described to give
students a good idea of the sorts of issues which interest sociologists
and of the sorts of things they have to say about them. As we
suggested at the outset of this chapter, however, we place more
emphasis on the *ways* or methodologies of understanding the social

world than on specific findings or results. After all, we have argued that 'results' are necessarily provisional, rather than final truths; they tend to become obsolescent over time. Consequently, we are suggesting that it would be more sensible to focus on ways of thinking sociologically in order to develop the ability and skills to be able, critically and constructively, to evaluate the ever-changing empirical results of sociological inquiry. Perhaps, too, the intellectual foundations might be laid for those students who wish to become professional sociologists and to produce warrantable findings themselves.

BRIEF OVERVIEW OF CONTENTS

In Chapters 2 and 3 we shall outline two distinctive approaches in sociology: consensus and conflict perspectives respectively. We shall see, however, that in one major respect these two perspectives have a common focus: they both stress the systemic nature of society. Although one perspective stresses the co-operative and harmonious elements in social life, while the other focuses on the coercive and divisive elements, they can both be seen to converge on some basic issues. In this way, both of these perspectives can be usefully labelled 'structuralism' in so far as they both focus on the whole society, the social structure and the relationship of its parts.

Chapter 4 contrasts structuralist approaches by developing inter-actionist approaches to understanding the social world. Although 'micro' or small group situations can be studied using structuralist assumptions, questions, and so on, interactionist studies sharply contrast with structuralism in that they stress the importance of investigating social action from the standpoint of the actors involved and hence the importance of the meanings that actors give to their actions.

Ostensibly, the ethnomethodological approach, outlined in Chapter 5, is also 'interactionist' in its focus on persons, language and social encounters. Proponents of this approach, however, take issue with all other approaches in claiming to study what other sociologists either take for granted or ignore, namely, the detailed study of the common-sense methods by which everyone, sociologists and laymen alike, make sense of their social world.

In Chapter 6 these sociological perspectives are examined and contrasted in terms of their distinctive methodologies. Throughout this book, we use the term 'methodology' to refer to a scrutiny of the basic assumptions, key questions, concepts and types of solution/ explanation found in any particular sociological perspective. In Chapter 6 we continue to use the term in this way, and examine general research strategies and their relation to specific research techniques such as questionnaires, participant observation, analysis of transcripts, and so on, which appear to be differentially used in the various perspectives. We examine why this should be the case and probe into the view of man and of social reality which underpin both research strategies and techniques. Finally, in Chapter 7, we conclude by returning to some of the basic issues raised in this introductory chapter and examine what value there can be in studying sociology.

Before we embark on the main body of the book, however, it might be helpful to give an extended example to illustrate how a particular area of social life can be approached and understood in different ways through the application of various perspectives. The area chosen is one which has attracted much sociological interest – mental illness.

PERSPECTIVES ON MENTAL ILLNESS

'Mental illness' is a comparatively new concept, although the sorts of behaviour to which it is commonly applied are as old as mankind. Today it is an accepted way of describing the behaviour of some of our fellow members of society. Most of us have some idea of what it means to say that someone is 'mentally ill'. We may even know people who are 'mentally ill'. The concept, then, is not unfamiliar to us. Yet when we begin to delve further into the nature of 'mental illness', we discover that there are several ways of understanding and explaining it. It soon becomes obvious that there is no 'one truth' to be discovered about it. We discover that its nature is very much a question of how it is looked at.

One common feature we do find is that the concepts of 'mental illness' and 'the mentally ill person' are usually applied to people who exhibit behaviour which the rest of us consider abnormal. Hearing voices, talking to oneself, having deep depressions, being unable to carry on normal conversations – these are some of the 'symptoms' we see as signs of mental illness.

The explanations of these behaviours are, however, numerous and various. We consider only a few examples to illustrate how it is possible for a common phenomenon to be understood and explained in several different ways.

We know that in the Bible madness was associated with out-of-the-ordinary, or abnormal behaviour. The usual explanations offered for the condition referred to possession by evil spirits. It was generally assumed that the unfortunate madmen behaved the way they did because evil spirits had control of their bodies. It was understood that supernatural powers inflicted the condition primarily as a punishment for sin. Madness was seen as a curse of God. For example, we read in the Bible that when Saul, the King of Israel, rebelled against God's command, 'the spirit of the Lord departed from Saul and an evil spirit of the Lord tormented him'.

We also know that Hippocrates, in Ancient Greece, explained the sorts of behaviour we are referring to by reference to his 'Humoral Theory'. He suggested that in the human body there were four humours or fluids which controlled our temperament, our emotions and moods. He considered that our behaviour was influenced by our moods and so in turn was controlled to a large extent by our bodily fluids. The fluids were known as *blood, phlegm, yellow bile* and *black bile,* and in the normal healthy body these fluids were present in particular proportions. But it was possible for excesses to develop, resulting in abnormal, unexpected behaviour. For example, an excess of black bile was considered to cause excessive melancholoy, or what today we might call a state of depression.

We have in these examples ways of understanding, ways of seeing and explaining particular forms of behaviour, which would not be acceptable today to the vast majority of us, but which were considered perfectly adequate in their time. Although the type of behaviour displayed by the King of Israel, or by the depressed Ancient Greek or by the modern-day neurotic businessman could be similar, the ways their behaviour and condition have been understood is very different.

However, this is not to say the ways in which these conditions are seen and understood is merely a question of history. Rather, we are saying that the variety of explanations can be viewed as a result of different basic assumptions about the nature of the world and life within it.

Today, just as in the past, the description and explanation of abnormal or odd behaviour can take a variety of forms. It is the case that most modern explanations are more likely to be scientific, although religious and supernatural explanations, in terms of possession by spirits, are still accepted by persons with particular religious convictions.

In modern Western culture scientific explanations, that is, explanations which are fundamentally testable in some way against empirical observations, are usually more acceptable to the majority of people. There are, however, a number of explanations both within and between such scientific approaches to understanding as biology, psychology and sociology.

Generally speaking, biological approaches rest on the assumption that human behaviour can be explained to a large extent by reference to the genetic composition and chemical processes of the human body. Assumptions of this sort have led to a variety of investigations and subsequent explanations of mental illness in terms of heredity and physical defects.

Psychological theories of mental illness have been even more common. Mental illness has been readily recognised as a problem of the mind and broad comparisons have been assumed between diseased bodies and diseased minds. Psychology, as the human science which focuses its study on the human mind and its mental processes, has naturally produced a variety of explanations of mental abnormality.

Within psychology, similar to most other disciplines, there are a variety of perspectives, each with its own bedrock assumptions about the psychological nature of the human being. Thus we find a variety of ways of seeing and understanding mental illness psychologically; but it is probable that the Freudian approach is the most well known and it provides us with an interesting example of a non-sociological, human scientific perspective.

The Freudian perspective on mental illness is founded on the assumption that the normal, stable personality develops through a number of stages in which the innate pleasure drive or libido is directed on to different objects. The normal personality passes through an oral phase, an anal phase and a genital phase. During this last phase an individual's sexual drives, which were previously directed to the parent of the opposite sex, are transferred to an appropriate other person. For a variety of reasons, mainly to do with inadequate familial relationships and early childhood experiences, a person may regress to an earlier stage of development or become fixed in a particular stage. Such fixations can result in abnormal behaviour. For Freudians, mental illness is seen largely as a pathological (that is, sick) condition of the personality brought about by experiences in early childhood which have hindered the normal development of the individual.

For sociologists, mental illness has been an area of investigation for several decades. Even since Durkheim demonstrated at the turn of the century how such an apparently individually motivated act as suicide can be explained by *social* causes, later sociologists have not hesitated to investigate and explain other aspects of behaviour which superficially have not appeared relevant to sociological consideration. Mental illness is one such typical area.

Following Durkheim's particular sociological tradition, some sociologists have sought the causes of mental illness in the structure of society. They, like Durkheim, have assumed that what an individual does is very much a question of what his social environment, what his society, structures him into doing. On the basis of this broad assumption, mental illness has been seen as a condition or attribute of the person like a disease or disability, produced by the person's societal environment. Consequently these sociologists have looked at the structure of various societies and particular parts of societies in order to discover what associations may exist between particular aspects of the social structure and mental illness.

An investigation typical of this approach is the study by Hollingshead and Redlich, *Social Class and Mental Illness*. In this study the authors seek to demonstrate that in the urban community of New Haven in the United States of America the incidence and type of mental illness vary according to position in the class structure. For example, they show that while social class 1 (High Status) contains 3.1 per cent of the community's population, only 1 per cent of all known psychiatric cases in the area come from it. Conversely they show that social class V (Low Status) includes 17.8 per cent of the community's population, but contributes as many as 36.8 per cent of the psychiatric patients. They also found that neuroses are concentrated at the higher levels and psychoses at the lower levels of the class structure.

An exact, detailed account of all the facts and figures they produce is not relevant to our purpose. What is important is that we recognise that this sort of sociological knowledge, this sort of generalisation, is the product of a particular approach, a particular perspective. It is only arrived at because the investigators started out with certain assumptions about the nature of mental illness and what causes it. The production of this sort of explanation is an example of the use of the 'structuralist perspective' in sociology. In this particular case, social class is assumed to be a feature of the structure of society. Members of the same social class are assumed to have similar roles in the economic order of society, similar attitudes and educational backgrounds, and similar life-styles. This broad economic and cultural similarity is assumed to differentiate large groups within the society and to produce different behaviours and conditions in the individual members of the groups. In this case, it is assumed to produce differences in the incidence and type of mental illness.

Similar broad structuralist assumptions lie behind studies which seek to discover associations between the incidence of mental illness and ecological factors such as area of urban residence. Studies of this sort imply that the style of life and the general organisation of different parts of a town or city can condition individuals into mental illness.

Durham and Faris, for example, have shown that in Chicago the incidence of schizophrenia varies in different parts of the city. They found that areas near the centre of the city had extremely high rates compared with other areas. The highest rates for schizophrenia were in the area they called hobohemia – the area of rooming houses and foreign-born communities close to the city centre. They suggest that these areas are locations of social disorganisation and as such constitute environments conducive to the development of schizophrenia. The implication clearly is that this particular form of mental illness is related to the ecological or spatial pattern of the city, which in turn produces different sorts of social organisation and environment. The condition of the person is assumed to be a result of the structural organisation of urban social and economic life, and in this way, this study presents an example of the use of a structuralist sociological perspective.

In contrast, the 'interactionist perspective' provides a rather different view of mental illness. Here, mental illness is not seen as a condition lying within the individual. Instead it is seen as a social status conferred on the person by other members of society. That is to say, instead of assuming that mental illness is something which persons can have 'within them', like a disease or incapacity which anyone can observe and recognise, it is seen as a state which is very much in the eyes of the beholder. A person is seen as mentally ill if other people say he is; the mentally ill person is one to whom that label has successfully been applied. Mental illness is seen as a label, a categorisation, conferred on to particular individuals by other individuals.

This way of understanding mental illness is not founded on the assumption that society is an entity with a structure which determines, or at least very strongly influences, individuals and their behaviour. Rather, it derives from a stress on the individual actions and perceptions of persons. Members of society are seen as active agents who construct their social action on the basis of the meanings and interpretations they give to their environment. They do not simply transmit or reflect a given structure, but in fact create it by their interaction. The world has to be interpreted, has to be made sense of and has to be given meaning. 'Mental illness' and 'mental patients' are neither 'objects' nor 'conditions' which are assumed to be 'out there', to be discovered. Rather, interactionists concern themselves with locating the processes by which people go about classifying others as 'mentally ill'.

Thomas Szasz has approached the study of mental illness from these basic assumptions and has attempted to show that there are some roles in society which have more power attached to them than most when it comes to the conferring of the label 'mentally ill' on to people. Although we may consider that we can recognise a mentally ill person when we are with one, psychiatrists are generally accepted as being the 'experts' in diagnosing persons in need of treatment. Szasz points out that the psychiatrist has considerable power; on the basis of his observations and analysis of an individual's behaviour, he can declare that the person is sick, that he needs treatment and that he should be put into an institution. The psychiatrist's diagnosis is likely to be accepted and acted upon by other members of society. In this way, the individual concerned becomes 'mentally ill' not simply because he does odd things, but also because the psychiatrist has put that particular label on him. If others try to apply the label, it is less likely to stick.

Some studies, starting out from interactionist assumptions, have shown how psychiatrists and others trained to identify the mentally ill person can disagree over the interpretation and meaning of the behaviours they observe. The possibility of disagreement shows how the differentiation of the 'mentally ill' from the 'normal' member of society can be largely contingent upon the circumstances of the social situation. An example of this work is the investigation by Thomas Scheff of the psychiatric screening procedures used in a Midwestern state in America to determine whether mental patients should be released. Scheff has shown how the diagnosis of a person as mentally ill, requiring involuntary confinement, can be affected by the financial, ideological and political position of the examining psychiatrists. He shows how these factors tend to predispose the court-appointed psychiatrists to assume that the subject is ill. The situation is defined as one in which the subject is presumed from the outset to be mentally ill and the psychiatrists then go on to interpret the behaviour and records of the patient on the basis of their prior definition of the situation. Scheff argues that without this prior definition, the records, behaviours and responses to the psychiatric tests can be interpreted differently.

The interactionist perspective also focuses on the individual's conception of himself. That is, it assumes that individuals have to interpret and give meaning to their own actions as well as those of others. It assumes that our self-conception influences whatever actions we may construct, and that this self-image is largely a result of the interpretations of other people's reactions to what we say and do. These assumptions have led to investigations into how people labelled as mentally ill see themselves and how, for example, the conferring of the label 'mentally ill' can subsequently produce abnormal behaviour by an individual because he constructs actions which he recognises others expect of him.

Thus we can see that the kinds of sociological analyses and explanations of mental illness produced by sociologists using the interactionist perspective differ considerably from those produced by the sociologists using a structuralist perspective. The events and behaviours in the world that both are observing may be 'the same', but because they start from different bedrock assumptions about the nature of the social world and make use of different conceptual frameworks, they produce different sociological analyses.

The questions which shape their research strategies and the actual methods of investigation they use tend to differ because they start from different views of the nature of the social world. Sociologists making structuralist assumptions such as Hollingshead and Redlich, or Dunham, tend to use questionnaires and survey methods, quantifying their data into statistical tables to produce analyses involving a heavy reliance on mathematics. Interactionists, however, are more likely to use methods of direct observation. They try to see the world from the same points of view as the mental patients, doctors and officials they are studying. Their research approach often involves living with their subjects over a prolonged period of time and sharing their day-to-day experiences. Neither the structuralist not the interactionist way of seeing, investigating and explaining mental illness is necessarily more correct than the other. They simply represent different ways of seeing the world sociologically.

Another way of seeing the world sociologically is represented by the approach known as ethnomethodology. Ethnomethodology can be seen as yet another sociological perspective because it asks questions and investigates the social world on the basis of different assumptions from those made in the structuralist and interactionist perspectives and, in so doing, uses a different conceptual framework.

The ethnomethodological approach assumes that the social world is being constantly created by members of society and that, for them, this continuous creation is largely unproblematic. It is unproblematic because it is seen as the result of members using their common sense. Through the use of their taken-for-granted, common-sense knowledge about how the world works and how they can get around it in acceptable ways, the members of a society are seen to be actually creating the society. But although ordinary members of society have no fundamental problems in living and achieving their daily social lives, the ethnomethodologist suggests that this everyday, mundane social activity is the product of complex methodic practices. He assumes that members of society do in fact continuously accomplish the social world through the use of common, albeit sophisticated, methods. Much of the effort to uncover these methods is directed to the analysis of transcriptions of natural conversations on the argument that members constitute their social encounters in, by and through such talk.

Thus the ethnomethodologist is not likely to investigate mental illness as a specific topic for study, given his concern with the more general and formal analysis of members' methods. Nevertheless, when his materials for analysis have reference to mental illness, the ethnomethodologist's approach can be illuminating. For example, Turner has suggested that former mental patients can be faced with particular problems when taking up conversations with acquaintances. His focus of study is in the way persons 'resume contact' after having been discharged from the mental institution. Turner suggests that in *any* subsequent encounter between *any* two persons, it may be the case that the parties to the conversation do some work of recognition. He argues that when persons engage in this 'resuming' work they offer identifications of themselves and the persons they are talking to, and in so doing they are suggesting a relationship between them. These identifications can be, and usually are offered without explicitly announcing that one is a friend, or a long-lost acquaintance. For example, by saying, 'Hi Chuck, how did it go last night? I sure wish I could've made it', as the opening utterance in an encounter the speaker is, without spelling it out word for word, probably identifying himself and the person he is talking to as 'friends'. Turner adds that part of this resuming work may involve bringing the parties to the conversation up to date, that is, filling each other in on newsworthy items which have happened to them individually since they last met. In the case of an encounter involving a 'former mental patient', however, Turner illustrates how troubles in everyday resuming work can be generated. For example, it may require the 'former mental patient' to accept unwanted identification.

After all, it is likely that such an individual wants to forget that he has been mentally ill; he may consider his 'former state' is as irrelevant to his current life as a broken leg. But when resuming involves bringing the parties up to date, it is often difficult to avoid the topic of his recent experiences. Turner appeals to his materials and to our common-sense knowledge of the social world to suggest that the identity 'former mental patient' is one which persons who have not been mentally ill are most likely to use, in preference to any other, when they are doing resuming work with someone they know to have been mentally ill. Thus, the ethnomethodologist, by analysing conversational materials, can show us how interactional troubles can be generated and managed in everyday encounters. In particular, Turner's work illustrates how such analysis can illuminate some interactional problems involving persons who have been 'mentally ill'.

CONCLUSION

We hope to have shown in this introductory chapter that whatever topic or problem we might choose to investigate there are a number of ways it can be aproached. Further, should we want to make a *sociological* investigation of the topic there is no *one* way to proceed. For example, it should be clear from the extended illustration we have chosen that it is not adequate to talk of *the* sociological approach to mental illness: there is no single, correct sociological approach. The sociology of mental illness constitutes different ways of seeing, understanding and explaining mental illness sociologically. How mental illness is understood and explained depends on the questions the researcher asks about it and the methods he uses to investigate it; both these in turn depend on the bedrock assumptions with which he begins. Of course, in our discussion of mental illness we have sought only to illustrate this point about the nature of sociological inquiry. It has not been our intention to make a thorough examination of sociological studies in the area of mental illness.

The possibility of applying a number of sociological perspectives is not tied only to the area of mental illness. Mental illness can be viewed as just one topic within the broader area of deviance, and just as this topic can be understood in various ways, so too are other topics such as crime, delinquency, suicide, and so on, open to a variety of sociological analyses. Just as there is no single sociological approach to deviance, so there is no single approach to the family, religion, education, politics, or, in fact, to anything else. Rather there are various sociological ways of understanding the social world and various research strategies for investigating it.

We are not suggesting that these different perspectives are distinct, watertight compartments which never overlap. In many sociological studies they often do. We do suggest, however, that they provide us with some organising principles for understanding the kinds of questions sociologists ask about the social world and the ways they set about investigating it. Furthermore, these organising principles tend to be used by sociologists in so far as they see themselves as operating from the basis of a perspective. In short, the notion of sociology as perspectives does reasonably accurately reflect the way sociologists organise themselves and do their work; it is a realistic way of describing the work done in sociology.

In the subsequent chapters we fill out these abbreviated sketches of the basic features of the major sociological approaches and show how they have developed to produce the different kinds of sociological analysis available to us today.

FURTHER READING

Sergeant, G., *A Textbook of Sociology,* 2nd edn (Macmillan Education, 1979).
O'Donnell, M., *A New Introduction to Sociology* (Harrap, 1981).
Bottomore, T. B., *Sociology: A Guide to Problems and Literature,* 2nd edn (Allen & Unwin, 1971). These are examples of books which provide alternative and now standardised ways of presenting sociology.
Spitzer, S., and **Denzin, N. K.,** *The Mental Patient* (McGraw-Hill, 1968). Selected readings illustrating different sociological approaches to the study of mental illness.

QUESTIONS

1 What do you understand by a 'way of understanding' or 'perspective'?
2 In what ways can scientific approaches to understanding the world be distinguished from other approaches?
3 Illustrate how the use of different concepts can influence our perceptions and understandings of some object, event, or social interaction.
4 How is it the various social sciences can be so 'different' from each other, yet still be scientific?

5 Discuss the differences between scientific and non-scientific approaches to the study and explanation of mental illness.
6 Discuss the differences between sociological and psychological approaches to the understanding of mental illness.
7 How is it possible that there can be so many different approaches to the study of mental illness which are at the same time all sociological?
8 Can some sociological approches be more scientific than others?

Chapter 2

Structuralism as a Perspective (I) Consensus

INTRODUCTION

Within sociology it is possible to identify a broad approach founded on the assumption that our actions are to a very large extent structured by our social environment. What values and attitudes we have, what activities and relationships we produce, are seen to be the result of, or at the very least to be greatly influenced by, the organisation and structure of the society in which we live. Such an assumption gives rise to a perspective we have called structuralism.

Within this broad approach, however, it is possible to identify two varieties of structuralism, each differentiated by the particular combinations of assumptions and the conceptual frameworks they use in their analyses of the social world. These two varieties are commonly known as the consensus and conflict perspectives. In this chapter we shall consider consensus as a perspective; we deal with conflict in Chapter 3.

THE CONSENSUS PERSPECTIVE AND THE PROBLEM OF ORDER

Most sociology in one respect or another can be seen as a contribution to our understanding of the ordered, patterned and predictable nature of the social world. However, the notions of 'order' and 'predictability' to which sociologists generally refer are not those which would imply that social relationships and events are fixed or inevitably predetermined. Rather the conception of order referred to derives from the observation that by and large both our expectations of our own behaviour and our expectations of the activities of others are generally fulfilled in our experience. That is not to say that we know exactly what others may do in any given situation, but generally have a good idea of the range of probable actions. We know, for example, that it is very unlikely for a grocer to start cleaning our shoes when we ask him for a tin of sardines. Just think how frightened we would be to leave our beds and our homes if we could not be fairly sure how the various people we meet are likely to behave!

A focus on the ways in which the 'ordered' nature of social life is organised is something all sociological perspectives have in common. Where the perspectives tend to differ is in their conceptualisation of the nature of the achievement and management of social order. Each perspective tends to give a different emphasis and attention to those aspects of social life which it considers contribute most to social order.

Those sociologists who have developed an approach in sociology which we are calling the consensus perspective have explicitly focused on the 'problem of order' at a societal level, that is, they have tended to concentrate on the order of total societies. Their theoretical and empirical analyses have generally been based on the assumption that societies can be seen as persistent, cohesive, stable, generally integrated wholes, differentiated by their cultural and social-structural arrangements. This assumption has generated a conceptual framework and mode of analysis which for the last few decades has been called structural functionalism. However, as we shall see, the development of this conceptual framework and mode of analysis has generated much argument and considerable differences in emphasis. We begin our consideration of the consensus perspective with two early sociologists who had considerable influence on the development of the subject, Comte and Spencer.

AUGUSTE COMTE: THE EMERGENCE OF SOCIOLOGY

It was Comte (1798–1857), writing in the first half of the nineteenth century, who gave sociology its name. He had seen the advances in physics and chemistry in the latter part of the previous century as evidence of man's decreasing reliance on explanations in terms of supernatural causes and metaphysical forces and claimed that the scientific methods of observation, experiment and careful comparison could be applied to the study of social phenomena. The application of these methods would enable us to discover the 'laws of social phenomena', which would provide us with a reliable basis of knowledge should we want to make our society a better place to live.

In Comte's view the new science of sociology was at the pinnacle of the hierarchy of sciences. Other sciences such as chemistry, physics and biology were all inadequate for the study of society. As a society was an extremely complex arrangement of institutions, traditions, knowledge, values, beliefs, and so on, its study required a new science with a new collection of concepts and analytical tools.

An important characteristic of any society, according to Comte, was its systemic nature. A society was a *system* of interrelated parts; it was something more than the mere sum of the individuals within it. The activities of the individuals could only be understood within the context of their particular societies. Total societies therefore were to be the focus of sociological study since any part, any activity, any institution could only be adequately investigated as an integral part of the total interdependent system.

Comte went on to state that like other sciences, the laws of social phenomena could be subdivided into two major fields of study: statics and dynamics. For Comte saw all sciences as divisible into 'statics', which was concerned with discovering 'laws of coexistence', and 'dynamics', which was concerned with discovering 'laws of succession'. Laws of coexistence governed the relationships between the parts of any phenomenon, be it a planetary system, a human body, or a society. Laws of succession governed the sequences of change that can take place in a phenomenon, again be it any physical object or a society. In sociology, therefore, statics was the analytical study of the interrelationships and functions of the various elements or parts of any social system. Its goal was to clarify the possible interconnections between such features of society as the family, religion, the division of labour and politics. Dynamics was the study of the changes and development of these connections and functions in particular societies.

The emergence of sociology was a necessity, according to Comte, because of man's growing awareness of the integrated nature of society and the inadequacy of available disciplines to deal with this new level of analysis, that is, the interconnections and functions of social facts and social arrangements. Sociology was also necessary because it could provide the scientific knowledge required for building a new society. Here it should be noted that Comte was writing in the aftermath of the French Revolution and he was unhappy about the state of the society in which he lived.

With these claims for the new discipline of sociology Comte laid the foundations for a consensus perspective and for the procedures to be used in empirical sociological investigations. Societies were assumed to be integrated wholes or social systems, and the most suitable methods for studying them were those already used by the natural sciences of physics, chemistry and biology.

In Comte's particular conceptual framework the concept of 'consensus' was used to refer to the total integration of the component elements of a society. As we shall see this is not the only way the concept has been understood and used by those subsequent sociologists who collectively have been responsible for the development of this perspective. Nevertheless, his focus on the nature of this interdependence or integration is a recurrent theme in the development of the consensus perspective. Herbert Spencer, writing in England a few years later, was one of the first sociologists to take up the development of these rudimentary ideas.

HERBERT SPENCER: THE EVOLUTIONARY ANALYSIS OF TOTAL SOCIETIES

In many respects, Spencer's (1820–1903) general sociological approach and his views on the nature of scientific knowledge were very similar to those of Comte. Both believed that all sciences rested on common philosophical foundations and could be brought together in a unified schema. Both believed that the fundamental laws which governed the natural world governed the social world; and that knowledge of these laws provided the most reliable basis for prediction and the guidance of effective social activities.

It was the concept of 'evolution' which provided the unifying principle for all sciences, according to Spencer. The totality of Nature comprises a variety of 'living forms' all experiencing a process of transformation or evolution. Every living form, whether it be a planet, a biological organism, or a society, is passing through a continuous process of development, all the time trying to maintain a state of equilibrium, that is, a stable state of relationships, both internally and with its environment. The general path of this process is from simplicity to complexity, from simple structures to complex structures, from homogeneity or sameness to differentiation, with a constant accompaniment of a changing equilibrium. The assumed evolutionary nature of all forms of existence is clearly present in

Spencer's conceptualisation of the social world and his model of society.

In order to outline his view of the nature of society and to show what he meant by saying a society can be viewed as a system, Spencer made extensive use of the analogy between a society and an organism. For example, he suggested that a society can be seen to be like an organism on at least five accounts:

(1) Both grow in size.
(2) As they grow both evolve, or develop more complex, differentiated structures.
(3) As their structures become more differentiated so there develops an arrangement of more specialised functions. For example, many parts of the complex, highly differentiated structure of a human body fulfil functions not required by the more simply structured amoeba. Similarly, many parts of a complex, highly differentiated social structure of modern industrial society fulfil functions not required by the simple social structure of a primitive, tribal society.
(4) Evolution for both societies and organisms involves processes of adjustment and adaptation to their environment.
(5) It is a characteristic of organisms and societies that should their unity be destroyed by a disintegration, or the loss of particular parts, it is usual for some remaining elements to continue to live, for a while at least. In an animal, for example, limbs or organs can be lost without the animal dying. Similarly, parts of a society can be destroyed or even a whole society can be conquered and absorbed into another, yet it is seldom that all trace of its cultural arrangements disappear. For example, the Roman Catholic religion is still practised in the Eastern European satellite states controlled by communist Russia; Red Indians can still be culturally distinguished in the United States of America.

Although sociologists today have little regard for the analogy between a society and an organism, its use by Spencer enabled him to make a considerable contribution to the development of the 'structural-functional' or consensus sociological approach. He used the concept 'consensus' in much the same way as Comte. For both it referred to the systemic nature of society. More specifically it referred to the overall, integrated interconnectedness of the various parts of a society.

Both considered this interconnectedness to be a characteristic of the very nature of a society. Given this generality, Comte and Spencer claimed that consensus must therefore be a necessary concept in sociological analysis.

In his particular development of the conceptualisation of society as an organism, Spancer was proposing that a society should be seen as more than a collection of individuals or parts. The patterned interconnectedness of its parts makes it into a distinguishable entity. Just as a mere collection of biological organs do not make a man, no more do a collection of individuals make a society. What makes one collection a distinguishable entity we call a man, and the other collection a society, is the particular arrangement of interconnections experienced by the component parts of each collection. What distinguishes a man or a society from the mere collections of their different component parts is the way the elements are assembled and function, or work together, as a system.

Sociology should focus its study on this systemic nature of societies. Societies like all other living forms should be analysed by identifying their component parts, the interrelationships between them and the functions they fulfil for the total society or social system

The parts of a society to Spencer's mind are what today are generally called its institutions. Those he identified included the family and kinship system, the political system, the military, religion, forms of social control, the economic system, the stratification system and education. He also included language, leisure and morals.

All were seen to be parts of a society, but parts which essentially functioned in co-ordination as integral elements of a unified system. They could not be isolated from each other and therefore should be studied as interconnected, non-separable elements. Thus he continued Comte's emphasis on the study of societies as wholes.

He did suggest however that, for analytical purposes, the various parts could be broadly organised into three groupings. The groupings were (*a*) those which fulfilled Regulating functions, (*b*) those which fulfilled Sustaining functions and (*c*) those which fulfilled Distributive functions. As societies evolve they have to manage their relationships with their physical and social environments. This management requires them to develop some forms of Regulatory control through the development of structural arrangements to fulfil political and military functions. In addition it requires that the elements which fulfil these functions are differentiated from those which are responsible for Sustaining the total system through the economic production of food, shelter and common comforts. Further, as these structural and functional elements became more and more specialised and differentiated in well-developed societies, the need increased for Distributing organs to arrange the allocation and distribution of resources.

Assumptions of the kind outlined above about the nature of society and the evolutionary processes of internal social change logically led Spencer (i) to focus his empirical investigations on the changing patterns of structural and functional characteristics of societies, which in turn led him to try to classify the various types of social systems, and (ii) to ask questions about the relationships of particular parts or institutions of a society to the whole system, especially focusing on the functions these parts fulfil for the total society.

ÉMILE DURKHEIM:
THE DEVELOPMENT OF FUNCTIONALISM

There is no doubt that Émile Durkheim (1858–1917) made a considerable contribution to the development of sociology in his own time, nor can there be any doubt that his contribution is still an influential force on the theory and practice of sociology today. However, although he claimed to be speaking for all sociology, taking it for granted that there was *one* sociological approach and *one* set of methods for doing research, it is more accurate to see his work as representing a major contribution to the development of the consensus variation of the structuralist perspective. In particular, he developed further the mode of analysis in sociology which today is generally called functionalism; and he outlined in more detail than Comte or Spencer a general research strategy to be used in the investigation of social phenomena.

DURKHEIM: THE MORAL NATURE OF SOCIETY

Following Comte, societies were 'systems', as far as Durkheim was concerned, made up of interrelated social elements. But, most importantly for Durkheim, these social systems were *moral* entities. Although it is true that both Comte and Spencer had implicitly noted this characteristic of a society, it was Durkheim who emphasised it.

For him it was a fundamental assumption; he believed it to be an irreducible characteristic of a society.

Durkheim argued that all human associations give rise to expectations of patterns of conduct. As persons associate, that is, develop relationships, with others they tend to develop common ways of perceiving, evaluating, feeling and acting. These new patterns of values, perceptions and action then give rise to expectations and constraints on how persons should or ought to behave. Thus as persons associate with each other, so there emerges a 'collective consciousness' which in turn constrains them and obliges them to behave in particular ways.

We know from our own experiences that it is quite common for people to talk of moral pressures coming from society. We speak of activities which society does not allow. We also speak of society having to protect itself against those who break its rules, and of wrongdoers having to pay their debt to society. Contained in these observations and ideas is the notion that society somehow exists over and above us. It was this notion which Durkheim appeared to be drawing on when he suggested that a society was a 'moral reality', a 'moral entity'. In his view, this moral reality included the collective values, the order of priorities on which the members of the society are agreed. He made the assumption that for any group of people to live together co-operatively, they must have some basic common agreements on what their priorities are as a group, and on how they ought to behave to each other and arrange their relationships.

Durkheim argued this case when criticising the ideas of earlier social and political philosophers and in particular the theories of Thomas Hobbes. Hobbes had suggested that societies were formed by men coming together and agreeing, or making a contract to live side by side in peace, rather than continuing to fight one another. He argued that men agreed to stop their 'war of all against all' and to organise themselves into a state, with ruling government, in order to ensure their collective self-preservation. According to Hobbes, men agreed to give up their freedom to fight each other, in pursuit of their own individual desires, in return for the security that the new state would provide in its control of, and protection against, the force of particular individuals.

Durkheim's argument was that for men to come together at all to make a contract, they must already have some common agreement on the value of such a contract and some common agreement to be bound by the unwritten rules of a contractual situation. This prior agreement represented for Durkheim a framework of order which is the essence of society. If men could make a contract with each other they were already members of a society because they held certain values in common. Thus a fundamental consensus or agreement on basic values becomes synonymous with an understanding of the concept 'society'.

Durkheim's emphasis on the moral nature of social relationships appears in all his work. For example, in his book *The Division of Labour in Society*, which he subtitled *The Study of the Organisation of Advanced Societies*, he claims that the division of labour itself is a moral phenomenon, rather than an economic one. In the study he focuses on the moral, legal and political problems of societies as they change from simple, traditional, agrarian systems to modern industrial societies. He suggests that each of these two types of society is characterised by different forms of social solidarity and by different social systems of morality.

Earlier Comte had argued that the division of labour would bring increased conflicts, as individuals and groups developed and protected their own interests. Spencer had suggested that the division of labour would bring greater interdependence through increased differentiation and if anything make modern industrial societies less vulnerable to collapse and disintegration than simple societies.

Durkheim takes something from both of them. He agrees that simple or primitive societies have little division of labour. He suggests that they have a segmental structure, that is, they are made up of similar units such as families or tribes. There is only a limited number of roles to be played by each group. Consequently, it is their *common* roles, practices, expectations and beliefs which bind them together. They experience what Durkheim calls a 'mechanical solidarity' because each part of the society is comparable to all the other parts. Each part can be seen in this sense as a microcosm of the wider society. In short, men are bound together by common values, based on shared and common experiences.

As the division of labour increases and new roles are required, there is an increasing differentiation of units or groupings. At the same time the uniformity of beliefs and moral ideas decreases, but the society does not disintegrate; instead a new form of solidarity, a new form of moral order develops to supplement the weakening influences of common values. This Durkheim calls an 'organic solidarity'. It is characterised by the interdependence of different elements, within a general acceptance of the need for differentiation. The differences are accepted and indeed become expected. For example, modern man comes to expect to depend on the unseen coalminer, the power worker, the Christmas card maker and the farmer. Thus the nature of the moral consensus changes. Commonly shared values still persist because without them there would be no society, but they become generalised, as they are not rooted in the totality of commonly shared daily experiences. Instead of specifying the details of action, common values tend to be a more general underpinning for actual social practices. It is in this sense that the division of labour can be seen as a moral phenomenon.

Durkheim argues that the change develops through the stages of an increase in population leading to an increase in the density of social interaction, leading in turn to competition and conflict which threatens the social cohesion. The creation of a division of labour becomes necessary to ensure the continuance of order. The differentiation brings with it an interdependence. In effect he is suggesting that a new form of social solidarity, a new form of morality, becomes necessary to prevent society from collapsing and disintegrating. This amounts to saying that as the nature of the moral consensus changes, so the nature of the society changes.

In this account of the division of labour in society, we can see Durkheim's acceptance of the systematic nature of society. Like Comte and Spencer before him, he is implicitly using an equilibrium model of society. Society is seen as a stable, orderly system which experiences change and which adjusts or adapts to the changed situation in some way to re-create a new order, a new state of equilibrium.

The concept of equilibrium is important in the consensus approach. In general, societies are assumed to be orderly and stable until some event or change occurs. When this happens, it is assumed that societies produce more changes as part of a process of adaptation to the new situation in order to re-establish an equilibrium. The use of this concept does, however, produce a tendency to reify society, that is, to give it the characteristics of a real object, to assume that it has a life or existence of its own. The roots of this assumption lie in assuming that society is like a living organism, and although as we have said, Spencer himself did not believe that society *was* an organism (he merely treated it *as if* it were one), there were others at the time who did.

Durkheim probably saw society as a special kind of organism. It was like no other. He claimed that society existed *sui generis*. That is, society existed in its own right as a separate independent entity. He was more prone to reifying society than either Comte or Spencer and possibly more so than any influential sociologist since. The extent to which he was convinced of the pre-eminence of society is clearly shown in his discussion of the research strategy, or rules of investigation, to be followed in studying society.

DURKHEIM: RULES FOR INVESTIGATING SOCIETY

In his *Rules of Sociological Method,* Durkheim primarily described the methods to be used in the study of society, but he also spent some time describing the nature of the phenomena to be studied.

The subject-matter for sociologists, the phenomena they were to study in a scientific way, were 'social facts'. 'Social facts' were different from any other facts; they were the very fabric of society which arose out of human relationships and human association. For example, he views a rate of suicide for a society as a distinct order of reality. A rate of so many suicides per thousand of population cannot be reduced to individual suicides or cases without losing the essential meaning of a *rate*. A rate per thousand is a collective phenomenon; it is a *social* fact.

Durkheim saw a direct connection between the social nature of a rate and the suicide statistics for different societies. Although the rates may very from one society to another, some societies having high rates, some having low rates, each individual society seemed to have a similar rate from year to year. This observation suggested to Durkheim that suicide rates emanate from the social conditions of a society. He saw the rate in any one society arising out of the underlying structure of social life of that society; out of the ways people interacted with one another, their attitudes and feelings about things, for example, the nature of their religion. Different social structures generated 'suicidogenic' currents of differing strength and intensity, thus producing different rates of suicide. These rates are the result of collective action, they are the end product, the symptom, so to speak, and as such represent social facts. (We shall be dealing more generally with Durkheim's study of *Suicide* in Chapter 6.)

Fashions are another example of a social fact. A fashion such as long hair, mini-skirts, or platform shoes cannot be reduced to individual cases without losing the essential meaning of fashion. A fashion is a collective phenomenon; it is something which involves the collective action and sentiments of many persons.

Durkheim argued that in their emergent existence, that is, over and above, or external to any individual case, social facts constituted a distinctive and separate reality. It was a *social* reality, the reality of a society. It was the reality that sociologists alone should study.

These 'separately existing' phenomena exercised constraints on individuals. They had a coercive influence over people. For example we can feel 'out of it', or even guilty or behind the times, when we are 'out of fashion'. Similarly, some unfortunate individuals are driven to suicide by the pressures and strains a society generates.

In *Rules of Sociological Method*, Durkheim outlined a set of procedures for doing sociology. No one had provided such a clear set of methodological directives in the same detail before, and they still greatly influence the way many sociologists conduct their research today. His main aim was to make sociological research as objective and scientific as possible. His own work shows, in practice, what difficult aims these are. He said the investigator should eradicate all his preconceptions, that is, he should approach the phenomenon under study with as open a mind as possible, he should try to forget his biases. He should concentrate on the external characteristics of social facts, that is, on those characteristics which other investigators will clearly be able to see, like rates of suicide. He should not use his own subjective interpretations. By concentrating on these observable and external characteristics, the researcher will be able to produce clear unambiguous definitions of the social facts he is investigating.

Social facts, according to Durkheim, are of two different kinds, and their differences need to be taken into account in any sociological study. There are 'normal' social facts and 'pathological' social facts. Social facts are normal when they are widespread or general in a society. He also argued that social phenomena which are general to all societies must be normal. For example, because crime is found in all societies in one form or another, it is a normal social phenomenon. The way in which he used the concept 'normal' implied that those social phenomena which could be so lab   re necessary for the operation of a 'healthy', well-ordered society. As crime can be found in all societies, it is 'normal', which in turn means that it is an integral part of any healthy society.

However, Durkheim also suggested that though some social facts may be general in a society, they may not really 'fit the conditions for that society'. It is possible, for example, for a social phenomenon to be out of date because it belongs to a past form of society. Therefore he modified the simple condition of generality with the condition that the social fact had to be 'bound up with the general conditions of the collective life' of that particular type of society, at that particular stage in the evolution or development of that type of society. By his use of the concepts 'normal' and 'pathological',

Durkheim appears to be coming close to making value judgements about what is 'good' or 'bad' for a society. By his qualifying conditions he also appears to be implicitly using Spencer's 'organic analogy', suggesting that certain social facts can be healthy or unhealthy for particular societies.

He continues his analysis of social facts by suggesting that some system of classifying societies is required in order to determine whether social facts are normal or pathological. Following Spencer, Durkheim suggested that societies can be categorised according to their degree of composition or organisation. At one end of the scale there is the 'simplest' form of society, the horde. Moving along, there is, in increasing complexity, the clan (two hordes), the tribe, the city, and so on. In each classification, further distinctions can be made between societies according to their degree of 'coalescence', that is to say, according to the extent that their component parts fuse together to produce an integrated arrangement of institutions. Ideally, the classification of societies was also required as a precondition for the use of the 'comparative method', which Durkheim saw as the most useful procedure for establishing sociological proofs. He was very concerned that sociological theories should be testable, and as experimenting with total societies was impossible, the comparative method should be used as a method of quasi-experiment, a method of indirect experiment. In making his investigations, the sociologist should compare his findings from one society with those of other societies of the same and of different types. To carry out a further investigation he should examine a social fact in as many different types of society as possible.

DURKHEIM AND 'FUNCTIONAL ANALYSIS'

One aspect of the consensus perspective Durkheim did develop considerably beyond the contribution of both Spencer and Comte is that of functional analysis as a form of sociological explanation.

In his *Rules,* he suggested that in explaining social facts investigators should (a) find the causes of social facts, and (b) find the functions of social facts, that is, the part they play in helping to maintain an orderly society. In the search for causes, the sociologists should look for antecedent social facts, that is, those social facts which precede and seem to produce the particular social facts under investigation. In the search for functions, he should look to 'the "general needs" of the social organism'.

This then is structuralism in its extreme. The phenomena to be studied are *social* facts, that is, some emergent phenomena which only arise from man associating with man. These phenomena cannot be reduced to psychological or biological factors. Although Durkheim assumed that men may have the same basic human nature and psychological characteristics, he was not interested in studying these. What interested him was the fact that, despite these probable similarities, men developed different social relationships and social arrangements in different societies. To explain any of these social facts, we look for the functions the facts fulfil in the maintenance of the social system in which they are found. In looking at the antecedent social facts, the furthest we can go is to the 'internal constitution of a social group', that is, to the qualities and conditions of social life which are characteristic of any particular social group. It is the social organisation – the nature of social ties and social solidarity of any group – which is the fundamental reality beyond which the sociologist need not investigate. Once he gets into psychological or biological factors, he is no longer doing sociology.

DURKHEIM: A FUNCTIONAL ANALYSIS OF RELIGION

We conclude our examinations of Durkheim's contribution to the development of the consensus perspective by looking at his functional explanation of religion.

Briefly, he suggested that religious activity is found in society because it has a positive function; it helps to maintain the moral unity of society. He analysed religious activity in a primitive tribe on the assumption that all societies have some basic characteristics in common and that understanding of religion in such a simple society would lead him to an understanding of the essential features of religion in any society.

He studied Australian Aboriginal tribes and concluded that the function of religious ceremonies was to reinforce the solidarity of the members of a society. The ceremonial activity helped to show them that although they lived separate and scattered lives in their different clans, they were all a part of the same society with the same fundamental moral rules, expectations and obligations constraining them. Within the tribes, the clan is the basic unit of social life and each clan has a 'totem'. The totem, which is usually the name of an animal, such as a lizard, is like a coat of arms, or an emblem, that is, a symbol which is considered sacred and has very special meanings for those who take it as their totem. This totem is a tangible means of expressing men's feelings that the society in which they are members is bigger and better than each individual. It serves to remind individuals of their tasks and connections with the whole tribe and how much they value those links. These feelings are reinforced by the whole tribe periodically assembling for feasting and dancing and religious ceremonies; each individual experiences feelings of joy, high emotions, which he can only obtain in the whole collectivity. The individual feels acted upon by outside and valued forces and he feels solidarity with his fellows. The totemic emblem, then, reminds him of the uplifting force of society.

Obviously the Aborigines do not themselves see the emblem as representing society. They feel they are worshipping it in its own right. It is Durkheim, the sociologist, who recognises its wider and hidden significance: the function it has for maintaining the moral order of Aboriginal society.

In his analysis and functional explanation, Durkheim compares the totem of a clan with the flag of a nation. National solidarity depends on sentiments of patriotism in the minds of the individual members of the nation. For national solidarity and patriotism to be maintained, some collective expression is required from time to time. Rituals pertaining to flags, monarchs, state leaders, and so on, all help to serve this function. These rituals enable the members of the nation to focus their feelings on to the collectivity of which they form a part and thus help to maintain its existence by reinforcing their social solidarity.

ANTHROPOLOGY AND THE CONSENSUS PERSPECTIVE

Anthropologists, whose primary task has been to study small and non-industrial societies, have contributed to the development of the consensus perspective by their extensive use of 'functional analysis'. Two anthropologists are of particular significance for sociology: Malinowski (1884–1942) and Radcliffe-Brown (1881–1955). It was Malinowski who explicitly used the term 'functionalism' for his own particular brand of the consensus approach. He accepted the view that societies could be seen as social systems, and he suggested that these systems of interrelated elements arose from the basic needs of all men. His bedrock assumption was that all men had certain fundamental needs such as food, shelter, protection and sexual satisfaction. To meet these needs, men produce and distribute food; they build dwellings; they group together; they develop heterosexual relations. But in fulfilling their basic needs in these ways, they produce secondary needs such as communication, co-operation, control of conflict, and so on. The satisfaction of these secondary needs, by the development of language, norms, rules, enforcement agencies, and so on, in turn gives rise to the need for co-ordinating, governing and integrating institutions.

On the basis of these assumptions, Malinowski produced a conceptual framework of society as an integrated, co-ordinated system, generated by the very nature of man. Every feature of society is meeting some need, and it is at the same time fulfilling some function. In general, the functions it fulfils are the needs of man in his social environment. In meeting the different levels of needs, the social system is maintained. For him, all cultural features of a society are fulfilling some function or serving some needs. The task of the researcher is to discover those needs or those functions. When these are discovered, the existence of the cultural item, be it a particular form of social relationship between in-laws in a specific tribe or some burial ritual, has been explained.

Radcliffe-Brown's contribution can be illustrated from his famous study of 'joking relationships'. These relationships, often found in 'primitive' societies, permit – indeed, often require – one person to tease and make fun of another, who, in turn, is not allowed to take offence. It is a relationship of permitted disrespect and to understand its function it is necessary to see it in the context of respectful social relations in the society as a whole. Joking relationships are commonly found between relatives by marriage, especially between a man and his wife's brothers and sisters. Radcliffe-Brown suggests that a marriage involves a readjustment of the social structure, in that both partners have to modify their relations with their own families and are brought into a special relationship with each other's family. The relationship involves both attachment and separation, or, in Radcliffe-Brown's words, both social conjunction and social disjunction. Social disjunction implies divergence of interests and the possibility of conflict; while conjunction requires stability and avoidance of strife. The joking relationship is seen as a form of social arrangement which combines the two in a stable ordered form. Any serious hostility is prevented by the playful teasing; the regular repetition of this muted antagonism serves as a constant expression or reminder of that social disjunction which is one of the essential components of the relation. At the same time, the social conjunction is maintained by the friendliness; persons take no offence at the insulting or disrespectful behaviour.

For Radcliffe-Brown, all cultural items were seen as interrelated and interdependent within a total, unified system of social interaction. He saw a society as a system of interrelated elements of social structure which he defined as a network of normative relationships. These normative relationships existed within a common system of values. Like Durkheim before him, Radcliffe-Brown assumed that it was a necessary condition for the existence of a society that the individual members recognise some common values. Here, Durkheim's influence on his work was marked. Radcliffe-Brown's first, and probably best-known book, *The Andaman Islanders*, was basically a study testing Durkheim's suggestion or hypothesis that the major function of ritual is to contribute to social cohesion, thereby helping to maintain a society's existence.

TALCOTT PARSONS: INTRODUCTION

No one who studies sociology seriously can avoid coming across the work of Talcott Parsons. He has written more than 150 published articles and books over the last fifty years. Most of this work is characteristic of the consensus approach in sociology. We have only to notice the titles of some of his books to recognise his interest in this perspective. In 1951 he wrote the very influential *The Social System*; more recently he has written books entitled *Societies: Evolutionary and Comparative Perspectives* and *The System of Modern Societies,* to select only two. Titles apart, however, it is generally accepted by sociologists today that Talcott Parsons has made major contributions to the development of the consensus perspective through his detailed elaboration of its fundamental conceptual framework, and his attempt to systematise into a coherent theoretical scheme the basic ideas and assumptions of other proponents of the consensus approach.

PARSONS: THE SOCIAL SYSTEM

Parsons suggests that societies can be analysed as 'social systems'. In his view, if *any* social system is to operate at all, four basic conditions have to be met or, alternatively put, four basic problems have to be solved. He calls these conditions or problems 'functional imperatives' or 'functional prerequisites' and they concern not only social organisation, but also the personality needs of members of society. These four basic problems are:

(1) *Adaptation to the environment.* Any society must meet the physical needs of its members if it is to survive. To do this, it must make the required arrangements with its physical environment. Food and shelter are the minimum requirements, and their provision usually involves some system of production and distribution.

(2) *Goal attainment.* Any society must have some common agreement between its members about their priorities and aims. Thus it must provide the necessary arrangements to identify, select and define these collective aims or goals and provide the required structural arrangements for their attainment.

(3) *Pattern maintenance and tension management.* Any society has to make sure that its members are sufficiently motivated to play the necessary roles required and to produce the necessary commitment to the values of the society. They also have to be able to manage the emotional tensions which can develop between members during day-to-day social interaction.

(4) *Integration.* In order to maintain its existence, any society has to ensure a measure of co-ordination and control between the internal elements of the various parts of the social system.

Of these four problems the first two, adaptation to the environment and achieving collective goals, deal with the conditions and demands made from outside the system. They can be seen as largely 'instrumental' in that they require the performance of tasks such as allocating means to the achievement of valued goals. The problems of maintaining, motivating and controlling tension, and of integrating the action of members result from the fact that there is always more than one person in a social system. In other words, it is recognised that social interaction itself produces problems from within society. These latter two problems are seen largely as 'expressive' concerns, that is, maintaining social values and controlling emotional development.

In order to solve these problems and thus maintain its existence, any society has to have four major structural features. For Parsons, these structural features are the major sub-systems of the economy, the polity (politics), kinship, and community and cultural organisations.

The economy is that part of the structure of a society which provides and distributes the material resources needed by the members of a society.

The political sub-system and institutions serve the functions of selecting the collective goals of a society and of motivating members to achieve those goals.

The kinship institutions serve the functions of maintaining the accepted and expected patterns of social interaction and help to control interpersonal tensions largely through the process of social-isation. It is the process of socialisation which produces competent and adequately motivated role players who are committed to the values of society.

The community and cultural institutions, such as organised religion, education and mass communication, serve the function of integrating the various elements of a social system. These institutions can create, demonstrate and reinforce social values. They may, however, require help from formal agencies of social control such as the police force and the military, or from the legal institutions of the courts and the judiciary, should they prove inadequate on their own.

The particular form these structural sub-systems or institutions take in any society is, however, influenced by the *value system* of that society. Parsons was greatly influenced by the work of Durkheim and, for both of them, a society is essentially a *moral* entity. When Parsons refers to the structure of a society, that is, to social structure, he is referring to a *normative* structure, that is, to the structure of expectations which is embedded in the playing of roles. The institutional sub-systems, such as kinship, economy and the polity referred to above, are all made up of roles.

In the economy, for example, there are managers, workers, bank clerks, factory hands, salesmen, and so on. These are all examples of some of the roles which can go to make up an economic sub-system. But role is a normative concept. It refers to the expectations which are associated with a particular position. According to Parsons, the particular expectations, which define the roles constituting a societal institution, are underpinned and influenced by the value system of the society. Diagrammatically Parson's conceptual framework of a society or social system can be represented as in Table 2.1.

The table shows society as made up of a number of 'institutional orders' such as kinship, religion, politics, economy and education. Each of these 'orders' is made up of specific institutions such as families, churches and schools. These institutions, in turn, are made up of particular sets of roles, which can be simply defined as

Table 2.1 *Society as a Social System*

INSTRUMENTAL FUNCTIONAL IMPERATIVES   EXPRESSIVE FUNCTIONAL IMPERATIVES

INSTITUTIONAL ORDERS

ADAPTATION	GOAL ATTAINMENT	PATTERN MAINTENANCE/ TENSION MANAGEMENT	INTEGRATION
ECONOMY	**POLITY**	**KINSHIP**	**CULTURAL AND COMMUNITY ORGANISATIONS**
(major sub-system) made up of	(major sub-system) made up of	(major sub-system) made up of	(major sub-system) made up of
INSTITUTIONS (e.g. Factory system, Banking system)	INSTITUTIONS (e.g. Political parties, State bureaucracies)	INSTITUTIONS (e.g. Nuclear family, Marriage)	INSTITUTIONS (e.g. Schools, Churches, Media organisations)
Each institution is made up of	Each institution is made up of	Each institution is made up of	Each institution is made up of
SETS OF ROLES Specific norms giving concrete behavioural prescriptions define roles. These concrete norms are underpinned by:	SETS OF ROLES Specific norms ... ... underpinned by:	SETS OF ROLES Specific norms ... ... underpinned by:	SETS OF ROLES Specific norms ... ... underpinned by:

FUNDAMENTAL VALUES

expected ways of behaviour. 'Mother', 'father', 'husband', 'priest', 'teacher' and 'pupil' are examples of roles. Although different individuals may play any single role, they are expected to conform to expected ways of behaving which are prescribed by the nature of that role. The specific norms which guide, influence and even constrain particular forms of behaviour are in turn influenced and underpinned by the general system of values which characterises a particular society. Societies have different value systems, and these can and do give rise to different forms of social structure.

For example, let us make some distinctions between the social structure of 'traditional' Chinese society and a modern industrial society. In 'traditional' Chinese society, particularly the period in the middle and latter part of the eighteenth century, values associated with family life were dominant. Loyalty to one's family was considered the highest loyalty of all. Even crimes of violence could be condoned if they had been committed to avenge wrongs done to one's family. Ancestor worship was a strong element in religious activities. In many respects the society could be described as 'family oriented', in the sense that most decisions were made with reference to family interests. Because the family was such a valued institution, and family life and loyalties were given the highest priority, family interests took precedence over those of other groups. The social structure of traditional Chinese society was to a large extent arranged around the family.

The average Chinese family was the basic economic unit. It was practically self-sufficient in both production and consumption. Even the families in the gentry who did not have the same degree of self-sufficiency as the peasantry minimised their dependency on non-family members by using servants. Their servants were treated as virtually members of the family. They were quasi family members.

The family in China was also the basic unit for the allocation of power and responsibility. Individuals interacted with their family more than with any other group, and were controlled primarily by the head of the family. One's own family was the most common hierarchy of power and responsibility any individual had to deal with. The family head was not responsible to someone over him in a wider social hierarchy, rather his responsibility operated downward to the kinship unit of which he was head.

Even the formal political arrangements like the neighbouring ruling councils (the equivalent of our local parish councils) and the imperial bureaucracy were not beyond the influence of the family. Although the neighbourhood councils were officially expected to prevent any blatant family self-interest, they often operated through the use of family pressures; and although in theory the bureaucracy was organised in such a way to overrule all family interest, in its practical operations it could never do so completely. In practice the ruling philosophy to which members of traditional Chinese society subscribed was that a proper government could not be unjust to any family. If a person was a good family man, inevitably he was a good citizen.

In modern industrial society, although family life and family loyalty is considered important and valued to some extent, the values of economic efficiency, individualism and effort for the good of the whole society probably have a higher overall priority. Political decisions are usually made with economic considerations of efficiency in mind. The political decisions about provision of schools and the length of time children should stay in them are usually made on the basis of the benefits to the economy. It is no coincidence that the provision of education has widened in societies which have developed industrial economies.

From these broad comparisons it is possible to see how the value system of a society can influence its social structure. Following Durkheim, Parsons considers the value system of a society to be one of its essential characteristics. For both thinkers, common agreement on certain fundamental values is an integral or constitutive feature of any society. For both, a consensus on basic values among the members of a society is an element of the definition of a society. Without such agreements there would be no society.

Parsons, however, has elaborated on Durkheim's more general statements and incorporates into his own theoretical analysis consideration of the relationship between norms specific to a particular situation and the general value system of a society. He suggests that the social system can be seen as consisting of individual members of society who perform different activities, or play a variety of roles, within the general framework of the societal division of labour. From this activity there develops a network of concrete, or 'situation specific' norms which in practice regulate the performance of the roles and define the obligations and prohibitions, the 'dos' and 'don'ts', for each social activity. Thus the norms prescribe appropriate concrete behaviours. For example, 'be faithful to your wife' can be seen as one of the norms defining the role 'husband' in Western societies. 'Do not favour any one child' can be seen as one of the norms which come to define the role of 'teacher' in our schools. They are concrete behavioural prescriptions. They specify appropriate role behaviour in particular identifiable situations.

From this approach, the problem emerges of maintaining an integration of the whole social system, given the necessary diversity of roles and norms, especially in modern society. It is to this problem that we now turn for detailed consideration.

PARSONS: EQUILIBRIUM AND SOCIAL INTEGRATION

The centrality of the normative nature of social structure in Parson's conceptual framework is also reflected in his use of the concept of equilibrium. Whereas the notion of equilibrium was largely implicit in the work of Comte, Spencer, Durkheim and the anthropologists, Parsons explicitly introduces it into his theoretical scheme. For him, a society in a state of equilibrium is one in which there is no conflict, one in which everyone knows what is expected of him in any role, and one in which these expectations are constantly being met. This is a condition of perfect equilibrium and, as such, in practice is never realised, but it is assumed to be a condition society is always striving to attain.

The key processes for attaining this theoretical state of equilibrium are 'socialisation' and 'social control'. Role players 'learn', that is, are 'socialised' into, the expectations attached to the role, and this process is backed up by the positive sanctioning (reward) and negative sanctioning (punishment) of role performances which do, or do not meet these expectations. The central problem is that of monitoring role players to meet the role expectations. In the perfectly integrated system the 'deeper layers of motivation become harnessed to the fulfilment of role expectations'. Thus there is a necessary relationship between the personality of an individual and the social structure of his society when it is in a state of equilibrium.

Socialisation is therefore an extremely important process for those who use this consensus perspective to analyse the nature and processes of social behaviour. It is the process through which individuals learn what is expected of them in various situations, it is the process through which members of a society become committed to the societal value system. In this process of social learning the role of parents is seen as crucial.

For Parsons, the mother and father are the important moulders of the child's personality and in his description of the mechanisms of the learning process he relies heavily on Freudian psychology. For example, he uses the concept of identification to explain the taking in, or internalising, of the values of a mother as a representative of society by a young child. The mother has the opportunity to exercise a tight control over this learning situation and can reinforce the tendencies of the child's behaviour which fit her own expectations of how the child should behave. The emotional attachment which the child has for the mother is seen as an important factor in the process of learning the societal values.

Parsons emphasises the acquisition of values and the plasticity and sensitivity of the newborn member of society, whose dependency involves it in deep emotional attachments. The child is seen as an empty vessel, which has to be filled with a culture, with orientations to values and with expectations about roles. In this way, the culture of the society is passed on to new members; the society is internalised in the new generation; it shapes and gives identities to the young. Here, Parsons assumes that individuals are natural seekers after gratification and approval; they are eager to learn and to conform to the values, norms and expectations of society. They are like 'empty vessels' because Parsons does not draw attention to any fundamental source of tension between the nature of man and the nature of society. In general, his theoretical approach emphasises the influence of prior or antecedent factors in the process of socialisation. For example, the low level of parental commitment to some societal values may be, for their children, an antecedent factor which adversely affects the quality of socialisation, thereby impairing the chances of the children meeting their teachers' expectations.

With this conceptualisation of the process of socialisation, Parsons also has a ready-made theoretical framework for the study and explanation of deviance. Basically, deviants are seen as those who have been inadequately socialised; those who are insufficiently committed to the values and norms of their society. It is this assumption about the nature and causes of deviance which leads sociologists using this perspective into investigating early childhood experiences, because it is in the family that the basic work of socialisation, of developing stable personalities and commitment to societal values, is seen to be carried out. Deviance is defined in terms of the dominant value system and is seen as a pathological state. At a societal level, it can also be interpreted as a disturbance of the equilibrium of the social system which requires the intervention of agencies of social control such as the police force, mental institutions and the prison service.

In considering the concept of equilibrium, Parsons also demonstrates his acceptance of the idea that the parts of a society's social structure are interdependent. For example, he, like other sociologists, has noticed changes in family structure, particularly the move from extended to nuclear family units. In extended family units, it was usual to have three generations of one family living together, either under the same roof or in close proximity. Today, in modern industrial Western societies, nuclear family units, comprising mother, father and their young children, are widespread. Parsons argues that this change in family structure is related to changes in the functions of the family. He claims that as society has changed, so the functions required of the family have necessarily changed, thereby altering the structure of the family.

With the development of industrialisation, specialised institutions, such as welfare services, education and political organisations, have developed, for example, caring for the sick and elderly, educating the society's children and deciding how the society's resources will be managed and distibuted. At the same time, a factory-based industrial economy has increasingly required high levels of specific skills and a certain amount of geographical mobility from its labour force. Increasingly, jobs have been distributed to members of society according to ability and merit, rather than by inheritance. Achievement has become a general social value and has, in the new industrial society, tended to be associated with financial success. Such changes in the values and structure of society have had their repercussions on the family.

The tendency has been for young families to move to wherever the husband can best use his talents in the industrial economy; and for families to reduce the number of children they bring into the world, and then to do all they can, including sacrificing some of their own pleasures, to encourage each child's potential development. With fewer children, more of the family resources, including a mother's time, can be so invested that each child's chances of making a success of his life are increased. As the family has given up some of its former functions to outside specialised agencies, so it has become more specialised in its functions of socialising children and of providing a social environment in which adults can develop and maintain stable, well-balanced personalities.

Explicit in this generalised analysis is the suggestion that the nuclear family structure fits the social and economic structure of industrial society very well, better in fact than the former larger extended family unit. Parsons sees the changes as an example of the process of 'structural differentiation'. He claims that kinship tends to dominate the social structure of primitive societies and, by comparison, in advanced industrial societies a far greater part is played by non-kinship structures, such as political organisations, churches, business firms and schools. Through the process of differentiation, certain functions are transferred from the family to other institutions and thus, with less functions to serve, the family becomes a more specialised social unit. What is emerging is a 'new type of family structure, in a new relation to a general social structure'.

We now consider Parsons's argument that norms can be in conflict in different parts of the social system and yet not upset the equilibrium of society. We can illustrate this argument with Parsons's analysis of education and its interrelationships with other 'subsystems' in the social structure, the family and the economy. He suggests that the development of a formal and compulsory educational system in industrial society can be viewed as society's way of attempting to re-establish an equilibrium following the social disruption caused by the development of an industrial economy. Industrial production and an industrial form of economic organisation require men to be employed according to their ability. The most efficient use of manpower requires that men be given jobs according to what they can do rather than who they are.

Sentiment plays little or no part in the employment of workers and favouritism is frowned upon. Specialisation is considered an efficient principle of manpower deployment. It is in keeping with the general aim of an industrial economy, namely, to produce as much as possible for the smallest amount of investment of both men and materials. In the family situation, however, other ways of behaving are expected and valued. It is usual for us to help members of our family and do what we can for them, because they are members of our family. Sentiment is considered appropriate in familial relationships. In modern society, such sentiment can generate a potential conflict of expectations between familial roles and expected ways of behaving in the economy.

The educational system provides a social mechanism for avoiding or reducing this potential conflict. In school, the child learns that favouritism is not appreciated and that people are rewarded mainly for what they can do and for what they can achieve. The young pupils also come to notice that as they progress through the education system from infant to primary, from secondary schools to further education, they come across more and more specialisation. In the infant school, they may have only one teacher who is like a mother to them in many respects; in the secondary school and thereafter they are not only taught by specialists, but they are even likely to go to counsellors for specialised advice on their emotional problems.

In this way, the educational system can be seen as acting as a bridge between the potentially conflicting relationships and expectations encountered in the family and economic systems. As a bridge, it can be seen as helping to maintain the equilibrium of society by giving members of society an opportunity to learn how to adjust to and cope with conflicting expectations in societally approved ways.

PARSONS: PATTERN VARIABLES AND TYPES OF SOCIETY

The importance Parsons places on norms and values is brought out by his concept of 'pattern variables'. This concept provides the basis for a classifactory schema for categorising the norms and values of any society. Furthermore, Parsons claims that this schema for pattern variables can serve to display a society's measure of equilibrium and integration. He suggests that any value, role, norm, institution, sub-system of society, or even the whole society can be classified via this schema; and that the fundamental importance of values is shown in the way they set the limits to the range of norms and other features of social systems. In particular, the sociologist can derive a measure of 'fit' between norms and values in any society by using this classificatory schema for pattern variables. The schema is shown in Table 2.2.

Parsons suggests that the fundamental value system of a modern, industrial, bureaucratised society can be characterised by the pattern variables in 'B', and the fundamental value system of, say, a small tribal society may be characterised by the pattern variables in 'A'. At a very general level of comparison, we see a link between Parson's two sets of pattern variables and Durkheim's mechanical and organic forms of solidarity. Parsons suggests his schema goes further; it identifies the potential conflicts of values and norms, which society must overcome in order to maintain its equilibrium, that is, to achieve its integration and stability. For example, in our society the family can largely be characterised by the pattern variables 'A', while institutions found in the economic and political sub-systems can be broadly characterised by pattern variables 'B'. But as there is an interchange of personnel between these system parts, a potential conflict arises. It has to be coped with by society through some integrating mechanisms for managing such tensions, in order to ensure the required degree of equilibrium for the maintenance of order.

Table 2.2 *Parsons's Concept of Pattern Variables*

Pattern variables 'A' Characteristic of 'expressive' values and norms, i.e. an emphasis on emotional satisfaction.	Pattern variables 'B' Characteristic of 'instrumental' values and norms, i.e. an emphasis on achieving goals, and accomplishing tasks.
Ascription Emphasising the qualities or attributes of actors, i.e. who they *are*.	**Achievement** Emphasising the performance of actors, i.e. what they *do*.
Diffuseness Emphasising broad relationships dealing with a range of purposes and interests, e.g. the relationship between a mother and a child.	**Specificity** Emphasising limited relationships for specific purposes, e.g. the relationship between a doctor and a patient.
Particularism Emphasising the organisation of particular relationships with particular actors, e.g. 'being loyal to one's mother'.	**Universalism** Emphasising the organisation of interaction according to general principles, e.g. treating every one equally before the law.
Affectivity Emphasising the gratification of emotions.	**Affective neutrality** Emphasising the deferment of gratification, i.e. disciplining oneself.
Collective orientation Emphasising collectivism, i.e. pursuing shared interests.	**Self-orientation** Emphasising individualism, i.e. pursuing private interests.

One such mechanism is that of role specialisation. As we have already seen, the family tends to develop into an 'isolated' nuclear structure in which most members are insulated from participation in extrafamilial institutions. Typically the adult male plays what Parsons calls the 'boundary-role' as he moves back and forth between family and non-family institutions. He also tends to concentrate on instrumental, task-oriented functions. The adult female tends to stay at home and specialise in expressive functions.

Similarly, the school can serve an integrating function by gradually socialising the child (who in his family situation has been experiencing the values and norms classified under pattern variables 'A') into roles and thereby norms and values which can be classified under pattern variables 'B'. Thus the school as an institution meets some of the problems of integration for the social system and thus helps to maintain an adequate equilibrium. The concept of pattern variables helps us to analyse and understand the nature of the possible relationships between various institutions and highlights the interdependence operating between the various elements of a social system.

Although we have been implying that Parsons's theoretical model of a social system refers to total societies, it is important to note that he claimed it was equally applicable in the analysis of institutional orders (for example, kinship), institutions (for example, marriage) and even to two-person role relationships, such as a husband and wife. This general applicability of his concept of 'social system' again illustrates how Parsons has provided sociologists with a more detailed set of concepts than had previously been available, to help understand the nature of social behaviour from within a consensus perspective.

In conclusion, Parsons has mainly been criticised for producing an abstract theoretical schema which is difficult to apply to empirical research. In the following sections we shall assess this criticism by examining some empirical work generated within the consensus perspective. We begin, however, with Merton's defence and proposed modification of the functionalist approach to sociological investigation.

ROBERT MERTON: FUNCTIONAL ANALYSIS

Robert Merton claims that theoretical schemas of the kind Parsons has produced do not help us to get on with the real business of sociology, that is, doing sociological research. Rather than trying to produce elaborate comprehensive theories, we should remember that sociology is not as old, nor as established, as the natural sciences and we should direct our energies into working on testable propositions from limited sets of assumptions, concerning specific situations. If we do this, we may be able to draw some of our findings together and move gradually towards some more general theory. Merton sees Parsons as being too ambitious, too keen to construct a great theoretical schema which does not help us very much with the practical problems of doing research.

Merton argues that functional analysis is a very promising sociological approach, but its promise has not been fulfilled because it has tended to lack methodological rigour. He sees this lack of rigour mainly in the form of muddled and imprecise concepts and assumptions. It is his aim to provide a checklist of 'dos' and 'dont's' when studying any phenomenon in a functionalist framework. He calls this systematic checklist of concepts and procedures a 'paradigm'.

There is a problem with the concept 'function' itself, he argues, because it has been used in many different ways. In common parlance, the word has several different meanings ranging through an occupation, a festive event, the activities done by a role or office and, more abstractly, it also refers to motives, intentions and aims.

Merton suggests that it would help considerably if, when it is used sociologically, it is reserved only for those observed *consequences* of social events or arrangements which make for the adaptation or adjustment of a given system (such as a group, a society). For example, the pattern of social arrangements in families or political systems should be studied to observe their consequences for meeting the requirements of the ordered and stable social system of which they form a part. Families, for example, may be seen to have the *functions* of providing new members for society and socialising them into competent role players with stable personalities.

There are also problems with the general assumptions made by functionalists. Specifically, Merton suggests there are three misleading postulates or assumptions in functional analysis which he attempts to remedy. These assumptions are:

The Functional Unity of Society

It is commonly assumed, especially by anthropologists, that all standardised beliefs (cultural items) or standardised practices (roles, institutions, social activities) are functional for the *entire* social or cultural system.

The problem with this assumption is that although it may be generally true for small, primitive societies, it is nonsense for large, complex societies. Many items may not be functional for the entire system, but only part of it, especially in a modern industrial society which is so complex and highly differentiated. So when looking for the function of a particular activity, arrangement, or belief, it may be sufficient to ascertain its consequences for only a particular unit or part of the total society. It is important therefore that when a sociologist says that any particular item is functional, he specifies the *unit*. It may be functional only for a particular institution or a group or one individual family or a school. For example, to say that religious belief and ceremonial activity are functional for society in that they promote solidarity for all the members of that society is inadequate in the case of Northern Ireland, where religious differences can help to split society.

Universal Functionalism

This assumption is closely related to and hard to separate from the functional unit of society. It is the urge to find positive functions for any social item whatsoever, that is, assuming that a practice must fulfil some useful function if it has survived for a reasonable period of time. For example, Merton cites Kluckhohn's argument that the buttons on the sleeve of a man's coat are not useless but fulfil a positive function because they preserve the familiar, the feeling of tradition. Merton argues that not all items necessarily fulfil positive functions, because if we accept that items may not be functional for the entire society then it follows that they can be functional for some units or parts and not for others. It is possible that some items may have a negative consequence for some parts, in that they make for instability and disruption rather than for the stable maintenance of the system. As Merton puts it, it is possible that some items may have *dysfunctional*, that is, disruptive, consequences for certain parts of a system; and have neutral or non-functional consequences, that is, neither positive nor negative, for other parts. What the sociologist should do, according to Merton, is to balance the positive functions against the dysfunctions before saying whether the item is functional or not and, of course, be careful to specify exactly what units he is referring to.

Indispensability

This assumption confuses the notions of (*a*) functional prerequisites, that is, there are certain basic functions that must be fulfilled if a given unit (a society, or group) is to survive or persist, with (*b*) social forms/institutions/practices. For example, a society must have some orderly arrangements for ensuring that functional prerequisites like the production and distribution of food and other scarce resources are fulfilled. But there are many ways, many types of actual, concrete social arrangements, for fulfilling these prerequisites, for example, self-sufficient agricultural units, hunting economies, slave-based economies, barter, money economies, capitalist or socialist economies. Thus it is nonsense to look at any particular activity or practice in any society and to argue that it is indispensable to that society because it fulfils a functional prerequisite. There may well be other social forms and practices which equally could fulfil them. We should recognise that for any social practice, there may be *functional alternatives* or substitutes. More than any other, this assumption gives functionalism a 'bad name' for being conservative, that is, seeking to justify the existing institutions in society. Thus functionalists misguidedly argue that something is 'indispensable for the well-being of a society', on the basis of this false assumption of indispensability.

Manifest and Latent Functions

A further elaboration, which Merton goes on to suggest for functional analysis, is that in our investigations we may distinguish between *manifest functions,* which are recognised and intended by the individuals involved, and *latent functions*, which are the unintended and unrecognised consequences of social behaviour. It is possible that some beliefs, actions and customs can have functions, or dysfunctions, for a part of society or for a whole society of which the individual participants may be unaware. For example, the rain-making ceremonies of the Hopi tribe have for the members of the tribe the recognised and intended purpose of producing rain, but a sociologist observing the activity may discover that these repeated rain-making ceremonies have the consequence of maintaining the Hopi society by reinforcing the feelings of solidarity among its members. If the Hopi are not aware of and do not intend this particular consequence and it can be shown to occur, then we call it the latent function of the rain-making ceremony. As we can look for latent functions, so we can seek latent dysfunctions. It is in these ways that the sociologist can be seen to 'look behind' the behaviour and activities of groups of people in society.

Merton suggests that a functionalist perspective can provide an illuminating approach to social life and can reveal fascinating information about ourselves and the way we organise societies. One famous and often quoted piece of empirical work is the study of factory workers known as the Hawthorne Electric studies. Initially, the investigation was concerned with the relationship between the lighting of the factory and productivity. Several experiments were carried out varying the lighting arrangements, but no consistent relationship was discovered. Instead, it was found that production increased during the experiments whether the lighting was increased, decreased, or kept constant. It was later discovered that the reason for this was that the presence of the investigator had latent, unintended consequences on productivity. It transpired that the social arrangements of the work system were much more important than the physical condition of the amount of light the workers had to work in. The fact that outsiders were taking an interest in them, were studying and watching them, resulted in them working at a faster rate. After this discovery, research was redirected on to the effects on production of social arrangements and behaviour.

Functional analysis can therefore provide us with a variety of types of explanations, although all of them will be within the broad general framework of indicating the consequences of particular social actions or arrangements for some identifiable social system or sub-system. Merton illustrates some points in his own analysis of the 'political machine' in American cities.

The question he asks is, 'How can the local political party organis-ations survive in the U.S.A. given that they are so widely regarded as corrupt and immoral?' His sociological answer is in terms of the functions they continue to perform.

From his investigations, he suggests that the 'official political administrtion' is characterised by general inefficiency, which leads to the generation of an unofficial or alternative structure in order to meet the needs of particular groups. The political boss organises his area or constituency through his precinct captains who develop personal relationships and links with the local people. In return for their votes, the members of the 'political machine' give the local inhabitants the services they require such as food, jobs, advice and practical assistance. In practice, the people tend to prefer this arrangement to having to deal with the impersonal official welfare workers. Merton concludes that the 'political machine' serves four major functions for the social system of which it forms a part.

(1) For the socially deprived, it satisfies wants which are not adequately met by the 'legitimate' social structure.

(2) For business, especially big business, the political boss provides political privileges which bring immediate economic gain. Business firms seek political deals which enable them to stabilise their situation and to meet their objective in maximising profits.

(3) The political machine provides jobs and career prospects for people who were socialised into poor and disadvantaged backgrounds. Those who work for the machine can have a chance to realise the 'American dream' of getting ahead.

(4) The machine supports illegitimate businesses, for example, drug-trafficking, prostitution, illegal gambling. These enter-prises provide services similar to those of legitimate businesses in that both types of business supply goods and services in response to a demand.

Thus the machine cannot be eliminated until a suitable functional alternative is devised which fulfils these functions.

In his attempts to sharpen and clarify the functionalist form of analysis, Merton does not lose sight of the basic conceptual framework of the consensus perspective. He does, however, tend to use it implicitly rather than explicitly. For example, he seldom explicitly refers to the concept of social system, although it is always implicit in his analyses. Similarly he tends to make the implicit assumption that society is primarily a moral or normative structure. Specifically in his article on 'Social structure and anomie', Merton makes the assumption that in societies there are particular goals which the members of the society can identify and which they aim to attain. He couples it with the assumption that there are in society acceptable ways or means of attaining the goals. Examples he uses from American society include the value of economic success and the acceptable way of attaining it through honest hard work. The valued goals and the norms regulating their acceptable attainment give rise to the patterns of interaction and social arrangements which comprise the social structure of a society. He suggests that at times different elements of the social structure can be in disjuncture, that is, they are not compatible, thereby creating structural pressure on individuals to make deviant responses. For example, working class children, through no fault of their own, may not get the necessary education to obtain jobs which will pay them handsome salaries. Thus there is a structural pressure on them to obtain money by illegitimate or illegal means. Although he does not actually use the terms or concepts in his analysis, Merton is implying that deviant responses arise when the total social system is in a condition of disequilibrium.

It is possible to see further influences of 'consensus theorists' on Merton's approach. His use of the concept 'dysfunction', for example, implies the notion of order, stability and even equilibrium. There is the suggestion that dysfunctions refer to disruptive elements in a social system. In that sense, they are conceptually linked to Durkheim's notion of pathological social facts. For all those sociologists we have so far considered, including Merton, there seems to be a basic assumption that societies are 'normally' orderly and stable and that disorder is an 'unnatural' condition. It is for this reason that consensus approach in sociology is often accused of being conservative. Although they have all claimed they are concerned to produce a conceptual framework for objective, scientific investigation, the very concepts they use – equilibrum, disequilibirum, normal, pathological, functional, dysfunctional, and so on, – do imply an evaluative view of society. That is to say, they do seem to have in mind an ideal arrangement for society.

Having set out the basic elements of the conceptual framework used by consensus approaches, and having identified the range of basic assumptions on which they are founded, we shall conclude this chapter by looking at some of the ways the perspective has been used by particular sociologists in their investigation and analyses of some specific substantive areas.

KAI ERIKSON: DEVIANCE AND SYSTEM MAINTENANCE

Erikson examines a seventeenth-century Puritan settlement in Massachusetts. He regards it as a self-contained 'social system' and tries to show how the 'crime rate' can serve a positive function in maintaining its integration over time.

To assume that societies can be viewed analytically as entities, or systems, existing in their own right, implies that they must have some boundaries which mark the limits of their operations and which distinguish them from other systems and from their environment. It is not unusual to hear people talk about drop-outs and criminals being 'outside society' and about society having to deal with them because they are seen as problems for society. The concept of a boundary implies that society has to build within it certain mechanisms which ensure that the accepted and expected ways of behaving are maintained. It implies a sort of social control system which comes into operation when members of society go beyond what is generally acceptable. The law, the police force and mental health agencies can be viewed as typical examples of social control agencies maintaining the boundaries of society.

In his study Erikson examines three different 'crime waves': the Antinomian controversy of 1636, the Quaker persecutions of the 1650s and the witchcraft hysteria of 1692. He saw each of them as attempts by the members of the community to redefine the boundaries of their society.

The first involved a group of dissidents who followed the teachings of a certain Mrs Hutchinson. She questioned the right of the community's clergy to identify those who were touched by grace, that is, the saved, or the elect, on the grounds that most of them were not competent to judge such a thing. In so doing she was challenging one of the cornerstones of the community's religious orthodoxy. 'Antinomians' was the name given to the heretics of Luther's day, and Mrs Hutchinson and her followers were soon to be identified as heretics, insurgents, seditious persons, who had to be dealt with. They were taken to court and convicted of various crimes, mainly sedition. Mrs Hutchinson herself was declared 'unfit for the society' and banished, being imprisoned until she was sent away.

The Quaker persecutions, about twenty years later, presented a similar example of boundary reinforcement. In this case the 'deviants' were banished and even put to death.

The third example Erikson deals with was the witchcraft hysteria in Salem Village. In this case a number of young girls were declared to be possessed by the devil because of their strange or deviant behaviour. These girls would scream unaccountably, grovel on the ground, bark like dogs and engage in all sorts of strange antics. They were asked to name their tormentors, to tell the authorities who had bewitched them. They identified three at first and then, flushed with the attention they were receiving and their new-found power, they went on identifying more and more agents of the devil. The hysteria was under way. Several people were brought before the courts, convicted of witchcraft and put to death.

Eventually, however, the hysteria died down, as the girls began identifying people at random, even accusing some of the community's respected persons, and suspicions grew about the validity of their accusations. Erikson suggests that this outbreak of hysteria on the part of the community's authorities, as they rushed headlong into executing all 'witches', is symptomatic behaviour of a community having some difficulty establishing boundaries, finding its identity. After all, the Puritan settlement had not long been established in that part of the world. It was probably a time, he suggests, when these settlers felt alone in the world, felt bewildered by the loss of their old destiny, but were not yet aware of their new one. During this particular period they were trying to discover some image of themselves 'by listening to a chorus of voices which whispered to them from the depths of an invincible wilderness'.

It is interesting to note that when the Puritans were in England they were seen by the rest of English society as a militant and dissident minority group. At that time they argued for their right to be different. They argued for their right to exercise a freedom of conscience. In their new situation, however, they were trying to establish a new society, a new social order, and were not prepared to allow others the freedom they themselves had previously claimed.

This observable change of priorities on the part of the Puritan settlers does seem to imply that running a society as opposed to operating in one as a minority group can lead people to change their value orientations, for 'the good of the society'.

Erikson claims that this society, in deciding what was deviant, was defining its own particular standards. By focusing on particular types of deviance, the Puritans were defining, for all to see, the boundaries of expected and valued ways of behaving. In so doing, the community's normative unity, its 'way of life', was being clarified. Through his analysis of these three different 'crime waves', the author suggests that as the community changed, as its boundaries of the acceptable and unacceptable changed, so the waves served to provide moments when the community members could look at themselves and reaffirm their shared values.

Thus it provides some evidence from a specific situation for the general explanation of deviance proposed by Durkheim. The analysis lends support to the idea that a society probably needs deviants because, as long as some members are considered deviants by the rest of society, attempts to control them set boundaries of acceptable, expected behaviour for all other members. If the deviance is publicly recognised and punished then it serves to remind the members of a community, or a society, what their proper standards are. It serves to spotlight the right, by locating the wrong. Thus it serves to maintain the societal consensus. Societies, then, will ensure that they have enough of it: they will produce a steady level of deviance to ensure the maintenance of their boundaries.

NEIL SMELSER:
A CONSENSUS APPROACH TO SOCIAL CHANGE

Smelser's work illustrates how a sociologist using the consensus perspective can study the problem of social change. By the use of such concepts as 'social system' and 'structural differentiation', he views the problem as concerning the 'adaptive adjustment' of society: the social system 'adjusts' or 'adapts' itself in order to re-establish an equilibrium, thereby overcoming any strains or tensions disturbing to its tendency towards stability and integration.

In *Social Change in the Industrial Revolution*, Smelser applied this theoretical framework in a detailed study of social growth resulting from industrial development of the Lancashire cotton industry during the period 1770–1840. He suggests that this period can be seen as a series of adjustments occurring in society, in contrast to the period before 1770 which was relatively stable, and which represented a period of equilibrium. He claims that a new sort of equilibrium was achieved in the years after 1840. He suggests that certain initial conditions led to the industrial structure being unable to meet productive requirements and it was through a process of structural differentiation, which he describes in terms of a general sequence of identifiable stages, that a new and 'better suited' structure emerged. He follows this up by suggesting that the same general process and sequential stages of adaptive structural differentiation can be seen to have taken place in the family as it became unable to perform its functions adequately as a result of the changes in the economy. He follows this further by analysing and describing the growth of processes of structural differentiation within a variety of institutions such as trade unions, savings banks, friendly societies, and so on. These are seen as providing in part the necessary specialist agencies to mediate between the family and the economy, since family life had become segregated from work.

His anslysis claims that throughout this period the various parts of British society were constantly adjusting to one another, thus demonstrating their interdependence and their collective tendency to produce an equilibrium.

In the elaboration of his model of structural differentiation, Smelser suggests that the value system is the primary source for evaluating possible structural change in society. The value system supplies the standards for legitimising and approving new arrangements and expectations. The value system thus limits the directions and degrees of change. He admits that values can change, but they generally change much more slowly than social structure. Thus to a large extent, the fundamental value system remains constant during a single sequence of differentiation and so, for that particular period, the criteria for assessing the performance of any unit of the structure do not vary.

DAVIS AND MOORE:
A FUNCTIONALIST THEORY OF STRATIFICATION

A functionalist theory of stratification has been proposed by Davis and Moore and by Parsons, but like so many forms of analysis arising from the use of the consensus perspective derives from the work of Durkheim.

Like crime, social stratification is recognised as a common feature of all societies. It is therefore seen as a 'normal' characteristic of society and is assumed to be serving some positive function or need for society.

However, these two sociologists make the further assumption that some of the tasks required by a society are more important than others. In particular, the tasks of administration and of governing the society are assumed to be very important. They also assume, along with Parsons, that it is necessary for a society to provide structural arrangement to motivate its individual members to fill certain positions in society *and* to motivate them to perform the duties attached to those positions. If all the positions and tasks were equally easy to fill and perform, and were all equally important to the survival of society, and if all the members of a society were equal in their abilities and talents in relation to the required tasks, there would be no problem. But such is not the case. Talents *are* differently distributed. Therefore a society *must* have some kinds of inducements or rewards available in order to encourage those with the most suitable abilities to fill the most important positions.

These inducements usually take the form of high rewards, both of goods and prestige, for the important jobs in society. They can also carry with them a not inconsiderable amount of power. The consequence is that the wealth, prestige and power which society has provided for these positions make those who hold them into a privileged class.

In this way, Davis and Moore explain why social stratification must exist in all socieites and, in particular, in any modern complex society. The division of labour inevitably produces inequality of reward because without these inequalities of reward, the continuity of the division could not otherwise be guaranteed. Social inequality is generated by, and is functional for, society. Not only does every society 'need' it, but social inequality can also be seen to be empirically present in all known societies. Social inequality is, therefore, both universal and necessary in society.

ASPECTS OF A CONSENSUS APPROACH TO THE FAMILY

'The family' is a well-worn area of sociological investigation and most students taking introductory courses in sociology spend some time studying it. The vast majority of studies of the family have assumed the consensus or functionalist approach although they may not always have explicitly identified their theoretical assumptions in these terms. A survey of the commonly quoted literature shows that changes in the structure and functions of the family is a frequent 'problem' investigated by sociologists, and a great deal of the work in this particular area is a development from, or reaction to, the analyses made by Talcott Parsons in the 1950s.

As we have seen earlier in this chapter, Parsons's approach emphasises the structural changes which have taken place in the family. He describes the broad change as being from the extended form to a nuclear form and sees this direction of change as being compatible with the demands of industrial society. At the same time, through the process of 'structural differentiation' the family sheds some of the functions and becomes a more specialised social unit concentrating mainly on socialising young children and providing a suitable social environment for the development and maintenance of stable, well-balanced adult personalities.

Sociologists interested in the family in more recent years have taken up various aspects of Parsons's account. In particular there have been several studies which have investigated the nature of any remaining extended family relationships. In America Litwak suggests, on the basis of evidence collected from 920 wives in the city of Buffalo, that it is possible for a modified form of the classical extended family to exist and operate in a modern industrial society. Although young married couples may move away from their parents geographically and socially, through an improved system of communications which the same industrial society provides, they are able to visit regularly and help in times of crisis or difficulty.

He also claims that the family has not completely lost its 'less essential' functions such as religious, political, economic and educational activities, but instead it tends to share them with other bureaucratic institutions. For example, children at school still need the support and encouragement of their family, and the selection of an occupation and the motivation to work can still be influenced to a large extent by an individual's family background. The development of specialised bureaucratic institutions which now perform some functions formerly associated with the extended family does not necessarily imply that these bureaucratic institutions enjoy a monopoly of those activities. The range of activities and functions which family groups can and do perform in modern industrial society is still very wide.

In Britain, the studies by Young and Willmott (*Family and Kinship in East London*) and Rosser and Harris (*The Family and Social Change*) are probably among the best-known and most quoted works which demonstrate the influence of Parsons on the study of the family.

As a result of their investigatins in East London Young and Willmott concluded that extended family relationships have not totally disappeared in modern British society. At least in this particular working class area of Bethnal Green there was still a strong tie between mothers and married daughters. The two frequently saw each other and gave each other emotional and domestic support. In many cases the tie was found to be sufficiently strong to discourage young married couples from moving out of the area, and thus had the effect of keeping alive some measure of extended family relationships.

Rosser and Harris explicitly regarded their research as a follow-up to the Bethnal Green study. For them it was another attempt to test the hypothesis of sociologists like Parsons, who had been suggesting that the disruption of the extended family and the development of the segregated nuclear family is increasingly likely to come about in Western societies because the extended family system is in fundamental conflict with a modern industrial economy. The evidence they collected from a survey of families in Swansea suggested that although young married couples may move away from the immediate vicinity of their parents' homes, they still maintain fairly regular contacts by weekend visiting and telephoning. Instead of disappearing, the extended kinship group has been modified by wider social changes and become a looser or more adaptable structure.

As a development of their earlier work, Young and Willmott in *The Symmetrical Family* have attempted to produce a more general survey of changes in the structure and functions of the family. They suggest that it is possible to see the family in our society as developing through four main stages or types differentiated by their changing functions and role relationships.

Stage 1 has a type of family found in pre-industrial times. The stage 2 family came about with industrialisation. This type began to decline in the early years of this century, but still persists in some areas. It was the kind of family represented in the earlier study of Bethnal Green. Currently in our society the stage 3 family predominates, that is, the Symmetrical family. This type is a nuclear family which is home-centred, and the marital partners, albeit in their differing conjugal roles, contribute equally to the maintenance of the home.

The stage 4 type of family is yet to come, but according to Young and Willmott there are signs that it is appearing in the upper areas of the stratification system, more particularly among managing directors. These families are more asymmetrical in their involvement in the home. The husbands are more interested in their work rather than the home; wives look after the children. The authors predict that as changes in technology generate more interesting jobs, taking away the routine elements, people will become more work-centred and through a process of diffusion downwards through the stratification system this form of family in which one partner becomes more interested in work and the other more interested in the home will become more widespread.

Studies of this kind illustrate the ways in which several of the major features of the consensus or functionalist perspective in sociology are embedded in research orientations. In these studies the family is assumed to be an institution, that is, a particular arrangement of social roles, which performs functions for the wider society in which it exists. At the same time, it is assumed that the family is related in ways to the other institutions which together with the family comprise the social structure of society. As changes occur in one element, adaptive changes occur in others, in this case in the family. Assumptions of this kind imply a particular model of society: a model which sees society as an integrated unit or system.

The concept of a social system has also been applied to the family in its own right. Using the Parsonian framework of functional imperatives, Bell and Vogel have suggested that the functional problems facing the family are analogous to those facing a society as a whole, in fact to those facing any social system. They change the terminology a little, although the concepts they use refer to the same general functional problems. Their equivalent to adaptation is 'task performance', their equivalent to goal attainment is 'family leadership' and they keep the terms 'integration' and 'pattern maintenance' for the other two problems.

The family has to fulfil certain tasks which involve it having contacts with external systems. For example, the provision of the necessary economic resources usually requires a member of the family to work, requiring involvement with the social or physical environment in which the family is located. Even within the strict boundaries of the family certain productive and servicing tasks have to be fulfilled such as cooking and maintaining the family's equipment and possessions. Technical childcare problems such as providing food and clothing are also examples of tasks the family has to manage.

The family also has to provide some means of selecting and

attaining the family goals; Bell and Vogel refer to this requirement as the problem of family leadership. It is usual for parents to be allocated this leadership role, but there can be variations depending on the particular activities and goals involved. Some problems, such as deciding on family size, deciding on the life plans for the children and organising family holidays, can involve several or all members of a family; and different members may be called on to provide the leadership in each case.

To the concept of integration the authors link that of solidarity and point to the functions of family rituals and family celebrations with regard to this functional problem. The coming together of families at meal-times, family holidays, weddings, funerals and the like are examples of social activities which can reinforce the solidarity of the family and help to integrate its various members.

Pattern maintenance refers to the problem of maintaining the family value system, and socialisation is the process which achieves it. The standards and general notions about what are good or bad activities and goals constitute the family value system. The values a family recognises provide principles for organising a heirarchy of goals and the basis for acceptable rules for attaining them. Although it is possible for children and their parents to have different values, there must be some agreement on certain basic values for the regulation of family activities; if there is not such agreement the family is likely to disintegrate. More generally, if the internal social structure of the family cannot cope with all of these four functional problems it will not be able to maintain its existence as a separate social group.

CONCLUSION

In this chapter we have been illustrating the view that how a sociologist approaches the study of social life will depend on the theoretical and conceptual assumptions he makes about society and social behaviour. We have suggested that one variety of structuralism may be called the consensus perspective because it is based on the assumptions that: (*a*) consensus on basic values is the main feature which holds a society together and keeps it orderly; and (*b*) a society can be viewed as an integrated system of interdependent parts. We have also suggested that this perspective produces explanations of particular processes or structural arrangements found in society in terms of the functions they fulfil for the maintenance of the total society, or any particular sub-system within it.

From this perspective, societies are viewed as integrated wholes which structure and coerce the persons within them. New members have to be moulded into the cultural expectations, the norms and roles, which the society requires for its persistence. The concepts of consensus, equilibrium, system, functions, functional prerequisites, interdependence, solidarity and integration form the core of this perspective and guide the form of inquiry by suggesting particular problems and offering particular answers. These answers may be described as functionalist or consensus theories.

We have traced the development of this perspective from the very first sociologists to present-day practitioners of the approach and have illustrated the ways in which they tend to approach the study of such substantive areas as the family, religion, social stratification, socialisation, deviance and social change. What we have presented here is in many respects an oversimplified account, in which we can see that even within this one broad perspective there are numerous variations which emphasise some particular aspects more than others. Since the days of Durkheim and Spencer, many modifications and elaborations have been made by such sociologists as Talcott Parsons, Robert Merton, Alvin Gouldner, Wilbert Moore, Marion Levy, William Goode and Kingsley Davis, among others. To date, the most sophisticated attempt to elaborate this perspective as a general sociological approach has been the work of Talcott Parsons. He has extensively used the concept of system, applying it not only to the structure of societies and particular elements within them, but to personality and culture as well. He suggests that societies, as systems of interaction, are made up of a complex interrelationship of all of these systems. He has set out in detail the characteristics of the structure and process of the social system, arguing that the concept is applicable to all possible societies. His work demonstrates at its fullest development the logic of functionalist thinking. As we have seen, it has stimulated both criticism and actual empirical research projects.

The perspective is widely used in sociology, although not always explicitly, and sometimes without acknowledgement that other perspectives exist or could be equally valid. We hope that when the reader comes across a sociological study which uses this approach, whether explicitly or not, he or she will be able to recognise it and pick out the particular emphasis or modifications which the authors may be using from the basic model which has emerged in this chapter.

FURTHER READING

Thompson, K., and **Tunstall, J.** (eds), *Sociological Perspectives: Selected Readings* (Penguin, 1971). For excerpts from Comte and Spencer.

Bierstedt, R., *Emile Durkheim* (Weidenfeld Goldback, 1969) Contains a summary of Durkheim's life and excerpts from Durkheim's major works.

Radcliffe-Brown, A. R., 'On the concept of function in social science' (Bobbs Merrill Reprint S.227).

Anderson, M., *Sociology of the Family: Selected Readings* (Penguin, 1971). Includes Parsons's essay 'The family in urban-industrial America', giving Parsons's structural analysis of the changing functions of the family.

Halsey, A. H., Floud, J., and **Anderson, C. A.**, *Education, Economy and Society* (Collier Macmillan, 1961). Includes Parsons's essay on 'The school class as a social system: some of its functions in American society'.

Davis, K., and **Moore, W. E.,** 'Some principles of stratification', giving a 'consensus' view of stratification; and M. M. Tumin's reply contrasts it with a 'conflict' approach. Both bound together as Bobbs Merrill Reprint S.68.

Smelser, N., 'Mechanisms of change and adjustment to change' (Bobbs Merrill Reprint S.629), for a functionalist/consensus view of social change.

Becker, H. S. (ed.), *The Other Side: Perspectives on Deviance* (Free Press Paperback, Macmillan, 1974). For Erikson's 'Notes on the sociology of deviance'.

Morgan, D. H. J., *Social Theory and the Family* (Routledge & Kegan Paul, 1975). For an analysis of Parsons's influence on the study of the family.

Leslie, G. R., *The Family in Social Context*, 4th edn (Oxford University Press, 1979). Chapter 4 describes the family system in China.

QUESTIONS

1 What do you understand by the problem of order'?

2 What are the characteristics of the consensus approach to the 'problem of order'?

3 How did the following thinkers contribute to the development of the consensus approach: Comte, Spencer, Durkheim and Parsons?

4 What are the advantages and disadvantages of seeing society 'as an organism'?

5 Do you think Durkheim's functional analysis of religion has any relevance for the analysis of ritual behaviour in modern society?

6 Why do you think some anthropologists have considered the 'functionalist' approach so useful for their studies?

7 What do you understand by the concept 'functional prerequisites' of society? Do you think that the presence of these prerequisites for society can be scientifically proven?

8 What is meant by 'a society in a state of equilibrium'?
9 Outline a possible functional analysis of some institution in society other than education.
10 Do you think Merton's attempt to clarify functional analysis succeeds in making the approach more scientific?
11 How can both deviant behaviour and social stratification be seen as positively functional for society?
12 In your view what are the positive benefits of using a consensus sociological approach to studying the social world?
13 What are the main characteristics of a functionalist approach to the family?

Chapter 3

Structuralism as a Perspective (II) Conflict

INTRODUCTION

'Conflict or consensus? In sociology there has been a tendency for theorists to take one side or the other, to see society as being better characterised and described primarily in terms of men's clashing interests or in terms of men's shared agreements. Generally, conflict theorists regard themselves as radical critics of existing society and view consensus theorists as appeasers of the existing system, the *status quo*. On the other hand, consensus theorists dismiss conflict approaches as merely political – an attempt to argue for a new society in terms of a set of values which masquerade as 'science'. Both groups of theorists tend to see their own approach as more accurately describing the way society works. In this chapter we will try to show that these two approaches are not diametrically opposed, but have much in common. Yet they differ sufficiently to enable us to distinguish two distinct sociological perspectives.

CONFLICT AS A PERSPECTIVE: THE CONTRIBUTION OF KARL MARX

Although Karl Marx died more than eighty years ago, his work is very much alive today and in fact constitutes the main body of conceptual and theoretical work within conflict theory. As anyone living in the twentieth century knows, his thought has had immense influence in shaping practical policies; Marxism is a living, powerful and practical body of thought and doctrine which shapes the destiny of millions of men and women. A substantial part of this body of thought provides sociologists with a systematic and rigorous way of analysing society and forms the core of the conflict perspective. We will, therefore, devote most of this chapter to Marx's sociological work as a 'conflict theorist' and then show how his work continues to give theoretical direction and significance to the work of later sociologists. To do so properly, we need to provide some detailed background of nineteenth-century capitalism as an essential back-cloth for understanding Marx's theories and concepts.

A SOCIOLOGICAL DESCRIPTION OF NINETEENTH-CENTURY CAPITALIST SOCIETY

By 1850 the social systems of European countries were changing and none at a faster rate than Britain which became the first industrial capitalist society in the world. We look at this society, largely using the basic approach for describing a whole society outlined in Chapter 2. A more detailed colouring of the description can be found in the *Condition of the Working Classes in England* written in 1848 by Marx's close collaborator, Friedrich Engels.

ECONOMY

Despite a trebling of population between 1750 and 1850, the proportion of workers employed in agriculture was dropping rapidly. The 'surplus', non-agricultural population was fed by means of a big increase in the productivity of land due to improved (though as yet non-mechanical) agriculture techniques and, by 1800, an increase in food imports. Industrial employment was provided by an expansion of domestic or cottage industry where rural workers used handicraft skills in their own homes to produce simple goods like woollen cloth and iron nails. Limitations and bottle-necks in the supply of various simple commodities such as spun cloth stimulated the introduction of new industrial technology which outstripped the confines of cottages as soon as artificial power was required to drive the machinery. At first the new machinery, being driven by water power, was located in rural areas where downward-running water could be obtained. Once steam power was introduced, then industry could move to the towns, resulting in a massive increase in their physical size and the number of people living there. The now familiar phenomenon of industrial urbanisation was clearly visible in Britain in the mid-nineteenth century.

These trends naturally brought about changes in the occupational structure of British society. Traditional work opportunities both on the land and in cottage industry declined rapidly in scale and importance. The work in the new town factories was largely 'semi-skilled' and could be done by the women and children who comprised the bulk of the workforce. New skills and trades were also developing (for example, machine-making, fitting) and some existing industries were quickly expanding (such as coal-mining).

The nature and sources of wealth were transformed by industrialisation. Land was being replaced as the major source of wealth by industrial capital, that is, factory buildings and the expensive machines that they contained. Industrial capital could yield larger returns (profits) because land and farm rentals were difficult to alter and depended on the vagaries of weather and crop production.

POLITY

The rapid growth of industrial capital made its owners, the new industrial capitalists, major contenders for political power in Britain. They had to dispossess the traditional power-holders, the landed aristocracy and the rich merchant capitalists, who made their money through farming, trade and banking rather than from the direct control of industrial production. Then the industrial capitalists could ensure that government policies and laws concerning prices, taxation, employment, imports and exports, and new industries did not interfere with their interests. There is no question that they matched their economic dominance with impressive political achievements. Examples are: the dismantling of traditional controls concerned with fair prices and the employment of apprentices; the 1832 extension of the franchise to include only well-off property holders; the persistent checking, harassment and stunting of the trade union movement through Parliament and the courts and the use of the agreed forces; the unwillingness to yield ground on the employment of women and young children, and on working conditions, in particular the length of the working day; the success of shifting the increasing costs of government on to the shoulders of the poor by using mainly indirect taxes levied on basic commodities, rather than direct taxes related to incomes. In fact, the success of the industrial capitalists in shaping the social system to conform to their interests is epitomised by the social, economic and philosophical ideology which served to legitimate and to justify their power position and which came to be known as 'laissez-faire'.

'Laissez-faire' has its intellectual roots in the economic writing of Adam Smith. In his *Wealth of Nations*, Smith argued that the best way to maximise individual wealth and happiness was for governments to abstain from intervening in economic affairs and to let individuals 'get on with it'. The 'laws' of supply and demand would ensure that poor judgement was met with bankruptcy, good judgement by fat profits. The public would not suffer high prices for very long because fat profits attract new firms into an industry, the supply of the commodity produced by that industry would increase and prices (and profits) would revert to a reasonable level. On the face of it, leaving economic affairs in the hands of countless individuals would seem to invite anarchy. On the contrary, Smith argued that the market mechanisms of supply and demand, if not messed about by government controls, would ensure that economic affairs were conducted in an orderly manner which ensured that the nation's wealth increased at a rapid rate. In his view, it seemed that 'an invisible hand' guided the destinies of men. Thus free enterprise, competition, the economic freedom of the individual and the profit rate as *the* criterion of economic success and efficiency were all extolled both to the detriment of more traditional forms of collective enterprise and also the government's traditional duty of securing economic justice in the form of a minimum wage or of fair price policies. By 1850 the British polity had fully absorbed laissez-faire doctrines: the government was reduced to two functions, foreign policy and the internal policing of society.

The agencies of the polity – Parliament, the courts, the judiciary and the local magistrates, the armed forces and the unreformed civil service – were in no sense bodies representative of the whole population. Members of Parliament, judges, justices of the peace, army officers and influential civil servants were recruited from the prosperous and propertied sections of society. The rare recruit coming from the propertyless masses, the great numerical majority of population, had to identify with the interests of the dominant minority to achieve social mobility and success.

KINSHIP

Urbanisation had profound repercussions on the pattern of family relationships that make up the institution of kinship. Clearly, the move to the towns to find work in the new factories necessitated the abandonment of a rurally based life-style where agricultural work and pursuits were intermingled to varying degrees with cottage-based industrial work. Most town families ceased to be economic units of production, no longer being able to produce goods like woollen cloth for the market or to grow foodstuffs for themselves. Instead they became solely units of consumption whose purchasing power was earned by selling their labour mainly in the new factories. Such employment tended to disrupt and to disorganise stable family life because women and children, being paid much lower wages, tended to be preferred to adult males by the industrial capitalists. For the capitalists were constantly trying to cut costs, especially labour costs, in an effort to bring down prices, beat their competitors and capture the market for their goods. With a working day of about sixteen hours, with the women and children in a family working in one factory and the adult males working (or looking for work) elsewhere, the home came to be no more than a dormitory for six days in the week. And as the home tended to be jerry-built, overcrowded, ill-lit with atrocious sanitation and other 'amenities', most workers in their sparse leisure time tried to seek entertainment and diversion elsewhere.

Thus families tended to be less secure economically. They were now entirely dependent on the vagaries of the employment market for work and income and could no longer fall back to some extent on the produce of their own land or gardens. Moreover, they no longer had the support of neighbours and 'extended kinfolk' such as uncles, cousins and grandparents. And the local community might well have been underpinned by the local church and local large land-owner or 'squire' taking some responsibility for local welfare. Conditions in towns in the first half of the nineteenth century militated against the development of new-style local town commodities.

Families were also insecure in their internal relationships. The traditional division of labour and allocation of responsibilities within families which shaped the nature and content of husband–wife, parents–children and child–child role relationships were obviously disrupted by the small time spent together as a family unit, by the husband's loss of the role of chief bread-winner, by the wife's need to return to work as soon after childbirth as possible. Given the long hours of work, the geographical separation of home and work, the ever-present threat of unemployment, the world of work, the economy, dominated the family life of the factory workers to an unprecedented extent.

VALUES

Values are concerned with standards of acceptable and unacceptable behaviour, notions of right and wrong conduct and, therefore, ways of seeking to justify or to legitimate behaviour. Different societies can be compared and contrasted in terms of the distinctive variety and range of values which are incorporated in bodies of religious, philosophical, political and other systems of thought. These values help to shape the workings of such major institutions of society as the economy, the polity and the family. In saying this, we are not necessarily agreeing with the consensus theorists that the regularities and uniformities and orderliness of social life stem from the agreement of all members of society on a basic set of shared values (that is, a 'Common Value System'). We are simply saying that values do play a part in shaping the actions of members of society in that they may be used as a resource for explaining, justifying and even motivating action. Consequently, it is important to be aware of the nature and range of values which are available to provide such a resource in a given society.

In nineteenth-century capitalist society the structural changes in the economic, kinship and political institutions of society outlined above were paralleled by equally far-reaching and significant changes in values. Whereas in pre-capitalist societies social action was largely justified and conducted within a framework of tradition, in the new capitalistic British society notions of rationality, of rational action, were becoming more and more influential and pervasive in the social structure. A good reason for engaging in social actions like, for example, obeying the political authorities, or cultivating the fields in a certain manner, or bringing up the children in a certain way, could not longer be accepted, taken for granted and justified on the grounds of tradition, that is, it had always been done like this. Instead, rationality involves a search for reasons and criteria to demonstrate that of all the alternative ways of doing anything, the 'best' way or means has been chosen. Thus, the relative stability of traditional thinking was replaced by rational thinking – the perpetual quest for the best means to achieve a given end of goal – thereby tending to open up social life to more scrutiny and questioning than hitherto. Traditional practices could no longer serve as a bulwark against the rapid change that can result from an unchecked appeal to reason, an unceasing search for criteria, for good, clear and logical grounds for action. Consequently, there was a growing opening up of goals and standards as well as of means.

In Britain, indeed throughout Western Europe, standards of value and goals of action were in process of being reshaped. Men's views of society and the natural world were changing. Men could no longer view themselves in a time-honoured order where, for example, social position, occupation and authority were 'given' and the range of possible changes in them were limited for all but a tiny handful of people. By 1850 men had witnessed drastic changes in the social position of individuals and in the real possibilities of widespread and sweeping changes in the very structure of society. Underlying these changes was the growing conviction that men could understand and, ultimately, master the forces that shaped both the natural world and society. Coupled with this faith in reason was the growing stress on individuality, the importance of the individual in society.

These beliefs had to come from somewhere; they were closely routed in recent experiences. Thus, economically and technologically, men were mastering the inimical and unpredictable forces of nature and, as we outlined above, major changes in the economy were taking place. Such changes did not consist only of massive increases in total production and in the reorganisation of the labour force, but also major shifts in values and attitudes.

In most societies there have been small groups of business men who have amassed fortunes by means of their 'capitalistic' enterprise. Once rich, such groups seldom persist in these enterprises. They prefer to switch to more traditional and more esteemed forms of wealth like landowning so that capitalistic notions seldom succeed in dominating the values of their society. The situation was very different for nineteenth-century capitalists, whose drive to make profits and economic gain was not simply a means in order to achieve other goals, but was a major, if not the major, goal in life. Success in business – measured precisely and rationally by the level of profits shown in the balance-sheet – dominated other goals and values in life. Moreover, the life-long pursuit of economic success as an end in itself was not a goal confined to the industrial capitalists. Gradually, the value which they placed on rationality, calculability and efficiency pervaded the attitudes of much wider sections of the society. As we have indicated, these values were related and systematised into a powerful ideology known as 'laissez-faire'. Here, achievement, the twin value to success, was sanctified. And achievement essentially meant the success of an individual in carving out and creating a career, ideally by his own efforts, unaided by the traditional advantages of birth, favour, or patronage.

'Laissez-faire' was as much a political as an economic doctrine. It focused on the individual, rather than on groups like families, local communities and even the state as the basic unit of society. This focus, reflecting changes in men's thinking, was brought about not only by industrialisation, but also by the great political revolutions of the late eighteenth and early nineteenth centuries. Of these, by far the most significant was the French Revolution of 1789.

The French Revolution highlighted and confirmed several major shifts in the range and variety of considerations out of which the basic values and attitudes of individuals and groups in society can be created. By attacking and, for a time, dismantling hitherto 'unshakeable' and 'unchallengeable' social institutions, the revolutionaries clearly demonstrated the novel idea that men *could* remodel society; and, even more radical, they *should* remodel society. Thus time-honoured and venerable institutions such as property, the church and religion, the monarchy and its divine right to rule, the family, and even the names and basis for the days, months and years of the calendar were attacked, reshaped and even replaced in the perceived interests of the 'people', the masses. The needs and rights, note *rights*, of the individuals who together made up 'the people' represented new criteria for social action. To achieve these 'self-evident' rights to justice, to freedom and to equality of opportunity required the development and application of the reason and intelligence seen to be vested in every man. Such development could occur once the shackles of superstition and ignorance maliciously and self-interestedly imposed by the religious and political leaders of the state were cast off. Hence not only did new values like individualism, the rights to count for something and to be heard politically and socially, emerge, but so also did notions for implementing and securing these rights. For example, the use of reason was to be encouraged through the provision of educational opportunities; social and political justice was to be ensured through democratic political institutions like freely elected Parliaments answerable and responsible to the people.

Needless to say, these new values were not institutionalised, built into, the normal social practices and culture of French society or any society in Europe for some considerable time. The practical institutional changes made by the revolutionaries were short-lived. Their importance derives from helping to motivate and inspire individuals and groups in the many social and political struggles which characterise the rapidly changing social structures of all societies in Europe thoughout the nineteenth century. Indeed, these values provide a fulcrum for conflict throughout the world today. Never again could tradition serve as a sole and sufficient reason to halt change; never again could the rights of individuals, the demands of the masses, be anything other than a major consideration in the working of societies.

MARX'S ANALYSIS OF NINETEENTH-CENTURY CAPITALISM

METHODOLOGICAL ASSUMPTIONS

Marx would broadly agree with the preceding sociological description of early capitalism. His concerns, however, go beyond description: his basic aims are to develop a sound scientific explanation of the 'mechanism' of stability and change of society as an indispensable prelude to revolutionising the capitalist system. In order to arrive at his distinctive concepts, theories and explanations, Marx, like all thinkers in all disciplines and fields, had to make a number of assumptions about the nature of man and of the world. We can distinguish the following six important and overlapping assumptions which underpinned his conflict perspective in the social world.

(1) The world, including the social world, is better characterised by flux and change rather than by stability and the permanence of phenomena.

(2) In the social world, as in the world of nature, change is not random, but orderly in that uniformities and regularities can be observed and, therefore, scientific findings can be made about them.

(3) In the social world, the key to this pattern of change can be found in men's relationships in the economic order, the world of work. Subsistence, the need to make a living, must be achieved in all societies. How subsistence is achieved crucially affects the whole structure of any society.

(4) Society can be viewed as an interrelated system of parts with the economy very much shaping the other parts.

(5) Men within a society are shaped, in both attitudes and behaviour, by its social institutions. Marx believed that underlying all the various and different kinds of 'social men' which are produced by different types of the society – primitive, ancient, feudal, oriental and capitalist – is a basic and essential human nature. For Marx, man is essentially rational, intelligent and sensitive, but these qualities can be warped and diverted into their opposites if the social arrangements of a society are so badly designed as to allow some men to pursue their own

interests to the detriment of others. Very few men can escape their historical and social circumstances and study their own society with the detachment and dispassion required of science. Marx, however, considered himself to be such a man.

(6) Finally, Marx's basic philosophical view of the nature of man and his relationship with the natural world is generally called *historical materialism*. Historical materialism incorporates most of the preceding points, but will be restated here in view of its crucial importance to Marx's sociological work.

With historical materialism, Marx tries to create a philosophical viewpoint which can produce a compromise between two opposite philosophical views on the nature of reality: idealism and materialism. An extreme view of idealism is to suggest that the world exists in men's minds; the world can be changed by changed thinking. Materialism, again pushed to an extreme, suggests that the world 'out there', the world of material or physical objects, shapes the thoughts and ideas of men. Marx decries both of these approaches. Clearly, ideas do not work in a vacuum, ideas are not produced in a vacuum. For ideas to have any influence, they must have some bearing and relevance to the historical context in which they are generated. Thus da Vinci might have been 'ahead of his time' in the sixteenth century with his drawings of flying machines; in the sixteenth century, however, such ideas were socially and historically irrelevant. The time was not 'ripe' for such ideas to have any chance of acceptance, development and fulfilment; they were 'ivory tower doodlings'. Ideas are important to social life and behaviour; but not *any* ideas. No one can think the existence of current social practices into extinction. Neither can sheer thinking power bring new social institutions into being. Ideas must have a sufficient bearing on existing social reality *in that particular historical context* if they are to inspire and move enough people to take *action*. Only by taking action can ideas serve to transform social practices. In this way, Marx attacks idealism. As for materialism, he argues that the material world is not simply 'out there' in a timeless and unchanging fashion. It has been, is, and will be, continually shaped and reshaped by men *acting* on their ideas and perceptions and thereby changing it. The material world of today is very different from that of the Ancient Briton, for example.

Thus it is Marx's view, as a historical materialist, that, of course, men's ideas and men's consciousness shape the social and material world if: (*a*) men act on those ideas; and (*b*) they realise that the material features of a particular society in a particular historical period must set limits on the extent to which ideas, even when backed by social action, can significantly reshape the nature of society.

Marx's analysis of early capitalist society draws heavily on these methodological assumptions.

MARX'S ANALYSIS

In broad terms, Marx viewed capitalism as a social system which was basically characterised by:

(1)   the naked exploitation of many people by a few people;
(2)   contradictions, strains and tensions within the system. These contraditions are, in fact, created by the system;
(3)   given (1) and (2) above, the certainty of drastic and violent change of the system.

In expanding and illustrating these points, we will in effect be giving Marx's distinctive explanatory description of capitalism. We will then proceed to isolate and examine the key concepts used in the Marxian analysis of capitalism.

Naked Exploitation
With the development of industrialism, institutions which helped to bind individuals into their society – extended families, local communities, the church and, above all, traditional ways of life (culture) and traditional values – were weakened. For Marx, their inadequate substitute was the 'cash nexus'. Under capitalism the major link between man and man was an impersonal cash tie. Social worth was replaced by economic standing and performance; and man's relationship to the market became the predominant relationship in social life.

Most people had only one marketable asset, their labour power. In sheer scale, they constituted a new category of people in the emergent industrial society, the free labourers. Owning no other assets, they were free to find work on the labour market, or they were free to starve. A much smaller group in society was made up of industrial capitalists. They owned the means of production, the factories, machinery, land and raw materials, which provided increasingly the main means of employment for the bulk of the population, the free labourers. The capitalists had their freedoms: to employ or not to employ. If they exercised their right not to employ and therefore to lose profits, then the free labourers *had to* exercise their 'right, not to work but to starve'. Clearly, then, the industrial capitalists had economic power over their employees. Economic power was supplemented and reinforced by political power; the industrial capitalists successfully used their economic wealth and standing to ensure that their interests were looked after by Parliament and the courts. Attempts by employees to defend themselves by means of collective organisation were greatly impeded by hostile Acts of Parliament and court decisions.

A situation where one group, the capitalists, had great social and economic advantages which derived largely from the toil of another much larger group, the free labourers, which received low wages and was ever threatened by the dire prospect of unemployment, could reasonably be described as exploitative. And even nakedly exploitative in that the only relationship between the two groups was in terms of cash. So that the vast difference between the cash return, the profits, to the capitalist and the cash return, wages, to the free labourers was obvious to all concerned. But the capitalist did not regard himself as an exploiter. He regarded himself as a benefactor in supplying work. Naturally, he could not possibly employ all those who wanted work; his workforce must be limited by his total production which in turn was determined, in the last resort, by the demand for his goods, his market. And, again naturally, he was in business to make profits; and to make profits he had to try to beat his many competitors by reducing prices. With his existing machinery, the only way to cut prices was to reduce his costs: his payments for land, equipment and raw materials, and labour. As his biggest single recurring cost was for labour, he had little option other than to try to reduce wages, to reduce the size of his labour force. He wanted as much work from as few workers for as little pay as possible. That was the system and no matter how developed his charitable and humanitarian impulses, he had to work it in this manner in order to survive.

Thus, Marx argues, exploitation was not due to the 'evil nature' of some men. Rather, it was a structural requirement of the whole social system. In a capitalist economy comprising many small, highly competitive businesses, capitalists had to screw down wages and depress working conditions in order to make the profits that ensured the maintenance of their social and economic position. Likewise in their economic calculations, capitalists had to regard their fellow human beings, their workers, as 'labour', as one of the three factors of production, as a commodity to be bought or not bought according to price (wage). Hence, the capitalist social system

'structured' a new major bond between men: a depersonalised, calculating cash relationship, unmitigated by welfare or other more
humane considerations. Moreover, this relationship reflected and
characterised a social system which generated the grossest, large-
scale inequalities yet seen in the course of human development.
Capitalism was a society rooted in naked exploitation of the many by
the few.

The Contradictions of Capitalism
Marx argued that the structure of the capitalist system generated
conflicts, troubles and tensions. In his term, the structure produced
'contradictions', which could only be resolved by dismantling the
system and reconstructing a new one.

For example, the capitalists were 'structured' by the system into
'cutting their own throats'. Their very existence as successful
capitalists demanded that they made profits. In a highly competitive
business world, they were perpetually trying to cut costs and thereby
lower prices in an attempt to undercut their competitors. Now,
clearly, if a single capitalist, or a few capitalists, could lower costs by
cutting wages while the majority of capitalists had to continue the
old, higher, uncut wage, then the wage-cutting capitalist minority
would successfully capture the market because they could now sell
cheaper goods. But no minority of capitalists could for long get
away with this manoeuvre. Very shortly, all capitalists would have
to reduce wages or be bankrupted. In this sense, their social actions
are determined by the system. Yet the process does not stop at this
point. For by cutting the *general level of wages,* that is, the total
amount of money paid out in wages, the capitalists are producing the
unintended consequence of cutting total purchasing power in the
economy. As their market, the demand for their goods, is made up
of the spending of the bulk of people in society, the free labourers,
whose wage comes from working in the capitalists' factories, then
clearly, sales and profits must drop. In order to try to regain higher
sales and profits, capitalists would then introduce a further round of
price-cutting by way of wage reductions. The result of such actions
was recurrent economic crises in the form of a constant succession of
booms and slumps which came to be called the 'trade cycle'.

The capitalist system, therefore, itself produced the tensions and
conflicts which threatened to tear it apart; conflict with wage-
workers over pay and conditions; violent competition between capitalists; and the alternation of euphoria and despair brought about by
the trade cycle. Further, Marx argues, these tensions would

intensify, given four major trends which he observed in capitalist society. These trends were:

Polarisation. Increasingly, industrialisation was undermining and even eradicating traditional skills, occupations and distinctions. Independent and self-employed people of all kinds – crofters, small landholders, master craftsmen and skilled artisans – were left stranded without land, usable skills, or marketable cheap goods as indistrialisation transformed the economy. There was, therefore, a tendency for the working population to be 'polarised' into two 'armed camps': the capitalists and the free labourers.

Homogenisation. As part and parcel of polarisation, individuals within each of the two main industrial categories, capitalists and free labourers, were becoming more alike or 'homogeneous', in several crucial respects. Within the category of capitalists, cut-throat competition tended to eliminate with time the 'small-fry', whereas the successful capitalists tended to expand their businesses. Thus the typical capitalist tended to become the owner of a growing and more complex business firm. He became wealthier. The free labourers, on the other hand, became more homogeneous in terms of their increasing dependence on the need to acquire the new skills dictated by the rapidly changing machinery in factories, rather than on their old reliance on traditional crafts and skills. The workers were also, of course, homogeneous in respect of their dependence on the capitalists' factories for work and subsistence.

Pauperisation. In their incessant drive for greater and greater profits, the capitalists tended to drive wages down to a minimal level – the bare level required for the workers' subsistence. This tendency was especially apparent in time of slump, but even in boom times the still large number of unemployed checked the rise in the level of wages even though the capitalists' demand for labour increased. Thus, over time, slumps became more protracted, booms shorter, as the capitalists discovered that, despite cutting wage costs, the rate of profits tended to fall. Thereupon they tried to cut wages even further, effectively cutting total purchasing power and therefore sales in their own market and the profit rate dropped again. The 'floor' to this process of wage-cutting must be the level of wages required to keep the free labourers minimally fit enough to turn up for work and to rear children. A subsistence level of wages was required to ensure the existence of the future supply of workers. In this manner, the wage-workers are made into 'paupers', that is, they are 'pauperised'.

Monopolisation. An aspect of the homogenisation of the capitalist business was the process of 'monopolisation'. As the smaller, independent concerns disappeared, forced out by the fierce competition, those remaining became larger units of production. The larger they grew the more they benefited from economies of scale, for example, buying materials in larger quantities and thereby getting them cheaper. Their resultant cheaper products enabled them to corner increased proportions of the market. In extreme cases, the sole producer of a particular commodity could exercise complete control over the supply of that product and over the employment of the relevant section of the labour force. The monopolist no longer had to compete. Thus competition, a driving force for efficiency in a capitalist economy, was no longer relevant to him.

These four trends are clearly interconnected and complementary. Many of their constituent features, for example, the obsolescence of traditional skills, the growth of machine-dictated work and skills, are inescapable features of any industrialising society as we can see from the experiences of modern 'underdeveloped' countries. But the misery and exploitation caused by low wages, (or even no wages for unemployed workers) are, for Marx, characteristics of capitalist society and are not inevitable conditions of industrialism. These characteristics are generated by the way capitalism is organised as a social system.

Another major contradiction Marx saw in the capitalist social system was a contradiction between 'objective reality' and men's 'social consciousness'. For Marx, 'objective reality', the 'facts' about capitalism, would include: the technological potential to meet basic human needs; the uneven distribution of goods with the relatively few capitalists receiving a hugely disproportionate share; the way this share-out is justified on the grounds that each person's income reflects his effort and his value to the economy, so that the 'enterprise' of the capitalist is and should be better rewarded than the labour of the worker because 'enterprise' is a scarcer commodity than labour in the economy; and, finally, the fact that the capitalists have effective political control of society.

Marx saw this contradiction between 'objective reality' and 'social consciousness' stemming from the way men in capitalist society, capitalist *and* worker alike, regard these facts about the social system and, indeed, the system itself as 'natural'. They are seen as 'natural', 'God-given' and hence inviolable 'facts of life' and are therefore taken as inevitable conditions of existence. Although workers may despair about low wages and terrible conditions and although some capitalists may genuinely wish to be more humane, neither social category can escape the thinking of the times. They can perceive their social world only through the distorting prism of the monetary system; goods can only be distributed if there is money to pay for them; workers can only be employed if there is a market for the goods they produce; businesses can be organised and run only if there are profits to be gained; slumps are caused by the impersonal and 'natural' and 'inevitable' mechanism of market forces (demand and supply) and are therefore outside the control of men. Instead of men using ideas and social inventions like money as tools or means to control their world, they themselves become the tools which serve to operate an impersonal system of their own invention! Such impersonal forces as the price mechanism, the market mechanism, demand and supply, the rate of profits, the general level of wages, are 'out there', above and beyond the control of men. Yet these 'impersonal forces' are nothing more than a codification or systematic summary of the ideas and actions of men in society. In this way, man can be seen to be controlled by outside, impersonal forces, that is, to be 'alienated' from his own social world.

Violent Change of the System – the Revolution

Marx argued that the capitalist system of society was doomed. The contradictions within the social system would itensify, bringing about ever-worsening crises in home and foreign markets and, hence, in most people's domestic and economic situations. This disintegration of capitalism, as polarisation, homogenisation, pauperisation and monopolisation intensified, would effectively open the way for the establishment of a new and alternative type of social system. A new system, however, would not *automatically* be generated out of the chaos of the old system. In stating that 'man makes his own history', Marx was clear that just as men created the capitalist system, so men would have to create a new order of society.

First, someone had to understand clearly and scientifically how the capitalist social system worked. Only on such a basis of understanding could a new system be constructed; a new system which would avoid building in the errors of the old system. Marx claimed to have achieved this understanding and to have diagnosed the fundamental basis for change, not only for capitalism but for other types of social system: *the private ownership of the means of production*. Marx argued that, throughout history, the basic character of a society was shaped by its economic institutions. The most important of these institutions was private property.

By private property Marx meant, of course, property or ownership of the means of production in a society; property which was crucial and directly related to the production and exchange of goods and services in a society. Regardless of whether this property was in the form of the slaves of antiquity (early Greek and Roman societies), or in the form of the serf-plus-land package of feudal society, or, as in the case of his major interest, capitalism, in the form of industrial capital (machinery, factories, and so on), the very ownership of such property necessarily created potentially far-reaching divisions within the social structure. By means of painstaking and voluminous studies, Marx claimed to show how the private ownership of the means of production vitally influenced the entire structure of a society.

He argued, however, that it was not enough merely to provide people with this analysis. What they also needed if they were to bring about an alternative society was the conviction that the alternative would be a *better* society. Part of this conviction would derive from the intellectual understanding of how society worked and how men produced unintended evils like the trade cycle which was universally deplored, but widely accepted as 'unavoidable'. Part, however, would also derive from developing new ideas, new values, which would underpin the sometimes new, sometimes restyled institutions of an alternative type of society. In fact, a new *ideology*, a 'counter-ideology', would have to be developed. For Marx, an ideology is simply a set of related ideas and values which reflect the interests of a group. The contents of a *counter*-ideology, therefore, would be ideas and values reflecting the interests of the workers; it would provide them with a blueprint for change. It would provide a set of standards for evaluating current social, political and economic events and for assessing whether or not these events assist or impede the development of the new society.

Even so, an analysis of the working of existing society and a blueprint for changing it are still not enough to bring about revolutionary social change. Not only must people know what to fight and what to fight for, they must also fight. By this, Marx emphasised·that men must act if they are to determine their own future society. Marx argued that the exploited non-owners of the means of production can only·develop consciousness of the counter-ideology which is suggested by his writings and supported by their bad experiences in capitalist society if they actively oppose the system. They should do so by organising themselves industrially into trade unions and politically by developing a political party which will further their interests. Only through struggle will the new consciousness develop and the old, false consciousness be eradicated. The old consciousness is false because it reflects the interests of the privileged groups and not the interests of the bulk of the people. 'True' consciousness for the bulk of the people can only come about when they develop an ideology (a *counter*-ideology in contrast to the owners' ideology) which actually reflects *their* interests. The capitalist owners, who try to make out that their way of seeing the social world is the one, the only, true way of seeing it, can only be overthrown if 'true' consciousness develops among the bulk of the non-owning people.

MARX'S BASIC CONCEPTS AND THEORIES

In the previous section, we have drawn on a number of Marx's major assumptions, concepts and theories to give a descriptive account of how he viewed and analysed nineteenth-century capitalist society. We are now in a position to be able to isolate and to analyse these concepts and theories in a more rigorous and systematic manner.

SOCIAL CLASS

Marx wanted to discover the principles of change for society. He was not interested merely in describing the stratification system of a society in order, for example, to show exactly how many layers or strata there were in society, to show which of them had high or low prestige, and to show what kinds of prestige they enjoyed. Thus he never produced a theory of stratification. Instead, he examined society for those key groups which either appeared to have a strong interest in maintaining the existing social system or which had a strong interest in trying to change it. Such groups are the social classes.

Members of a social class may be distinguished by two sets of criteria:

'Objective' Criteria

People may be seen to comprise a social class if they have one attribute in common: namely, if they share the same relationship to the means of production. Marx claimed that feudal serfs, for example, can be seen to form a social class in that all serfs share the same relationship to property. The rights and obligations they have in relation to the owners of the land and to the land itself are common to all serfs as holders of that position or role in the division of labour of society. Similarly, the owners of industrial capital may form a social class in that they are similar, as owners of industrial capital, in their basic social, legal and economic relationship to the non-owners of capital. In short, Marx suggests that the basis for social classes might be located in the different relationships of people to the means of production. Such relationships are crucial in determining the life-chances and the life-style of the individuals concerned.

'Subjective' Criteria

Marx suggested, however, that having a relationship in common, even this kind of relationship, is not of itself sufficient to be able to call a number of people a social class. To classify a number of people merely in terms of having some common attribute is to do no more than to create a *category*. There is an infinite number of such categories, for example all red-headed people, all people over six feet tall, and so on. Such attributes as red hair may be significant for the individuals concerned, but may be of no significance for the social structure. However, relationships to the means of production *do* have great social significance. And this significance becomes even greater if members of a category based on the relationship to the means of production become so *conscious* of this membership that they use it as a basis for organising social action. Thus, for Marx, a category may only be a 'latent' or potential class until it is transformed into an active social class by men's consciousness of the importance of that category, of that way of seeing or identifying themselves.

Marx summed up these distinctions by remarking that it was not enough for a class to be class *in* itself; it had also to be a class *for* itself. For example, Marx suggested that in history, serfs and peasants were usually not a social class, but only latently or potentially a social class. In terms of social action, they were no more than a 'category' of people. Occasionally, however, when times were especially bad, when the harvest failed or when rents suddenly soared, the widely scattered peasants would unite and form a short-lived avenging army, seeking to put right the injustices they felt. For a short time, such common action transformed a latent social class (in itself) into a viable social class (for itself). Men became conscious of the similarities of their *common* plight, became conscious of the *shared* identity, that is, 'peasant', and, in this way, transformed a statistical category into a meaningful and active social force, a 'social class'.

THEORY OF SOCIAL CHANGE

The concept 'social class' plays a vital part in Marx's theory of social change. He sees social class as the crucial mechanism for changing social systems. Although he is fully aware that, in any society, there is a large number of categories and groups, he suggests that for the purpose of understanding how the social structure changes in major ways, only two groups are of significance: a group having a strong interest in maintaining the existing system; and a group having a strong interest in changing it. Social change comes about through the struggle – political, legal, economic, possibly even military – between these two groups.

For example, Marx explains in fine detail how the downfall of feudal society came about through the struggle between the new rising group of industrial and mercantile town-dwellers and the traditionally powerful group of landed aristocrats. For their survival and development, the town-dwellers had to wrest power from the feudal lords in order to create better conditions for mercantile and industrial enterprise. Laws which tied men to the land and laws which made land unavailable for buying and selling had to be changed. Such laws had been created in the past by the feudal lords to suit their own particular interests. They were now an obstacle to the development of the new forms of wealth in the towns.

Marx develops this analysis with the aid of some additional inter-related concepts: the 'forces of production', the 'relations of production', the 'economic base' and the 'superstructure'. By 'forces of production', Marx is referring to the way the production of goods is done in a society; to the sorts of technological 'know-how' in operation, the types of equipment in use and the type of goods being produced. The forces of production shape the nature of the 'relations of production'. Here Marx is referring to the social relationships found in production, that is, the nature of the economic roles permitted by the state of development of the forces of production and, further, relationships that exist between these roles.

Together, the 'forces of production' and the 'relations of production' make up what Marx terms the 'economic base', sometimes called the 'substructure' or infrastructure of society. His theory is that changes in society stem from the economic base/substructure. The other parts of society, such as religious, familial and political institutions, are in effect shaped by the nature of the economic base. These other parts he calls the 'superstructure' of society. Figure 3.1 demonstrates in diagrammatic form how these concepts are related. Social change can be represented as starting at the bottom of the triangle and working upwards to the top of it. We will illustrate these concepts by continuing with our example about the downfall of feudal society.

In feudal society, the prevailing and major forces of production were concerned with agricultural production. Most people worked on the land, using primitive tools. The farmer-worker himself was the main instrument of production. In a situation where land was relatively plentiful and workers scarce, the main problem for land-owners was to secure and to maintain a sufficient supply of workers on their land. The relations of production in feudal society reflected the need of landowners for a secure supply of workers. These workers, known as serfs or villeins, were effectively tied to the land by a complex set of relationships with the landowners, the feudal lords. In a sense, the serfs were owned by the feudal lords in that they were not free to work elsewhere, even having to pay a forfeit or fine if a daughter married and moved to another lord's territory or manor. There was a 'fit' or congruence between the forces of pro-duction and the relations of production in feudal times. The sorts of

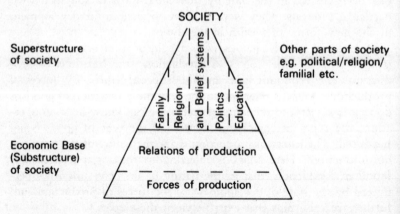

Figure 3.1 Marx's Model of Society

problems created by the state of technological know-how, the available tools and equipment and the way agricultural production was carried out generated a set of social relations which solved these problems, namely, the serf–lord relationships.

With the development of new forces of production in the towns, such as the growing industrial production by artisans and the growing monetary and exchange facilities, the old feudal relations of production limited the freedom to hire labour, the freedom for labour to be geographically mobile and the freedom for town-dwellers to buy and sell land. Thus there was a contradiction between the new forces of production and the old relations of production.

Changes in the social structure were not, however, automatically brought about by this contradiction. The town-dwellers had to perceive what and who were blocking the pursuit of their interests and they had to act concertedly and vigorously to do something about it.

Critics of Marx often accuse him of being an economic determinist, that is, of arguing that changes in social structure are basically brought about or determined by changes in the economic base. This accusation is true in as much as Marx is convinced that major changes in society must concern men's vital interests. Economic relations are paramount in that a person's relationship to the means of production can shape not only his consumption pattern, but also his life-style and the life-chances of both himself and of his children. Nevertheless, as Marx is only too fully aware, *men must take action* if changes in the relations of production are to occur.

This awareness of the need for men to take action is further demonstrated in Marx's application of his theory of social change to capitalism. Although the inherent contradictions of the capitalist system created ever-worsening crises and although the relationships sanctified by capitalistic deals concerning the individual's right to private property and his right to compete with others became increasingly irrelevant to the newly developing forces of production, Marx argued that these factors alone could not bring about social change. In order to bring about a new type of society, the bulk of the population, the free labourers, had to become aware of what was happening in their society. They had to see the common bonds, the common plight, which linked them in their common identity of 'free labourer'; they had to become an acting social group, a social class. The workers, organised as a class in and for itself, Marx called 'the proletariat'. By taking common, concerted action in the factories, in the streets and in the courts, by forming organisations like trade

unions and political parties, members of the proletariat could begin
to develop their own ideology and begin to work for a society which
could serve their interests. With capitalism, then, as with previous
historical types of societies and epochs, there was no inevitability of
social change for Marx.

As we can see, Marx's theory of social change is complex and
incorporates a number of further theories. We now turn to a brief
outline of the most important of them. Marx did not fully spell out
or explicate any of them himself because his major concern was to
describe and explain the workings of the capitalist system and to
show how it might be changed, rather than to tidy up all aspects of
his thinking for the future use of academic sociologists.

THEORY OF POWER AND THE STATE

Marx argued that power, the ability of some people to exert their
will over other people, derived from the economic base of society.
Thus in capitalist society, the owners of the means of production
(whom Marx called the bourgeoisie) clearly had industrial power;
they could determine what to produce, how much to produce,
whom to employ, how many to employ and where to employ them.
Equally clearly, their incomes could shape a distinctive life-style for
themselves and their families; they could purchase opportunities for
their children in business, in careers and in education. Furthermore,
Marx points out that an examination of laws passed, court decisions
made, arrests made, and so on, showed that the influence of the
bourgeoisie in the defence and extension of their interests was far-
reaching. He felt that if decisions in Parliament and the courts were
scrutinised in terms of the key question, 'In whose interests are these
decisions made?', the answer almost invariably would be, 'In the
interests of the bourgeoisie'. In this way, he argued that the state
could be seen as 'the executive committee of the bourgeoisie'. Time
after time, laws and their enforcement tended always to penalise the
proletariat in the interests of the bourgeoisie. Only after massive
struggles could the proletariat achieve any favourable decisions
which improved their lives under capitalism. Without constant
vigilance, concessions and improvements tended to be quietly
removed over time. The treatment of the proletariat in this manner
was not due to any massive conspiracy on the part of the
bourgeoisie. Rather, in pursuing their own interests and ideals and in
ensuring that people in key and official positions would do likewise,
the bourgeoisie were genuinely convinced that their way of thinking

about the world was right. To their minds, it was 'the only true way' of thinking about the world. Thus industrialists genuinely believed that industrial production was threatened and the country was in danger when the workers succeeded in reducing the working day to fourteen hours, and when eventually women and children were forbidden to go down the mines.

THEORY OF KNOWLEDGE

Marx believed that knowledge was historically and culturally relative. In every society, people believed that their knowledge, their perceptions of the world, their values, their standards of behaviour, their way of going on – all of which we can loosely term 'their culture' – represented 'the best' in some absolute sense. They failed to see how their culture was in fact shaped by their historical circumstances. For Marx, the culture was decisively shaped by the type of economy and the sort of prevailing relationships to the means of production, that is, by the economic base. The leading ideas in a society are those which the dominant group finds congenial and acceptable in terms of its basic economic interests. The dominant group, the owners of the means of production, are thus not only the rulers of the state, they also are the rulers or arbiters of approved and acceptable ideas and knowledge.

Here, Marx might be seen to be posing a dilemma for his own work. If ideas are relative, there being no absolute standard of truth, why should anyone listen to what he has to say? For how can anyone criticise with any conviction one ideology in terms of another? To these objections he might answer as follows. First, the ideas and standards of the bourgeoisie did not 'fit' reality in that the bourgeoisie could neither explain nor control the recurrent crises of capitalism. Second, Marx did believe that the truth could be discovered by means of scientific work. He believed that as his own work was scientific, then he produced 'true' findings. This point will be taken up further in Chapter 6 when we examine positivistic approaches to studying the social world.

THEORY OF ALIENATION

In treating alienation, Marx's key concept is 'fetishism'. By fetishism, he means to suggest that men somehow come to dissociate themselves from their own products, whether these be material things or ideas. Somehow these man-made things and ideas obtain a life of their own, become more important than their inventor, man, and end up by dominating him. These products of man's own creativity are treated as 'fetishes': they are treated as objects of mystery, objects which are outside of man's control. Such objects are thus set apart from man, they are *alien* to him and come to dominate him. Examples of such objects in the realm of ideas are the 'laws' of supply and demand which impersonally determine what should be produced, how many should be employed, and so on. Man fails to see that such laws are the products of his own thinking, thinking which is historically and culturally relative. Instead, they are regarded as 'the truth' – which is 'out there', permanent and inviolable. Similarly man sets apart from himself the machinery that he operates, the products that he makes.

In short, Marx argues that men are alienated from one another; they are alienated from their products, material and ideal; and they are also alienated from their society. The root cause of these forms of alienation is to be found in the way man's social relations are structured by a social system which is organised around the sanctity of the private ownership of the means of production. In capitalist society, such a system dehumanises man into a mere commodity, labour, which can impersonally be bought and sold on the labour market. In such a system, the alienating effect of the cash nexus extends beyond economic institutions to shape man's attitudes and behaviour in all of his social relationships. Though alienation exists in all societies which have private property of the means of production, Marx argued that only in capitalist society had it reached its fullest, most crippling development.

THEORY OF RELIGION

Marx's theory of religion is simply an illustration of his more general theory of alienation. He argues that in primitive societies man resorted to magical–cum–religious explanations to deal with phenomena which were beyond his understanding. With the development of the institution of private property of the means of production, these explanations gradually took the shape of justifications and legitimations of the rights of the dominant groups of privileged property-owners in a society. Religion as a way of thinking about the world was itself one of the alienating products of the social system. It was alienating in that both God and the scriptures were the products of man's own creative imagination. These products became divorced from man to become not only independent of his control, but also to exert control over man himself. Thus man looked for solace and guidance from a source seen as external to him and, in this way, failed to realise that he and he alone could shape his future and his society.

In Marx's view, religion served to siphon off potentially revolutionary thoughts and actions by focussing man's attentions on to the next world and by exhorting him to put up with the world for the sake of his immortal soul. Thus religious leaders promised a redress of this world's ills in the next world with such doctrines as 'the last shall come first' or 'it is easier for a rich man to get through the eye of a needle than to get into the Kingdom of Heaven'. In effect, these promises for the next world reversed the social order in this world. In this way religion presented a mirror-image of society.

For Marx, religion was 'the opiate of the people'. It distracted man's attention from the possibility of taking action to improve his social world by making false promises about a next world and by attempting to offer comfort and solace for the troubles in this world. He believed that scientific knowledge would dispel the mysteries of religion and expose it as the useful ideological tool of the dominant group or groups in society. Man had no need of religion and should realise he has only himself to rely upon.

MARX: CONCLUSION

It is Marx's great achievement to have synthesised all of these theories in his analysis of the capitalist social system. Though we may find the intellectual origins of most of his concepts and theories in the work of earlier thinkers, none of these thinkers was able to produce such a penetrating and wide-ranging body of work which could serve to sustain and stimulate later workers in the field of sociology. It is for this reason that so much space in this chapter on the conflict perspective has been devoted to Marx's sociological work.

We shall now turn to the work of later theorists in order to show how they have attempted to develop and to refine the concepts and theories provided by Marx as a systematic way of trying to understand the social world.

MAX WEBER

Max Weber (1864–1920) is in his own right a giant in the formation of sociological thinking. More than most great thinkers, his work straddles a number of sociological approaches. Here we focus simply on those aspects which seem to be particularly relevant to our discussion of conflict as a perspective. These aspects are:

(1) his attack on economic determinism, that is, an attack on the idea that major social change necessarily derives from the economic base;
(2) his refinements of the concepts of power and class.

ECONOMIC DETERMINISM AND THE PROTESTANT ETHIC

It has been said that Weber spent his life having a posthumous dialogue with the ghost of Karl Marx. Certainly in *The Protestant Ethic and the Spirit of Capitalism*, the first of a number of major works on the world religions, he attacks what many believe to be a major tenet of Marx's thinking: economic determinism. As we have seen, Marx's stress on the need for social action in order to produce change in society means that his position is more complex than that of a crude economic determinist. Nevertheless, many of his followers, the Marxists, adopted the straightforward position that only changes in the economic base can change society and Weber can thus be seen to be attacking this position of the Marxists, rather than Marx.

Weber's basic methodological position is that many factors must come together to produce social change. In *The Protestant Ethic* he declares that although he is investigating only 'one side of the causal chain' in the formation of capitalist society, other causes, including economic causes, are also very important.

Weber's basic problem is to explain why capitalism first developed in the West. His basic hypothesis is that a major cause of Western capitalism was the kind of religious ideas which developed in the West, but not elsewhere in the world.

In *The Protestant Ethic* he notes that capitalism developed first in Protestant countries. More specifically, it developed in countries where a particular variety of Protestantism, namely Calvinism, was strong. He argues that the sort of attitude to the world which was shaped by Calvinistic ideals provided individuals with the right sort of attitudes and motivations for bringing about a very major social change, the development of capitalist society. The sorts of attitudes individuals required to bring about a capitalist society were the very attitudes inculcated by Calvinistic religion.

Whereas most religions promote an other-worldly approach to life, stressing the importance of life in the next world, Calvinism, as a set of religious doctrines, made individuals focus their attention on life here-and-now. The basic reason was the doctrine of predestination. Calvinists agreed that God was all-powerful and all-knowing. He knew therefore who were the Elect, that is, those people who would be saved. Thus everyone's ultimate fate was predestined in the light of God's absolute knowledge. As this knowledge was in existence even before someone was born, there was nothing anyone could do in his lifetime to achieve salvation or to avert damnation; his fate was predestined. Unlike other forms of Christian religion, the individual could not achieve salvation by faith alone as in Lutheranism, or by doing good works and truly repenting his sins as in Roman Catholicism. Moreover, the individual was isolated, on his own; neither his family nor the organisation of a church could help him to achieve salvation. All a church could do was to bring like-minded people together. It could not forgive sins, wash the slate clean, or intercede on behalf of an individual.

In the seventeenth century, when the expectation of life was low, when death was an ever-present reality and when religion played a much larger part in people's awareness of the world, salvation was a very important concern. For the Calvinists, the doctrine of pre-destination might seem to make salvation a hopeless matter. They had no certain way of knowing if they were among the number of the Elect, because the Calvinists did not accept the authority or special powers of priests to know God's will. The Calvinists avoided the despair of hopelessness, however, by arguing that anyone whom God had elected would lead a pure and fruitful life. Thus they looked at individuals for signs of God's grace. If an individual prospered in his work, if he led a virtuous life, if he avoided temptations such as lavish expenditure, selfish adornment and aggrandisement, and if he practised his religion conscientiously, then it was very likely that he was one of the Elect. For why should God allow the unworthy to prosper? In this way, individuals could overcome the psychological uncertainty and insecurity, the spiritual isolation of the individual, induced by the doctrine of predestination.

Weber is arguing that a new set of religious ideals can transform people's daily behaviour, including their behaviour in the economic sphere. The religious ideals of Calvinism motivated individuals to apply to daily life and work a religious intensity. In effect, they became 'God's tool on earth' by working as hard as they possibly could at their work, instead of unproductively (in the economic sense) detaching themselves from the everyday world to pursue their religious interests. By trying to work harder, to produce more, to prove that they were favoured by God, they began to think in terms of the best means of doing their work and of ways of maximising their efficiency.

For them, traditional ways of doing things were less important than efficient ways. Thus, they began to think rationally rather than traditionally – all with a view to being efficient servants of God's will on earth. As they wished to avoid lavish 'irreligious' expenditure, they devoted more and more time to work, less and less to leisure. Their profits were ploughed back into their work, as it would be a sign of spiritual unworthiness to spend them on pleasures of the flesh. In these ways, they applied to daily work the fanaticism and asceticism which in other religions are usually focused on non-worldly affairs. Moreover, they made of their whole lives a sort of economic calculus: good, fruitful work must be done every day. Given the doctrine of predestination, they could not cease these efforts, for in such a case they could find themselves to be spiritually weak and hence, in all likelihood, damned by God.

The description of the religious view of the world produced by the doctrines of Calvanism is what Weber means by the 'Protestant ethic'. He compares it with a description of what he considers to be the essential features of the way capitalists think about the world, which he calls 'the spirit of capitalism'. He shows that both descriptions have much in common, especially the calculating, rational way of viewing the world in terms of maximising output by the best possible means. He suggests that there is an 'elective affinity', that is, a causal link, between them. In Chapter 6 we shall examine why Weber talks about an 'elective affinity' rather than a 'causal link'. He gives two basic sets of reasons for this link.

First, Weber suggests that a major social change, such as the rise of capitalism, requires a number of people who are tough enough to reject and to replace existing ways of thinking and behaving. The emergence of new technological know-how is not sufficient to ensure that it will be put into operation. Some groups of people must be motivated sufficiently to oppose existing vested interests in order to develop these new technological ideas. The Calvanists, with their fanatical attitude to work, with their disregard of anyone or anything which might distract them from their life's purpose – proving themselves to be members of God's chosen Elect – seem to Weber to be such a group.

Second, Weber seeks further support for his hypothesis by exploring the relationship between religious ideas and economic ideas and behaviour not only in the West, but in a number of historical cultures: India, China, Israel and Islam. In these cultures, he shows that in some major world civilisations, many of the 'ingredients' for the development of capitalism were present, for example, technological know-how, free labour and monetary institutions. Nowhere, however, was there also present a this-worldly religious ethic which also stressed that the way to individual salvation was by ceaseless work in everyday life.

Thus in his work on the world religions Weber attempts to show how religious ideas – the superstructure for Marx – can affect economic behaviour, Marx's economic base. This work has stimulated much controversy and argument not only among sociologists, but also historians, and provides a good example of how Marx's work has stimulated further thinking on these very complex issues.

POWER AND CLASS

Like Marx, Weber saw the social world in terms of groups and group interests. In the clash of competing groups, he too drew attention to the importance of power in determining which social groups would dominate over other groups. He did not agree, however, that power solely derived from economic relations, the relationship to private property of the means of production. For him, there were three dimentions to any analysis of power: class, status and party.

By class, Weber is referring to the economic order of society where man's 'market relationships' were of the utmost importance. By market relationships, he means no more than the relationship of individuals to property. Do they own property? If so what kinds? If not what is their bargaining position on the market for the goods and services they can offer? Clearly, this conception of class is very close to the 'objective' part of Marx's concept of class.

Weber also distinguishes two other dimensions of power: status and party. By 'status', he is talking about the way the organisation of society produces different amounts of prestige or social honour for different groups of individuals. Social honour is not achieved simply by the ownership of property or of a skill or attribute. Rather, it derives from a style of life practised by a group in a society. Status groups can be distinguished by their attempt to develop exclusive practices, for example, their own rituals, their attempt to control the marriages of their children to the right kind of people. For Weber, the caste system of India provides a good, extreme example of status groups. Status groups endeavour to maintain and to extend the privileges which distinguish them from other groups.

By 'party', Weber is referring to the way groups may organise themselves to achieve a goal or an objective. Parties may be trying to achieve positions, honours, or outright control of the social order. Clearly, parties may be formed on the basis of classes or status groups or some sort of mixture of both. Parties are found only in societies which are complex enough to have a clearly discernible 'staff' of power-holders who can be influenced or replaced.

Weber argues that these distinctions allow us to analyse the acquisition and retention of power in society in a sensitive manner. For example, we can see that classes organised in market terms are in some sense opposed to status groups which, in trying to preserve and extend their privileges, may act against the market principles of supply and demand.

For him, then, the struggle for power and the retention of power in a society are not simply a reflection of the 'economic base'. Although the class or material position of status groups greatly influences how they can operate in the world, perhaps as a party for the extension of their privileges, there is some independence of class, status and party actions. For example, in Classical China the highly educated scholars, the literati, were the dominant status group. Other groups, such as rich merchants, endeavoured to associate with the literati by encouraging their relatives to pass the necessary examinations, by selling up their trading interests in favour of the more respectable ownership of land and by trying to adopt the general life-style of the literati. Wealth alone did not guarantee the merchants either high social honour or the power to run the society. Care should be taken, however, not to separate out too sharply these aspects or deminsions of power, for we should note that most of the literati were recruited from wealthy landowning families. And, of course, the literati could and did use their power positions to secure more wealth for themselves and to increase opportunities for their children and families.

Control of the society, then, is likely to be wielded in the interests of class and status groups which are organised as a party for the purpose of influencing or running the machinery of the state. The aim of controlling groups is not merely to secure power, but also to establish their *right* to wield such power in the eyes of subordinate groups. In Weber's term they want to *legitimate* their power. If they can do so, if they 'legitimate' their 'power', then they achieve *authority* over subordinate groups. That is to say, they achieve the right to dominate them, where the right to dominate, and thus to have authority, is freely given to them by the subordinate groups. For Weber, there are three basic sources for legitimating power, that is, securing authority to dominate or govern. Authority can come from tradition, where ruling groups may rule because they have 'always done so'; from charisma, where leaders of ruling groups have the personal magnetism or charisma to induce people to follow them; or from rational means, where ruling groups secure power by using the legal and judicial machinery of the state. Once in power, ruling groups have to ensure that their legitimacy is maintained in the eyes of subordinate groups. They can do so partly through the control and dissemination of leading ideas (ideology); partly through the more open use of power by way of the state machinery of laws, courts, police, and so on.

In these ways, Weber has attempted to develop and refine Marx's basic concepts of class and power and also his conception of the relationship between 'base' and 'superstructure' in the explanation of social change. Clearly the core ideas and concepts of Marx continue to frame these modifications and refinements.

We can now turn to examples of the work of current sociologists who make a great deal of use of the intellectual apparatus provided by Marx.

RALF DAHRENDORF: THE NATURE OF CONFLICT IN 'POST-CAPITALIST' SOCIETY

Dahrendorf, in his book *Class and Class Conflict in Industrial Society,* examines the usefulness and applicability of Marx's sociological work to the study of modern industrial society. He argues that Marx's analysis of capitalist society was largely correct and his concepts and theories were valuable. However, these concepts and theories require to be modified if they are to be applied to *'modern industrial society'* because they refer too specifically to 'capitalist society'. There have been highly significant changes in the social structure since Marx's writing. In fact these changes have been great enough to produce a new type of society: 'modern industrial' or 'post-capitalist' society. Dahrendorf wishes to generate a body of concepts and theory which will be general enough to explain both capitalism *and* post-capitalist society. He endeavours to generate his new theory directly out of Marx's analysis, preserving, modifying and, occasionally, abandoning some concepts.

First Dahrendorf suggests that the following changes of the social structure have been sufficient to produce post-capitalist society:

The Decomposition of Capital

With the growth in the scale of business companies due to technological advance and to the development of the joint stock limited liability company, the link between the ownership and control of industry has weakened. Much control is now exerted by salaried managers who tend to legitimate their position in industry and in society rather differently to the old-style capitalist. Capitalists, too, play a somewhat different role as shareholders or as company directors.

The Decomposition of Labour

Like the controlling groups, the workers have become more differentiated. The proportions of both skilled and semi-skilled workers have grown and the proportion of unskilled workers has fallen. Far from becoming homogenised in terms of class consciousness, the workers are becoming increasingly aware of the differences between themselves.

The Development of a New Middle Class

This term is misleading in that it refers to a large and growing collection of different groups which have been created or expanded with the industrialisation of society. It is a category rather than a class in terms of Marx's use of this concept and is made up of 'white collar' workers such as teachers, accountants, surveyors, nurses and clerks.

The Growth of Social Mobility

There is much more intergenerational mobility between occupations, and self-recruitment (where the son follows his father's occupation) is great only in the very top and very lowest occupations.

The Growth of Equality

Over the last 100 years, social and economic inequalities have been reduced as the state has guaranteed a minimum standard of living to its citizens and has heavily taxed those on the highest incomes and those with the greatest wealth.

Dahrendorf concludes that society can be characterised correctly in terms of conflict between competing interest groups. In post-capitalist society, however, conflicts have become institutionalised, that is, orderly, patterned, predictable and controllable. Workers now have the right to express their interests legitimately through socially acceptable machinery such as collective bargaining which is conducted through their own *bona fide* organisations like trade unions. Conflict is not now so bitter and potentially disruptive of the social system because the changes in social structure listed above give everyone some stake in the system. Interests are pursued according to the 'rules of the game'. These 'rules' require a use of the established machinery for dealing with conflicts created by competing interest groups.

In the light of these arguments, Darhendorf points out what he considers to be the weaknesses of Marx's theories and suggests ways in which they can be modified in order to give a useful basis for analysing both capitalist and post-capitalist societies. For him, the basic weakness of Marx's approach is in tying power – economic, social, political – to the ownership of the means of production. He argues that social classes are not necessarily and inevitably economic groups; that social conflict is not necessarily rooted in property relationships; that the policies and operations of the state are not necessarily shaped or determined by the 'economic base'. For Dahrendorf, authority relationships represent the key feature of society. In any society some individuals have the right or authority to give commands to others. These others have, in turn, the duty to subject themselves to these orders, that is, the duty to obey. Thus individuals who share the identical interest of commanding or of obeying in some sphere of activity, whether it be political, economic, or industrial, may be described as a 'quasi-group', that is, a potential group. If these interests are articulated so that members become conscious of them and shape their behaviour in this sphere of activity in terms of them, then these interests become 'manifest' and become the basis of organised and self-conscious 'interest groups'. Dahrendorf defines social classes as organised or unorganised categories of people who share manifest or latent interests arising from their positions in the authority structures in which they find themselves. For him, then, class conflict is merely any conflict of groups arising from authority relationships.

Dahrendorf argues that most people in society are unlikely to be engaged in one mighty political–economic–social–industrial conflict which is generated from one structural source, property relationships. Instead, changes in social structure (that is, those listed above) create the social structural basis for a plurality of interest groups and hence a plurality of bases for conflict.

In this way, Dahrendorf attempts to refine and develop Marx's approach to understanding the social world. Clearly, his work shows strong continuities with that of Marx. Not all writers, however, share his view that a new type of society has succeeded capitalism. For example, J. Westergaard, in his article 'The withering away of class – a contemporary myth', suggests that, despite some changes, modern industrial societies are still similar in basic structure to capitalist societies. Though certain changes since Marx's time have obscured the visibility of the workings of the social system and have made the growth of class consciousness harder to achieve, the system is still largely built around the private ownership of the means of production and social life is therefore shaped in most respects by this fact.

With Henrietta Resler, Westergaard 'fleshes out' the argument in a full-length book, *Class in a Capitalist Society: A Study of Contemporary Britain*. The 'flesh' is provided by more than 400 pages of argument, supported by over forty tables and diagrams, all showing a wide range of inequalities in the distribution of income, share-ownership, tax benefits, pension schemes, social and educational mobility, trade union membership, involvement in strikes, and so on. Nevertheless, the class-based revolution for which all these inequalities provide an 'objective' base has not materialised.

LOCKWOOD AND GOLDTHORPE: CLASS IN MODERN SOCIETY

In his study *The Blackcoated Worker*, Lockwood explored the links between the 'factual' or 'objective' aspect of class and the 'subjective' aspect of class. He argued that, according to Marx's theory, clerks (or blackcoated workers) are potentially members of the proletariat because they are not owners of the means of production. Yet, by and large, clerks do not regard themselves as on a par with manual workers. They see themselves as different, even superior. Are they then, asks Lockwood, 'guilty' of 'false class consciousness', that is, do they have 'false' perceptions of their 'true' class position?

In answering this question, Lockwood makes use of Weber's adaptations of Marx's concept of class. First he examines the clerks' *market situation* and agrees that as the clerks do not own the means of production and as they have to sell their labour on the open market, they are in this sense potentially members of the proletariat. Indeed, this point seems reinforced when we note that the earnings differential between clerks and manual workers has been eroded over the last fifty or so years; now clerks receive only as much as the *average* manual worker. Secondly, Lockwood turns to the *work situation* of the clerks. Here he found significant differences between clerks and manual workers. For example, clerks usually enjoyed much better working conditions and greater access to pension funds and to sick benefits. They were also treated more as individuals because most of them worked in organisations where they were thin on the ground compared to the other types of worker employed. In fact, in many offices, individual clerks were differentiated in terms of level of salary and also in terms of internal status distinctions like number of telephones, size of carpet and desk, and so on. Generally, clerks identified with the management side of industry and displayed commitment to their work.

Lockwood concluded that the whole situation of clerks showed many significant differences from that of manual workers. It provided a sufficient basis for clerks to form different attitudes towards, and perceptions of, the social structure. Moreover, in so far as clerks tended to derive their values from middle class groups such as white collar professional workers, whom they sought to emulate and with whom they wished to identify, the *status aspirations* of clerks also differed. These status aspirations were reflected in a somewhat different life-style adopted by the clerks. Only in work situations where there were large numbers of clerks working together and where they had few privileges and individual distinctions did the perceptions and attitudes of clerks resemble more those of manual workers. Such situations occur, for example, in the large governmental offices of the Civil Service. Here the clerks formed trade unions and developed a militancy largely unknown to the bulk of clerks.

Thus most blackcoated workers do not develop a consciousness of belonging to the proletariat. Lockwood argues that they perceive themselves and their place in the social world differently because their work situation is different from that of manual workers. It is misleading, therefore, to call their perceptions 'false consciousness' because such terminology implies that there *must* be a fit between non-ownership of the means of production, that is, Marx's 'objective' aspect of class, and social awareness or consciousness, that is, Marx's subjective aspect of class. By showing that the objective or factual aspect of class can include the work situation as well as property relations, Lockwood suggests that the clerk's different, non-proletarian attitudes do in fact 'truly' reflect differences between them and manual workers. Moreover, if clerks do in fact base their aspirations and life-styles with reference to how they perceive middle class groups, that is, they take the middle class groups as their 'reference group' for standards and styles of behaviour, then their consequent consciousness of society is as 'real' as any other. In fact, he argues that what Marx is doing with his concept of false class consciousness is to confuse his view of how people *should* think and act with an account of how they *actually do* think and act. In short, he confuses prescriptions (value-statements of what *ought* to happen) with descriptions (factual statements about what *is* happening).

In collaboration with Goldthorpe and others, Lockwood pursues similar concerns in a series of studies of the political, industrial and class attitudes of Luton car workers. Given their very high level of earnings, the authors call them 'affluent workers' and ask if their affluence means that they are becoming 'embourgeoisified', that is, members of the middle class. Such an inquiry raises questions concerning the extent of their class consciousness, the nature of the working class, or proletariat, in modern industrial society and, therefore, the extent to which society is becoming polarised into two major social classes. As we have seen, Marx posed similar questions in his analysis of capitalist society.

In these studies, the authors examine three aspects of social class: the economic, normative and relational aspects. An examination of the economic aspect reveals that while the affluent workers' market situation is such that they receive very high earnings, they are still worse off relative to white collar workers when it comes to pensions, promotions, other fringe benefits, working conditions and security of employment. The relational aspect concerns patterns of social mixing and social relationships and here the available evidence shows little mingling of affluent workers and middle class groups in membership of clubs, societies and home-visiting. Finally, the normative aspect of class refers to the values, attitudes and behavioural norms or standards of groups. Here again, the affluent workers do not appear to be developing middle class standards by, for example, placing a high value on the entertainment of friends at dinner parties.

The authors argue that an increase in income does not automatically generate the new attitudes and values required to qualify for membership of a new social group. Moreover, an increase in income does not necessarily generate the desire to do so. If affluent workers are to become middle class they have to work hard socially. The authors suggest a possible route which the affluent workers might follow to become accepted into the middle class. First, workers must abandon their traditional views and attitudes. To do so isolates them from their fellow workers, that is, they become 'privatised' workers. Then they must aspire to become middle class by trying to adopt middle class life-styles, attitudes and behaviour. Only if they succeed and are accepted do they become middle class.

The authors find little evidence that such a process is happening. The attitudes and behaviour of affluent workers might be changing, but they are not being 'embourgeoisified'. Furthermore, they suggest that the middle class groups are themselves changing in modern society. Faced by a lessening of individual prospects and by erosion of living standards, these groups are becoming similar to working class groups in some ways. For example, teachers, local government employees, nurses and even doctors have tried to improve their prospects via trade unions and strike action. Thus there may be a *convergence* or coming together of middle class and working class groups. For example, both the 'new' working class and the 'new' middle class tend to be home-centred and family-centred and to pursue individual aspirations by way of collective action through trade unions. The authors do not suggest, however, that such a convergence represents the emergence of Marx's proletariat. The convergence is not creating a class-conscious and revolutionary group bent on reshaping society on the basis of a set of different organising principles for society.

BEYNON: AN ALTERNATIVE VIEW OF CAR WORKERS

For a richer, more gripping and less mechanistic view of car workers, we turn to Huw Beynon's *Working for Ford*. His approach is methodologically much closer to Marx because he does not simply document and refine concepts in a detached and academic manner. Rather, he plunges himself and the reader into the excitement and turmoil of an actual class struggle on the factory floor of Ford's plant at Halewood, Liverpool. By focusing on the struggle of the shop stewards with their own trade unions as well as with management, Beynon brings out the dynamic nature of Marx's concept of class. He shows how the ordinary shop floor workers develop a strong *factory* consciousness, but also how difficult it is for them to expand it into a wider class consciousness which would transcend Ford and other car firms. In fact, Beynon regretfully concludes that even when the shop stewards succeed in making their own trade unions responsive to the shop floor, there are still severe limits to these organisations as revolutionary bodies. They are so locked into the capitalist system that they sustain rather than help to overthrow it. In effect, both workers and management share a common ideology, the profit motive, in that they are both concerned to ensure that the factory continues to produce more cars and more sales, that is, more profits *and* more wages. Consequently, Beynon comes round to Dahrendorf's notion of institutionalised, rather than revolutionary, class conflict, though he is far from Dahrendorf's position of seeing this state of affairs as stable.

FRANK PARKIN: VALUES AND CONFLICT IN MODERN SOCIETIES

In his book *Class Inequality and Political Order – Social Stratification in Capitalist and Communist Societies,* Parkin uses Marx's original concepts to examine the social sources for the stability of modern societies. Why, he asks, do not the 'disprivileged' rebel more often against the privileged? He responds that usually the disprivileged are not socially controlled by naked physical force, but by a number of more subtle mechanisms. These include social mobility, low expectations and resignation inculcated by the educational system. Religion and gambling provide 'release' for individuals and can be seen to be alternatives to political radicalism, that is, the demand for revolutionary changes of society. In these ways, the serious inequalities which persist in modern societies do not generate revolutionary class consciousness.

Parkin goes on to examine the normative order in modern societies. He argues that there are differences in values and in consciousness between groups in society. He distinguishes three meaning-systems or ways in which values are organised. (i) Dominant groups in society have a 'dominant value system', which provides the moral framework, the leading ideas, for society. (ii) The 'subordinate value system' is generated in other (subordinate) groups and provides members with ways of accommodating to the unpalatable facts of inequality and low status without necessarily accepting them. (iii) The 'radical value system' provides an alternative moral framework for society; it provides a blueprint for reorganising society on the basis of a different set of principles. He sees workers' participation in trade unions, their willingness to utilise what Dahrendorf calls the 'rules of the game' and their struggle for higher wages as reflecting a subordinate value system, because they are trying to secure improvements *within* the present system. A radical value system involves thinking of ways to *change* the system.

Parkin moves on to discuss inequality and political ideology in capitalist societies. In particular, he examines the extent to which social democratic parties, for example, the Labour Party in Great Britain, have influenced the reward structure in society by reducing serious inequalities. He looks at available statistical information, such as the extent of social self-recruitment (that is, how many sons follow in their father's footsteps), the amount of upward mobility, the percentage of grammar school children of working class origin, changes in the average earnings of occupational groups over a period of time, and welfare expenditure as a proportion of total production. From these sources he concludes that they have not brought about any basic change in the class nature of inequality.

Parkin then turns to countries of the 'Soviet or socialist type' and compares them to capitalist societies, again by means of a variety of available statistics. He concludes that the socialist type of society is more fluid and open than capitalist societies. On this basis he argues that its inequalities are therefore not accurately described as a class system.

One aspect of the 'open-ness' of the socialist-type society he cites is the contrast between 'Command Systems' and 'Market Systems'. In socialist societies, the distribution of rewards is basically performed by the political machinery, that is, the Command System, whereas in capitalist societies, the market mechanisms of supply and demand dominate the distribution of rewards in society. Parkin suggests that though the Command System obviously creates some powerful political positions for individuals, it is nevertheless clear to subordinate groups in such systems where power resides, and who is responsible for the distribution of rewards and the creation of inequalities. In Market Systems, there is no such open-ness of responsibilities or decision-making; dominant groups can operate more easily because they are more secretive, in their own interest.

Thus, as we can see, Parkin employs Marx's intellectual apparatus, in virtually unamended form, to analyse the working of modern capitalist and socialist-type societies.

CONCLUSION

In this chapter we have tried to show the way in which conflict theorists attempt to describe and analyse the social world. In this approach, social life is viewed in terms of divisiveness, conflict, hostility and coercion which are inevitably generated by the fact that social organisation creates different involvement and interests for people. These interests provide a basis for the formation of groups which seek to preserve, to extend, or to realise them by taking action against other groups. Social changes come about as a result of groups acting in these ways. This approach to understanding the world may be contrasted to the 'consensus approach' of the previous chapter where we saw that consensus theorists tended to emphasise the cohesive and solidary aspects of social life. Society is seen to be based on the reciprocity and co-operation between people and to be generated by their adherence to an integrating system of norms and values. Thus for consensus theorists, social life is strikingly characterised by the persistence rather than by the change of the system.

As we have already suggested, however, these approaches may not be so radically different as they might, at first, appear. For in both approaches, sociologists are interested in finding out how the whole society works, what are its key parts, how they are related and how the social structure might be seen to shape and to delimit individual action. Above all, they both endeavour to study social structures as wholes and, in so doing, must inevitably make assumptions about social structures being systems of some kind; with parts of some kind; where these parts are related in some way; and where a sufficient change in the nature of these parts will constitute a change of the social structure as a whole. The differences between the conflict and the consensus theorists, and hence between their approaches to understanding the social world, revolve around their respective views as to the nature of the system, the nature of the parts, the kind of relationships between the parts and the importance, therefore, of certain parts. In their common stress on viewing the social world as a system, both consensus and conflict theorists might reasonably be described as '*strucuralists*'. In the following chapters other approaches in sociology will be contrasted to 'structuralist' approaches. Such a contrast will point up the similarities between consensus and conflict approaches.

FURTHER READING

Béteille, A. (ed.), *Social Inequality: Selected Readings* (Penguin, 1969). For a key excerpt from Dahrendorf's *Class and Class Conflict in Industrial Society;* for W. G. Runciman's 'Three dimensions of social inequality'; and for Béteille's 'The decline of social inequality'.

Birnbaum, N., 'Conflicting interpretations of the rise of capitalism: Marx and Weber' (Bobbs Merrill Reprint S.26).

Bottomore, T. B., *Classes in Modern Society* (Allen & Unwin, 1965). Discusses Marx's theory of class and examines its relevance in modern Britain, the USA and USSR.

Bottomore, T.B., and **Rubels, M.,** *Karl Marx: Selected Writings in Sociology and Social Philosophy* (Penguin, 1963). Useful for the introduction and a wide selection of readings on basic concepts and theories.

Jordan, Z. A., *Karl Marx: Economy, Class and Social Revolution* (Michael Joseph, 1971). Has an informative long introduction to Marx and a wide selection of readings from Marx's work.

Marx, K., and **Engels, F.,** *Manifesto of the Communist Party* (Foreign Languages Publishing Co., Moscow, n.d., or Bobbs Merrill Reprint S.455). Provides a lively and polemical exposition of many of Marx's leading ideas and concepts.

Thompson, K., and **Tunstall, J.** (eds), *Sociological Perspectives: Selected Readings* (Penguin, 1971). Especially for Weber's 'Class, status, party' and articles by Parkin and Goldthorpe. Also contains useful readings from Marx on a wide range of concepts and topics.

Westergaard, J. H., 'The withering away of class: a contemporary myth' (Bobbs Merrill Reprint S.774).

Worsley, P. (ed.), *Modern Sociology: Introductory Readings* (Penguin, 1970). Part 8, 'Social Stratification', provides a rich selection of readings for showing the relevance of the concept of class for studying modern society. The excerpt from J. Rex, 'Power, conflict, values and change', in Part 9, is also useful for consideration of a 'conflict model' of society.

Westergaard, J. H., and **Resler, Henrietta,** *Class in a Capitalist Society: A Study of Contemporary Britain* (Penguin, 1976).

Beynon, H., *Working for Ford* (English Universities Press, 1975).

QUESTIONS

1 Outline the main features of structural change in nineteenth-century capitalist society.

2 What are the main features of 'laissez-faire' as an ideology?

3 What are Marx's basic methodological assumptions? How do they influence his basic sociological concepts?

4 What do you understand by 'historical materialism'?

5 What, for Marx, were the main characteristics of capitalist society?

6 What do you understand by 'contradictions' in the capitalist system? Give examples. Are these 'contradictions' the same as the 'tensions' of the social system discussed in Chapter 2?

7 Outline Marx's concept of class. What is the importance of his emphasis on the subjective aspect of class for his theory of social change and revolution?

8 Contrast the views of Marx and Weber on (a) power, (b) the influence of ideas in society.

9 Does Weber refute Marx's notion that religion is the 'opiate of the people'?

10 Do you agree with Dahrendorf that capitalist society has been succeeded by a new type of society, namely, 'post-capitalist' society? Detail your reasons.

11 With reference to work by Lockwood and Goldthorpe show your understanding of the following concepts: false class consciousness; proletariat; 'bourgeoisification'.

12 Contrast and compare the descriptions of car workers produced by (a) Beynon, (b) Goldthorpe *et al.* To what extent do they throw light on Britain as a 'class ridden' society?

13 Outline Parkin's distinction between 'Command Systems' and 'Market Systems'. Contrast his description of modern Western society with Dahrendorf's description. In your view, which description most adequately portrays modern Britain?

14 What are the similarities and differences between conflict and consensus models of society?

15 'Ideology in the conflict model fulfils the same function as the common value system in consensus model.' Discuss.

16 'Britain is now a classless society.' 'Britain is the most class-ridden society in the world.' Both of these statements are frequently made about modern Britain. So, in your view, what would count as decisive evidence for choosing between them? How would you go about obtaining such evidence?

Chapter 4

Symbolic Interactionism as a Perspective

INTRODUCTION: THE DEMAND FOR 'SOCIAL ACTION' THEORY

The very format of this book, an exposition of a set of more or less self-contained perspectives, shows the current state of sociology. The discipline is characterised by the basic divisions in the ideas on how we should go about things. The basic division concerns recurrent demands for the development of a particular sort of alternative which takes 'an action approach' or works within an 'action frame of reference'. The fact that there are recurrent demands suggests that those demands are not usually satisfied. It also suggests – quite correctly – that those who call for the adoption of the 'action approach' are usually within a minority, which looks upon 'an action approach' as providing a corrective alternative to undesirable tendencies which predominate within the discipline.

Originating largely with Weber, the central idea of an action approach is that the sociologist should proceed by seeking to 'understand' those he studies. He should attempt to look upon the world in the same way that they do, should seek to appreciate how the world looks to them. He should, additionally, seek to grasp the ideas, beliefs, motives and goals which move people to act. Knowing how things appear to people and what sorts of thoughts, impulses and wants those people have, the sociologist will be able to see that they act as they do because they are seeking to realise their ends and desires as best they can in the face of circumstances as they see them. This emphasis upon 'understanding' the social factor has resulted in this approach being known as *verstehende* (or understanding) sociology.

There is a problem, however, in determining what this approach looks like in any detailed and coherent form. All kinds of different ideas about sociology have been represented as deriving from an action approach. We cannot hope to catalogue the wide diversity of views on the proper nature of the action 'frame of reference', but will discuss some of the major ways it has been invoked.

The demand for an 'action approach' has often reflected the view that available modes of sociological analysis leave much to be desired. The 'action frame of reference' is, therefore, often formulated in opposition to some other position. For example, Weber himself, Popper and Rex have all advocated such an approach against organicist or holistic doctrines. Such doctrines hold, in their most extreme form, that society is itself a living entity and, more moderately, that society exists in some sense independently of its individual members. As we have seen, functionalism is a good illustration of this view.

Weber thought that the development of *verstehende* sociology involved beginning from the definition of the basic forms of action, working out what forms of relationships people could create out of such basic modes of action and, moving 'upwards', specifying all the forms of group, association, organisation and institution which could be compounded out of those relationships. In Weber's view, even the most complex forms of social organisation – the massive world civilisations – should be looked upon by the sociologist only as a complex made up of relationships among its members.

A similar view is expressed by Karl Popper. He argues for the use of the idea of situational logic and the principle of methodological individualism. Popper's arguments are directed particularly against Hegel and Marx, whom he regarded as expounding holistic doctrines which treated the social whole, that is, society, as though it were a real entity, which is independent of, and more important than, its members. Popper regards such holistic doctrines as conducive to totalitarianism, to the oppression of persons, supposedly for the 'sake of society'. His opposition is, therefore, politically motivated, though his arguments are not solely political. He too argues that the sociologist should seek to 'understand' human behaviour. For Popper the process of understanding requires analysis of ways people relate ends to means in particular circumstances. Such analysis will provide explanation revealing the 'logic' in human action, even when that action is, apparently, quite bizarre.

We take as an example of the nature of this argument the case of the 'cargo cults'. Cargo cults were religious cults which sprang up in various Pacific island areas. They involved the believers in the expectation of the sudden, almost imminent arrival of a material paradise. The islanders believed, simply, that very soon they would, by one means or another, be provided with all the material goods they could want. They were often required, as part of their preparation for the arrival of 'the cargo', to destroy or abandon their homes and property. This willingness to do away with their possessions, on the basis of an unfounded expectation of new ones, might seem to us to be quite irrational. Nevertheless, an analysis stressing situational logic shows them to be behaving rationally. Looked at in the light of what the natives want (wealth of the kind possessed by their European colonisers), what they know about the ways Europeans come by their wealth (very little), and in relation to the conceptions that they have of effective means (religious and magical), it is hardly surprising that they believe that the cargo will come.

In Popper's view, situational logic is associated with the principle of methodological individualism. Situational logic emphasises the understanding of social life through a grasp of the way the (typical) *individual* looks upon and reacts to his situation. The policy of methodological individualism is simply an extension of this approach. It argues that all statements about 'wholes', for example, 'the state', should be reduced to statements about individual behaviour. The sociologist should not say 'the state does this' or 'a class does that' without recognising that such statements are a kind of shorthand for the actions of individuals.

The intense controversy generated by the principle of methodological individualism ignores the simple fact that it is *methodological* individualism. It is not saying that 'social wholes' do not exist. It merely recommends a *methodological* policy of trying, whenever some social whole is mentioned, to substitute explanations in terms of individual behaviour. The success of such a policy must be judged from the kinds of results produced by empirical studies.

Goldthorpe is another proponent of an 'action approach'. He uses such an approach to argue against those who see a 'logic' in the technology of industrial society. This logic is not the same kind as situational logic. It refers to the view that there is a kind of compulsion in society arising from the needs and constraints of its technology, that is, technology *imposes* certain kinds of social relationships and experiences on people, at factory level and at the level of society. At the level of the factory, it has been argued that the attitudes of workers and the organisation of hierarchies of supervision are predictable simply from a knowledge of the technology of the industry. For example, motor manufacturing processes will entail different hierarchies than those involved in a chemical plant (Woodward). At the level of the society, it is argued that all industrial societies are becoming alike. No matter whether they are capitalist or socialist, these societies are *industrial* and the necessities of industrial production require certain sorts of social relations. Hence as Kerr, for example, has suggested, industrial societies will tend to become more alike in respect of their stratification systems, political arrangements and the like. In reply, Goldthorpe has asserted that 'too great a weight has been given to technology as a determinant of attitudes and behaviour in the work situation; and too little attention has been paid to the prior orientations which workers have towards employment, and which in turn influence their choice of a job, the meaning they give to work and *their definition* of the work situation' (Goldthorpe, 1966, p. 228). He also points out that too much attention is paid to the fact that the societies are industrial and not enough to the fact that they differ in values, culture, political policy, and so on.

The relevance of the concept of 'action' for sociology has also been examined by a number of philosophers, particularly Winch, Louch and MacIntyre, who all use it to attack behaviourism and causal explanation. In extreme form, behaviourism holds that scientists must *only* study things which are movements of material bodies. They cannot deal with unobservable and intangible things like ideas and states of mind. Critics like Winch agree with Mead that in order to understand 'what people do' it is not adequate simply to observe the movements of material bodies; adequate explanation *must* make reference to ideas and feelings. The difference between a 'twitch of the arm' and a 'friendly wave' does not reside in some difference in the movement of the arm but in the fact that in the case of the wave the movement of the arm is *meant* to signify the *recognition* of the other person. Without reference to thought and feeling the wave is only a twitch.

Similarly, causal explanation is attacked for its inappropriateness as a way of describing human action. A commonly used example of causation is to explain the movement of one billiard ball as 'caused' by being struck by another. This model of explanation might be perfectly adequate for the movement of billiard balls but it is completely inadequate for human action. Pursuing ends, selecting means, shaping intentions, finding rules – none of these typical human actions is in the slightest like being compelled by an external force in the way that the ball is moved.

We note that the 'action frame of reference' is attractive to a range of theorists operating within various sociological perspectives. Even functionalists want to use 'action theory'. Thus, Talcott Parsons's structural functionalism has as its official title 'the general theory of action'. It has this title because Parsons seeks, like Weber, to begin from the elements of action and to build, from there, up to the most complex forms of organisation. After an attempt to do this Parsons decided, however, that he could not understand actions without reference to the system of organisation in which they were implicated. He therefore launched upon a structural functionalist programme, in the effort to show how actions, and the motives, thoughts, and so on, which organise them, are generated in and organised by the social system. Action theory is enmeshed with the very holism that action theorists regard as anathema. Unlike Parsons, many proponents of an 'action frame of reference' have not carried their argument forward into a full blown sociological schema. Neither have they done very much in the way of extensive empirical studies. As we have seen, however, Symbolic Interactionists can be fairly characterised as not only stressing social action, but also developing a programme for research which has resulted in a large output of empirical studies.

For our purposes here we shall concentrate on only two of the various strategies which could be counted as an attempt to develop an action approach, namely, Symbolic Interactionism in this chapter, and ethnomethodology in the next chapter.

INTRODUCTION TO SYMBOLIC INTERACTIONISM

It can be argued that Symbolic Interactionism is *not* a unified perspective in that is does not represent a common set of assumptions and concepts accepted by all those who practise the approach. Many of those we count as Symbolic Interactionists only reluctantly accept that label, preferring to see themselves as independent researchers rather than as supporters of a perspective. For our purposes, however, it is possible to identify a number of characteristics of the approach which make it distinctive.

Although we may identify some parallels between Symbolic Interactionism and a European tradition of sociology stemming from Max Weber, and now known as 'action theory', Symbolic Interactionism is an American product and for long periods its organisational focus was the University of Chicago. In lectures delivered at that university between 1894 and 1931 George Herbert Mead (1863–1931) articulated the main ideas. Herbert Blumer, a student of Mead at Chicago, in a series of papers written over many years, sought to show the sociological relevance of Mead's teaching. Everett Hughes and his associates, again over a long period since the 1930s and commonly from Chicago, have given empirical significance to those ideas.

Although the basic ideas of Symbolic Interactionism date back towards the beginning of the century, they have remained relevant because they have served to provide a minority tradition, at odds with the prevailing doctrines of American sociology.

GEORGE H. MEAD: THE BASES OF SYMBOLIC INTERACTIONISM

THE DISTINCTIVE NATURE OF HUMAN BEINGS

At the heart of Mead's approach is the assumption that there is a difference between animal *reaction* and human *conduct*. Conduct, as he understands it, requires the possession of a mind; the possession of a mind is something distinctive to the human species. Further, Mead also argues that man is distinctive in that he has a *self*. He is *the* creature which is capable of being *both* subject and object, that is, man can *both* undergo experience and be aware of this experience.

In Mead's understanding, the life of most species of animal is dominated by the stimulus–response relationship. This relationship involves an automatic association between the circumstances of behaviour and the behaviour itself. When something happens, the animal automatically and invariably responds in a fixed way, whereas human conduct does not involve that kind of fixed inter-connection of action and occasion. There is a much greater degree of 'flexibility'. A man may behave in a given set of circumstances in one way at one time, in a completely different way at some later time, and differently again on a third occasion. Human beings are not tied down to the stimulus–response relationship. They can plan their conduct in the light of their expectation as to how things will happen. They can consider in the aftermath of an occasion how their projected actions turned out and can revise their anticipations and future practices in the light of what they have learned from past experience.

If human beings are to anticipate the future, to plan their actions and to reflect on past conduct, they must be able to reflect on themselves, to look on themselves in the same way as they look upon any other object. They must not only be aware of other things (including other people) which make up their environment, they must also possess some awareness of themselves as things in the same environment. It is this capacity for self-consciousness, this capacity for reflection upon themselves, which is the outstandingly distinctive characteristic of the human animal in Mead's account. In his view, self-consciousness depends on the ability of the individual human being to take the same attitude towards himself as others take towards him. From the point of view of other people, he is quite literally an object in their environment. To look upon oneself as an object is to see oneself as others do.

Mead's favoured example is the development of the child. In play, the child engages in the imitation of the behaviour which it sees around it. It acts now like a postman, now like a parent and now like a policeman. The child's engagement in play gradually develops into participation in games with others, where competent involvement does not just require imitation of behaviour. It demands that the players appreciate the viewpoints of one another. We can only participate effectively in games if we can assess their circumstances not only in terms of our own interests but relative to those of other players. In competitive games, for instance, we can only hope to win if we can estimate what our opponents are going to do and anticipate their moves. We must grasp how we appear to them, since they too are trying to plan their moves in relation to what we will do. For example, to be at all effective in chess, we must be able to look upon our pieces as they appear to our opponent, and see the potentialities and weaknesses of our position as it appears to him.

For Mead, the transformation of the child from a creature capable only of engaging in the imitations of play into one manifesting the self-consciousness required by games displays in microcosm the general process of human development. It is not only in games that human beings must possess self-consciousness; they must do so in all social activities. Of course, the individual cannot work out exactly how he looks to each and every other person in the world; there are too many of them, the task is too complicated. Instead the individual responds to 'the generalised other', that is, he reacts to his sense of the general, typical and predominant views of himself shown by others. This grasp upon the attitudes and views of others is only possible because human beings share 'the significant symbol', that is, human beings can engage in meaningful communication with one another through the medium of language. It is through dialogue with others that the individual becomes aware of the views and attitudes of others. Through such exchange, he can come to learn the ways of acting that others require of him and acquire the self-consciousness that is essential to the co-ordination of the collective life.

SCIENTIFIC STUDY OF THE MIND

One of Mead's central concerns is to solve the philosophical problem of the relationship between mind and nature. This problem acquires relevance for social science when it is posed as the question: Can those techniques which have been successful in the study of nature, that is, the techniques of natural science, be usefully applied to the study of mind, to human social activities? Mead seeks to show that there is no need to set up a sharp separation between nature and mind in the way that some thinkers have done. This sharp separation is improper, Mead argues, because mind is *part* of nature. To make his case he appeals to the doctrine of evolution, which is generally recognised as 'belonging to nature'. To show that mind is a product of a certain phase of the evolutionary process is to show it is just as 'natural' as anything else thrown up by that process.

He argues, for example, that capacity to master language, which is critical to the entire development of mind, is dependent upon the physiological development of the human organism, that is, the development of the vocal apparatus. The development of the mind itself requires the central nervous system to evolve to such a degree of complexity that behaviour is freed from the constraints of the 'reflex arc', that is, from the automatic linkage of a stimulus-response association. In short, the development of the vocal chords and other aspects of human physiology create the *possibility* of the human mind. In this way, Mead shows how the development of the mind is one aspect of general evolutionary process. It is an aspect, however, that differentiates the human species from other animals. He thinks we need a 'behaviourist' account of the evolutionary origins and development of the human mind. Rather than continue to struggle with difficulties created by a narrow conception of 'nature', Mead seeks to broaden that conception so as to allow mind to be included within it.

In identifying the account he intended to give as 'behaviourist'. Mead is not proposing, as others who have used the same title have done, that only the physical and organic characteristics of human existence should be studied without any concern for the reality of such things as thought and feeling. Mead was very firmly of the opinion that thought, consciousness and experience must be studied.

The label 'behaviourist' as used by Mead does not serve to identify his *subject matter* (that is, that he will deal with organic things but not states of mind), but rather his manner of proceeding. His account is built upon the observation of the ordinary activities of social life, upon publicly available and commonly observable facts that any of us might notice about our lives together. If the hallmark of science is not the material nature of the phenomena it studies, but rather the public availability of its observations, then Mead's behaviourist account is fully compatible with the requirements of science.

HERBERT BLUMER: SYMBOLIC INTERACTIONISM AND SCIENCE

Symbolic Interactionists are often regarded as holding the view that the methods of the natural sciences cannot be freely applied in sociological study. Our account of Mead might appear to contradict this view. For Mead tried to show that the social and natural sciences are continuous because mind is as fitting a subject for scientific study as any other aspect of nature. The whole issue, however, very much depends upon what we mean by 'the methods of natural science'. Some sociologists seem to think that following the methods of the natural sciences means impersonating the very specific procedures followed in, say, physics. Herbert Blumer has persistently attacked such ideas in sociology. Though he has argued against them from many angles, Blumer's views can be fairly represented by his criticism of 'variable analysis'.

Variable analysis requires that the relationship between two or more 'variables' be identified and specified. To take an imaginary example of the sort natural science might provide: for any gas, pressure varies directly with temperature. Here, we have two variables, pressure and temperature. They are variables in that their values may vary, may increase or decrease. We may have a finding of some scientific interest if we can find between such variables some stable relationship of values, for example, if we can show that an increase in pressure is *always* associated with an increase in temperature. It is even better if we can quantify such relations by showing, for example, that an increase of one pound in pressure is associated with an increase of two degrees in temperature. We may be able to go even further and show the 'direction' of the relationship between the variables, by finding that a change in one variable *leads to* a change in the other. In our imaginary example, a change in pressure *leads to* a change in temperature. In this imaginary case, we can talk of one variable, pressure, as the 'independent variable' and can regard temperature as the 'dependent variable'. Blumer says that the transfer of this procedure, without modification, into sociology, is unacceptable. He goes on:

> The conventional procedure in variable analysis is to identify something which is presumed to operate on group life and treat it as an independent variable, and then to select some form of group activity as the dependent variable. The independent variable is put at the beginning part of the process of interpretation and the dependent variable at the terminal part of the process. The intervening process is ignored, or what amounts to the same thing, taken for granted as something that need not be considered. (Blumer, 1969, p. 133)

We can illustrate the point Blumer is making in this comment with another imaginary example which attempts to show that the level of intensity of propaganda favouring birth control might affect child-bearing practices in a society, leading to rises and declines in birth-rates. Such a study might find that increasing intensity in propaganda favouring birth control *leads to* a decline in birth-rates. The general strategy such a finding would represent can be shown in this way: Change in independent variable *leads to* change in dependent variable.

The sociological findings could look like those in the natural sciences on which they are modelled. Unfortunately, the kind of understanding of the organisation of social activity which they express looks very much like this: Stimulus *leads to* response.

Following Mead, Blumer attacks this conception of human conduct. Such a conception may be adequate for studying the behaviour of animals, but it is not adequate for the study of human conduct. Blumer does not say we *cannot* apply such a variable model, or that we *can never* obtain any findings through its use. It can and does produce 'findings', but findings which, though interesting, are quite bare. Such findings give us no picture of the people to whom they refer *as human beings* in the world they inhabit. In short, they do not tell us anything about how human beings 'work'. They cannot, because the model of conduct they employ is of a lower level of organisation than that appropriate to an understanding of human conduct. For even if we do find that people modify their reproductive behaviour following their exposure to propaganda on behalf of birth control, we still

> do not know the run of their experiences which induced an organisation of their sentiments and views, nor do we know what that organisation is; we do not know the social atmosphere or code in their social circles; we do not know the reinforcements and rationalisations that come from their fellows; we do not know the defining process in their circles; we do not know the pressures, the incitants, and the models that come from their niches in the social structure; we do not know how their ethical sensitivities are organised and so what they would tolerate . . . (Blumer, p. 131)

The 'human' things are not just 'left out' of a given variable anlaysis; we cannot correct matters by including them. We cannot expand our findings so that they look like;

> an increased exposure to propaganda on behalf of birth control
> *plus*
> support and favourable rationalisations from fellows
> *plus*
> a social atmosphere of positive enthusiasm for birth control
>
> automatically leads to a reduction in the birth-rate.

To accumulate more and more variables does not lead to a solution of the problem. Complicating the relation among variables does not bring us nearer to a better understanding of *how* and *why* the things that we show to be associated are connected. If propaganda on behalf of birth control leads to a change in the birth-rate, it does not do so because people react automatically to exposure to propaganda. Any change in behaviour is due to the ways in which propaganda affects the circumstances of their lives, affects their sentiments and attitudes and enters into their reasoning about the arrangement of their affairs. Rather than finding out about the correlation of propaganda and birth-rates, we might more profitably occupy ourselves in finding out about the circumstances of people's lives. Blumer suggests:

> In order to act the individual has to identify what he wants, establish an objective or goal, map out a prospective line of behaviour, note and interpret the actions of others, size up his situation, check himself at this or that point, figure out what to do at other points, and frequently spur himself on in the face of dragging dispositions or discouraging settings. (Blumer, p. 64)

The stimulus–response model emphasises the primacy of external events; human actions are seen as a response to stimuli which occur in the outer world. Blumer points to the fact that human beings can *initiate* lines of actions, they can set out to do things without having to wait for external events to stimulate them into motion. He emphasises, too, the extent to which human action is *purposive*. It is taken in pursuit of some end that the actor has in mind, and towards which the organisation of action is a means. The stimulus–response relation not only leaves little room for conceptions of purpose, but it also offers a view of behaviour as automatic, as a reflex which is inexorably tied to the occurrence of a stimulus. Blumer reminds us, however, that action may be both deliberative and creative. It is deliberative in that the actor *thinks* about what he is doing, recognises, assesses and chooses among alternative courses of action. He makes plans prior to acting and revises them as he encounters changing or unforeseen circumstances. It is creative in that the actor is often engaged in 'putting together' his actions as means to ends— he has to organise his actions to get things done. He may put those actions together in novel, innovating and unprecedented ways.

Blumer's attack is, therefore, directed against the idea that action may be treated as *mere* reaction but it involves, too, the complementary argument against the treatment of circumstances as stimuli. For human beings, circumstances do not exist 'in themselves' as stimuli to which we must react in the manner of a mindless, instinct-dominated organism. What 'the circumstances' are for us is dependent on the purposes, plans and knowledge that we 'have in mind'. For example, how we respond to rainfall differs according to whether we are horticulturalists concerned for the welfare of our crops, or whether we are on holiday and in search of sunshine. The 'same' stimulus is different – blessing or curse – relative to our purposes and preoccupations. In Blumer's view, both terms implied in the stimulus–response relationship are misleadingly invoked if they are extended to the systematic description of human action: circumstances are not stimuli, actions are not mere reactions.

Blumer's objection to variable analysis is rooted in his conviction that its claim to provide the approach found in the natural sciences is largely spurious. Thus he calls this approach, as it is used in sociology, '*so-called* variable analysis' since the things which it identifies are not clear and discrete 'objects' with the unitary make-up that genuine variables should have. Rather, they are typically nothing more than 'abbreviated terms of reference' for complex patterns of social organisation which the researcher has not described and, usually, is not able to describe. The things which sociologists *call* variables cannot reasonably be described in this manner. Except in the barest manner they do not express quantifiable relations between known dimensions of phenomena. Sociologists cannot say *exactly* what sorts of activities will, in any empirical case, be instances of such abstract categories as, for example, 'social cohesion', 'authority', 'group morale' and most of the other technical expressions which make up the jargon of sociology. Such expressions, according to Blumer, typically lack any 'fixed or uniform indicators. Instead, indicators are constructed to fit the particular problem on which one is working. Thus certain features are chosen to represent the social integration of cities, but other features are used to represent the social integration of boys' gangs.'

Blumer's critique of variable analysis stresses the immensity of our ignorance. Despite the appearance of knowledge and sophistication which we can give to social science by the imitation of more complex disciplines, he suggests that social life is very complex, being made up of elaborate and multifarious processes about which we have only the most limited findings. The 'inner' workings of social life are likely to be no less complex than the processes they give rise to, but, again, we have only a sketchy understanding of their nature. In essence Blumer's general recommendation for the development of the discipline is that we aim to acquire a more detailed, leisurely and intimate knowledge of the diverse phenomena that we encompass within our discipline. Rather than pursue the (perhaps) inapplicable examples set by other sciences, we are better employed in seeking to develop our own discipline so that it can be responsive to those things which are distinctive of social life.

More specifically, Blumer advocates a 'naturalistic' approach to research. It involves the examination of particular instances of social life as they occur in their usual settings. They should be studied with some care and in some detail. The researcher should aim to see the world in the same way as those people he is studying. He should be prepared to live along with them throughout the course of their daily routines and to expose himself to those experiences which they typically encounter. He should aim for a sympathetic and sensitive understanding of their general outlook on the world. He should aim, too, to see how those processes which we talk about through our sociological abstractions (birth-rates, social roles, systems of authority, and so on) can be seen as organised patterns of conduct and social interaction across the span of daily experience.

This kind of advice does not tell anyone who feels inclined to follow it exactly what they should now do. It gives a rather clearer sense of what to avoid than what to value and pursue. For example, it does imply that the kind of contact between researcher and subject in the administration of a brief questionnaire is unlikely to be of the kind, duration, or quality that is desirable. In this view, the kind of sustained association and cohabitation involved in field researches would be preferable, but this advice provides the fieldworker with no specific guidance as to the manner, aims and techniques of his work in the field. The work of Everett C. Hughes and his associates, however, has commonly been viewed as providing an excellent indication of the kind of product towards which the pursuit of Blumer's policies might lead. To this work we now turn.

THE SCHOOL OF EVERETT HUGHES: DEVELOPMENTS IN SYMBOLIC INTERACTIONISM

The work of Everett C. Hughes and his many associates represents the kind of research policies Blumer has broadly indicated that sociologists might try to develop. Generally, this work emphasises the careful, naturalistic and detailed inspection of the particular case in a manner which follows Blumer's proposals. Our subsequent discussion is organised in terms of seven major and interrelated characteristics we have identified as reflecting the basic assumptions of Symbolic Interactionism as an approach to studying the social world.

INTRODUCTION: A FOCUS ON OCCUPATIONS

Since the 1930s, Hughes and others have conducted a series of studies predominantly focusing on various aspects of occupational life. This emphasis upon the institution of work, however, has not arisen by chance, but derives from a sense that work is one of the central areas of contemporary society and that it is within the world of occupational life that the individual's sense of self is often formed, defined and affirmed. The individual's sense of his own worth and self-esteem can be critically dependent upon his occupation and its status. Moreover, many of the individual's dealings with his society are carried on through the exercise of his occupational membership. We note, however, that while the approach consists substantially of studies of occupations it is by no means rigidly confined to them. Although work is a central and critical institution in contemporary society, in some ways it may not be vastly different from other aspects of social life. Hence we may expect to observe within it, just as well as in any other location, the operation of those processes through which *any* institution operates. We can, therefore, turn the study of an occupation into an opportunity for learning about things which are of general sociological interest and application. Some of our examples in the following discussion will therefore be taken from other areas in order that we may see that Hughes's tradition offers a general approach to sociology.

A PREFERENCE FOR FORMAL GENERALISATIONS

Symbolic Interactionists are interested in making general statements about the world. In their veiw, however, such statements cannot be usefully derived from variable analysis and a quantification of human conduct. Instead, they aim at producing 'formal' generalisations which derive from a detailed qualitative study of particular occasions. Indeed, very often they are more concerned with describing these particular occasions than producing generalisations. Generalisations are often more implicit in their work , rather than spelled out as primary objectives of research endeavour. This preference for 'formal' generalisations reflects the influence of the German sociologist Georg Simmel (1858–1918) whose work Hughes studies and some of which he translated.

Simmel thought that a vital part of sociology should be the formal analysis of social relations. By formal analysis he intends a distinction between the 'form' and 'content' of social phenomena. Thus for social phenomena like economic relations, kinship ties, political dealings, religious associations and friendship groupings, Simmel suggests that although the 'content' of these phenomena is different, they may have the same (formal) structure of social relationships. For example, he might have a general concern with 'social conflict' and examine how it can be found in such varied settings (of highly different 'content') as a business firm, a football club and a boys' gang. He might then discover that these varied settings all display in common the same formal properties or structural arrangements. These might be generally describable as 'opposition', 'affiliation' and 'co-operation', and can provide the basis for formal generalisations about the general nature of social conflict.

This distinction between 'form' and 'content' is not one which can be sustained too long nor pressed too far. It does, however, give some idea of the direction taken by Symbolic Interactionists. In general, they have tended to concentrate on the location of social processes which they take to be descriptive of, and applicable to, a variety of different social settings. This direction can be illustrated by their use of the notion of 'career' as developed by Hughes and his associates.

The concept of 'career' is familiar in the world of occupational – and particularly bureaucratic – life. It usually refers to a progression involving a series of differentiated stages, each having its distinctive titles, rewards, obligations, associated experiences, tasks and problems. The university teacher in England, for example, typically begins in his early 20s as a lecturer and may later become a senior lecturer and then possibly a professor. His movement up the scale is associated with increases in salary, obligations to do different sorts of administrative tasks and rights of access to different resources and gatherings (for example, committees) at each level. A person taking up such work knows that these stages represent a possible career path for him.

Symbolic Interactionists have applied the notion of a 'career' to a much wider range of activities than those conventionally described in this manner. For example, they regard the criminal, whose life might be thought the very paradigm of disorganisation, disorder and unpredictability, as also having a career. Thus, he is arrested, charged, remanded, tried, convicted and incarcerated in a series of stages provided by the legal system. Each of these stages takes place in a chronological order: arrest precedes charging, trial precedes conviction in the same 'formal' ways that, for example, lectureship precedes senior lectureship within the university system. The steps are predictable, and each one brings its typical experiences, tasks and problems.

Another example of the wide application of the concept 'career' is its use with mental patients. Again, mental patients can be seen to follow a progression, moving through a regular succession of stages from a 'pre-patient phase' through an 'in-patient phase' and into a 'post-hospitalisation phase'.

The preference of Symbolic Interactionists for formal generalisation is illustrated by their use of the concept of career. They try to identify generally operative social processes and find them in spheres of life which are normally thought to be quite distinctive and discrete. Thus although the notion of a career conventionally finds its application within the sphere of occupational life, Symbolic Interactionists have shown it can be applied to other areas of social life.

PARTISANSHIP

Symbolic Interactionism has been accused of sentimentality about 'underdogs'. Many studies conducted by Symbolic Interactionists have been sympathetic to the plight of those low down in organisational and social hierarchies and critical of those who are better placed. This accusation may be true, but there may also be good intellectual reasons for such 'bias'. For if we agree with Symbolic Interactionists that society is a continuing tussle among diverse groups, then we may well conclude that: (*a*) the more powerful groups control the means of communication in society; (*b*) that they disseminate favourable images of themselves through the channels of communication while conveying relatively derogatory pictures of other groups; (*c*) the lower status groups, therefore, are not able to speak for themselves to the public at large in the way the powerful can. The implication of these conclusions for the sociologist in search of discoveries about society is that there will be a likelihood of showing newsworthy and previously unappreciated things about the disprivileged. Such things can be discovered, for example, by simply finding out how those of low status look upon themselves and by observing carefully what they commonly do. By contrast, persons with power are likely to have already publicised anything favourable about themselves. Hence any sociological news about them is likely to be 'bad' for it will consist of the revelation of 'dark secrets'.

One of the targets of unsympathetic attention from Symbolic Interactionists has been the professions. In the world of work, one of the dominant groupings in American society is made up by the professional occupations; and Symbolic Interactionists have tended to probe into their claims about themselves. These occupations tend to project an image of themselves as dedicated to the service of the public and as putting aside preoccupations with monetary reward in favour of the interests of their clients. But professions, like all other groups, include those who are corrupt, dishonest and indifferent to the concept of service. The sociological student of professional work inevitably stumbles upon materials which will be discrediting to the pretensions of the professions. The sociologists' revelations often concern just those matters which professionals themselves would rather conceal or underemphasise.

Nevertheless, the less privileged, less powerful groupings in society hold a more promising prospect for sociological study since they offer a greater likelihood of the discovery of 'news'. We do not, as a matter of course and in the general run of our daily lives, have access to the viewpoints of the less powerful sections of our society. In so far as we are aware of such groupings, it is often only through derogatory accounts provided by more powerful groups.

Newspapers, television, judges, the police, criminologists, psychiatrists and other officials have their say about criminals and mental patients; everyone *except* the criminal or the mental patient is allowed a say in the public formation of his image. Consequently, the 'popular image' of disadvantaged groups is likely to be grossly unfavourable. The sociologist may be able to bring news to his society by showing that 'popular conceptions' are unjustifiably unfavourable. The sociologist might therefore provide a corrective by doing nothing more than by showing that the socially dis-privileged are not a subnormal species and by showing that 'deviants' and 'outcasts' are in truth only 'normal human beings' in particular kinds of circumstances.

Such research has an inbuilt tendency towards sympathy for those in the weaker positions. No reasonable person can expect them to live up to the unpleasant image others have created for them, any more than they could expect the socially dominant to live up to the splendid image that they have created for themselves. The tendency is, however, conducive to a clash of opinion with powerful groupings. Even to suggest, for example, that a mental patient has a 'point of view', which might be worth the sociologist's attention and study, can be to dissent from the 'official line' given out by dominant institutions. The mentally ill are popularly believed to be those who should be excluded from our ordinary social life and discourse because their minds are disordered. They are thought not to have the cognitive or emotional capacities to operate in the ways expected of full members of the society and they cannot therefore be expected to think clearly, coherently, or realistically. They are subject to distortions of perception, are out of touch with reality and are inclined to fantasies and hallucinations. How is it possible to call their ideas 'a point of view', how can they sensibly be said to see things differently from the medical and psychiatric practitioners who have to deal with them?

Such questions are, of course, critically related to the occupational competence of those who manage such people. Those who staff such institutions as mental hospitals (and welfare agencies, schools, courts and many other institutions) take it as a part of their work to become 'expert' in the handling of those over whom they have charge. They 'know' their inmates because they have detailed, direct and day-to-day experience of them. They *have* to understand such people and the ways in which they think. Above all, they have to be able to 'see through' them and their attempts at deception, at beating the system. For the sociologist to claim that he wishes to, and can, identify some *independent* point of view which those inmates possess and which is *not* known to the staff is directly to challenge the occupational pride of the staff. They *already know* what their charges think and how to work with them.

The entire rationale of the position presses towards a kind of partisanship. It is not that kind of partisanship which says that the poor, the oppressed, the marginal and the deviant are better than the conventional, the powerful and the dominant. Rather, it arises as a result of taking the line that the supposedly 'socially worthless' are actually *very much like* those who fall within more conventional moral boundaries and who are usually assigned a high social value. Indeed, the low esteem accorded to 'underdogs' may largely be a question of the conventional, the powerful and the dominant deciding what standards are to be applied to other people. The relative placement of groups within the social process of communication ensures that the researcher will, in general, have more revelations of a flattering and favourable kind concerning 'underdogs' than he will have about the privileged. The researcher, therefore, ends up taking the side of the 'underdogs' in so far as he seeks to explicate the elements of 'normality' present in their lives, thereby inevitably 'upgrading' their public image.

THE REVELATION OF RATIONALITY

Symbolic Interactionists often demonstrate 'rationality' in unexpected places. Nowhere has this demonstration been more emphatically made than in the examination of 'mental illness'. The very idea of 'mentally sick' persons involves the belief that their rationality is impaired, that they are incapable of conducting themselves in a rational way. Yet a number of researchers have tried to show that there is, in the behaviour of so-called mentally ill persons, a large and previously unrecognised element of rationality.

In 'Paranoia and the Dynamics of Exclusion', Edwin Lemert attacks the notion of the 'paranoid'. Supposedly, a paranoid fantasises that he is being subjected to persecution. Lemert claims that the label 'paranoid' usually involves us in a gross underestimation of the extent to which that person *is* subjected to persecution by a well-organised conspiracy.

Lermert argues that a kind of vicious circle develops between the 'paranoid' and other people. The 'paranoid' is usually a person who does not fit too well into his social relations with people, particularly people with whom he would normally relate informally in his working life. Because he does not fit in too well, other people begin to exclude him from informal association with them. Then the excluded person (the 'paranoid') becomes aware of his exclusion and reacts to it. His reactions provide others with yet further reasons to exclude him. They may in turn become cautious and afraid, suspecting that he is becoming mentally ill. Afraid of the 'paranoid's' reaction, they conceal their fear and suspicion and discuss among themselves the best way of dealing with this extraordinarily difficult person. Thus the 'paranoid' *is* correct; those around him *are* conspiring against him. His reactions against this 'conspiracy' confirm their suspicions that he is mentally ill and needs treatment. They involve a psychiatrist who, in trying to treat the 'paranoid' serves only further to corroborate the existence of the 'conspiracy'. Thus attempts to help a supposedly sick person serve only to add to his difficulties. He is now locked away as a paranoic.

A similar approach to mental illness is taken by Erving Goffman in his book *Asylums*. Goffman conducts his study of the social situation of the mental patient on the assumption that the individual is psychologically perfectly 'normal'. His aim is to show that the behaviour of the hospital inmate is a rational response to the way life is organised in the institution that encompasses him. Goffman characterises mental hospitals as 'total institutions'. The concept *'total institutions'* is another example of the formal generalisation towards which much of Symbolic Interactionism is directed. It is a concept designed to capture certain formal aspects of organisational life present in organisations which have the most diversified 'content', for example, organisations involved in such different tasks as transporting goods and passengers (ships), conducting the religious life (monasteries), preparing people for military careers (military schools), encapturing and exterminating people (concentration camps), curing and taking care of the sick (hospitals). They are all total institutions; they all encompass the entire daily round of their inmates: sleeping, working, eating and taking leisure must be done within the same physical confines and in the same company.

In Goffman's view, the fact that these organisations encompass their inmates' daily rounds is enormously and pervasively consequential for their social life. They impose upon their inhabitants the necessity for behaviours which may seem quite bizarre to people leading 'ordinary lives', but these behaviours are almost inevitable in the context of a 'total institution'.

Consider, for example, the 'hoarding' behaviour of patients. Some patients constantly keep all their possessions about their person and, as a result, carry about with them all sorts of 'trivial' and 'useless' possessions. These patients can, therefore, be seen as suffering from an overdeveloped possessiveness which might be seen to betray anxieties and insecurities developed beyond normal levels. They may, therefore, be seen as emotionally disordered. Goffman disagrees with this view. He takes the line that psychiatric ideology focuses attention upon the personality and emotional states of individuals without regard for the situation and circumstances within which they are located. The psychiatric orientation of the staff of the mental hospital inclines them to look upon the hoarding behaviour of the inmates as symptomatic of their mental condition. The staff do not take into account the kind of environment which *their own psychiatric orientation* and the nature of the institution provide for the inmate.

In Goffman's view, this environment is essentially 'depriving'. To see many of the possessions which the inmate keeps about his person as 'trivial' or 'useless' is to be unappreciative of the 'depriving' character of the institution. It is 'depriving' because not only are many ordinary, mundane things in scarce supply, but also because the inmates additionally lack privacy and security. The fact that patients keep many of their possessions about their person is perhaps only a sign of their lack of access to secure storage facilities; they are likely to lose any possessions left lying about.

This alternative explanation of many seemingly strange aspects of patient behaviour can be found in the odd circumstances under which patients live. Such an explanation, however, is not sought by the staff of the hospital. Since they subscribe to psychiatric ideologies, they are inclined to reject this sort of 'circumstantial' or 'contextual' explanations. They prefer explanations formulated in terms of 'personality' and 'states of mind'. Further, they attempt to force these explanations upon the patients. Psychiatric ideologies often have a self-sustaining feature of requiring those identified as mentally sick to accept psychiatric definition of themselves as a condition of 'getting better'. In other words, if the patient is unwilling to accept that his behaviour is attributable to his own personal deficiencies, then his refusal to do so is taken as 'another sign of his sickness'. Only when the patient begins to agree that his conduct can be explained by his own mental disorder can the staff accept that he is 'coming to terms' with his illness and beginning to get better. Since the staff control the release of inmates, they are in a strong position to impose their viewpoint on their charges.

On the basis of arguments such as these, it is therefore possible to claim that there is an unrecognised rationality in the behaviour of hospitalised mental patients. In the circumstances of the 'total institution', their behaviour is well adapted and, perhaps, the only kind possible. Indeed, it may be the very circumstances themselves which impose both the behaviour upon patients and the appearances of irrationality displayed by such behaviour.

DEFINING THE SITUATION

An important characteristic of the Symbolic Interactionist approach is summed up by W. I. Thomas's frequently cited slogan: If men define situations as real, they are real in their consequences. This statement emphasises a common focus of Symbolic Interactionist researches upon the processes by which the members of society *define* their circumstances and respective identities.

The implication of such a 'definitional' approach is that the Symbolic Interactionist disbars himself from making external judgements about the people he studies. Instead he must get close to them and describe *their* circumstances as *they* see them. He may not take on the peculiar and special task of saying what is 'really' happening in the society, regardless of the understandings people actually have of what is happening in their lives. He adopts the position of describing the competing and conflicting claims men make about what is 'real' and 'what is happening'. He does not seek to arbitrate between these claims, to say which ones are correct.

The case for such a definitional approach has been extensively and explicitly made by what has come to be known as the 'labelling theory of deviance'. The labelling theorist argues that in dealing with 'deviants', the sociologist is not usually studying the whole class of persons who have committed an act of deviance. Instead, he is merely studying those persons who have been seen to commit such an act and have been labelled accordingly. Consequently, any attempt to discover 'underlying causes' of deviance, such as hereditary traits and social background, simply by focusing on those persons identified and labelled as 'deviant' is bound to be faulty. To produce such findings necessitates a proper sampling of *all* of the people who have perpetrated the deviant act, not simply those who have been apprehended. The labelling theorist suggests that it is rarely possible to make such a sampling. Instead, he prefers the view that usually people who transgress moral rules are ordinary people who are motivated in quite conventional ways. They are not special, not set apart from 'normal people' by peculiar hereditary traits or other 'basic' and 'underlying' causes. For example, if people drink despite prohibition, that is, laws forbidding sale of alcohol, it is not perhaps because there is something about them which is peculiar, but because *everybody* drinks despite prohibition. If some of them are arrested for drinking, it is not because they are different but because they are unlucky.

The sociologist should, therefore, recognise the nature of the data with which he is dealing when he studies 'deviants'. Taking 'criminals', for example, he cannot know whether they 'really' do the things for which they are convicted. After all, even the massive investigative apparatus available to the police and the courts cannot provide certainty. Instead, he should realise that he is dealing with a population which has been *defined* by the society at large as different and which has publicly been labelled 'deviant'. Consequently, he should examine the ways in which the community defines some of its members as unworthy of continued participation in its daily life. To understand why some people are in prison, he must understand how the police are organised in their daily work, how they come to make arrests, why some cases to go to court and others do not, how courts are organised to lead to convictions, and so forth. Of course, some of the characteristics of prison inmates may have a good deal to do with their incarceration because they are the sorts of character-istics to which policemen, judges and jurors attend in making deci-sions about likely guilt. For example, if he finds that many prisoners are recidivist, that is, have previous convictions, he should not con-clude that this characteristic derives from 'underlying weakness'. Instead, he should notice that policemen, judges and jurors hold the theory that crime results from recurrent compulsions. The credibility which the police will extend to a suspect's denial may well depend upon the existence of a previous conviction for a similar offence.

TAKING THE ACTOR'S STANDPOINT

The idea that we need to look upon circumstances 'from the actor's point of view' is by no means distinctive to Symbolic Interactionism. The appeal that sociology should try to 'understand' the outlook, attitudes and beliefs of those whom it studies has been made on many separate occasions. Max Weber is the best-known exponent of the view that sociology should seek to study not the movements and reflexes of human bodies, but the actions of people in terms of their understandings and beliefs. The idea underlying an insistence upon an 'action approach' is not simply that it might be interesting to know what people think, but, rather, the idea that unless one knows what people think, we *cannot* understand why they behave as they do. People act as they do on the basis of the circumstances as they define them, they act as they do *out of* their beliefs and understandings.

The idea that the sociologist should 'understand', should 'take the actor's point of view', is not universally popular and there are many who regard it with considerable suspicion. They view it as a mystical notion whose application must be antithetical or opposed to the possibilities of rigour in sociology. By attempting to apprehend someone else's point of view, by trying to understand someone else's state of mind, we may seem to be trying to 'put ourselves in his place' and to be engaging in a kind of emotional speculation about him. As emotional speculations cannot be checked or verified, we may be seen to be operating in an unscientific manner.

Such objections, however, betray a continuing acceptance of just the sorts of views against which Mead was arguing, that is, views which maintain that the body and the mind are essentially separate. Such views rest on the assumption that we can observe the behaviour of the body for that is material, tangible and available to any observer, but we cannot observe the thoughts and feelings of the mind because they are intangible, immaterial and hidden within the confines of the body. We recall, however, that the implication of Mead's position is that the 'behaviour' of the body *is also* the 'behaviour' of the mind. Our living body is a mindful entity which *expresses* what we think and feel. Smiles and tears are not the sort of things we treat as 'physical' (in this narrow sense). We do not ordinarily think of tears as 'leaks from the eyeballs' or smiles as 'twitches of the mouth'. We do, in general, treat them as expressions of pain, distress, grief, pleasure, satisfaction, amusement, and so on. We treat the things people do as expressions of their thoughts, feelings, emotions and views. We do so without hesitation or difficulty. There is no reason why sociologists – unlike ordinary people – should pretend to be incapable of ascertaining the states of mind which activities express.

All that is involved in 'taking the standpoint of the actor' is an attempt to record and describe the ideas and impressions which persons express in social interaction; followed by an attempt to understand these ideas and impressions from the standpoints of the persons involved, rather than from the standpoint of an outside observer. For example, it might be the case that in our society

someone observed smiling may be assumed to be expressing amusement, whereas in another society, in a different cultural environment, the action of smiling may be more likely to express something
else, say, embarrassment. Such cultural variations present no
principled difficulties. After all, part of the sociologist's task is to
identify the different conventions present in different social settings.
He can presumably learn them just as he has previously learned the
conventions of his native society and just as the natives of other
societies learned the conventions of their own society.

A PREFERENCE FOR QUALITATIVE METHODS

One implication of the policy of taking the standpoint of the actor is
that research should be both intensive and typically accomplished
through the acquisition of a detailed and rich acquaintance with the
life, circumstances and ways of those being studied. Consequently,
qualitative methods are likely to provide the most congenial ways of
applying such a policy. (We leave a fuller discussion of this characteristic of the Symbolic Interactionist approach until Chapter 6.)

THE INDIVIDUAL AND SOCIETY IN SYMBOLIC
INTERACTIONISM

Throughout the earlier sections of this chapter we have touched
upon various elements and assumptions which make up a fairly
coherent conceptual framework or model of social organisation. In
this section we spell out this model more explicitly.

The Symbolic Interactionist approach rests on the assumptions
that the organisation of social life arises from within the society itself
and out of the processes of interaction between the members of
society. It does not accept the idea that the form of social organisation is determined by the influence of external factors, for example,
geographical or economic. Of course, it does not entirely discount
such factors in the shaping of social life; but it argues pragmatically
that their impact depends upon the kinds of intelligent adaptation
man makes to them. External factors do not 'in themselves' have any
kind of direct implications for action. As we saw in our earlier
example, the implications that some physical occurrence such as, say,
rainfall will have for action will depend upon the understandings,
beliefs and interests that people have. For Symbolic Interactionists,
although the organisation of society arises from within, it does not

take on the kind of systemic and autonomous character that we found in our examination of structuralist approaches. To treat the needs and operations of a social system as the determinants of the organisation of the lives of people in society is once again to propose that individuals merely react to external forces. As we have seen, this view is incompatible with a Symbolic Interactionist approach.

Symbolic Interactionists do not see society as some kind of well-defined, tightly integrated system of parts. Rather, 'society' is assumed to be a relatively loose arrangement of quite heterogeneous groupings – occupational, organisational, ethnic, class, status, political, religious, and so on. No particular kind of group is seen to be most 'basic' in the way, for example, Marxian theory insists upon the fundamental character of classes. The working of society involves the interplay of these heterogeneous groupings. This interplay is characteristically competitive in that some of these groups (or some alliance of these groups) may acquire a measure of predominance and may take a particularly advantageous position within the processes of social control, organisation and communication. There is no *a priori* theoretical reason, however, to expect any given group to take such an advantageous position.

ANSELM STRAUSS: SOCIETY AS 'NEGOTIATED ORDER'

This conception of the organisation of society and its component parts has been crystallised most sharply by Strauss and his colleagues in *Psychiatric Ideologies* with their concept of a 'negotiated order'. The concept, 'negotiated order', emphasises the fact that society is continuously organising. It is not the case that an organisation is established and then proceeds to operate in an unvarying way. Rather, society is constantly being organised and reorganised. Its arrangements are constantly being 'worked at' by those who live within them; they are constantly being arranged, modified, rearranged, sustained, defended and undermined. The members of society are, therefore, constantly involved in a process of 'negotiation' with one another as they make agreements on how they will conduct themselves and as they reaffirm, revise and replace these agreements over the passage of time.

The concept of a negotiated order was specifically devised to cope with explaining the nature of the division of labour in psychiatric hospitals. We might expect these organisations to have a well-defined, clear and stable division of both labour and authority for those who operate within them, that is, doctors, nursing staff,

patients, medically unqualified aides and the public. This expectation, however, was not realised in those organisations studied by
Strauss and his colleagues. Instead, the situation was fluid and constantly changing; lines of alliance, responsibility and speciality were
continually revised and modified, and quite different 'balances' in
different parts of the same hospital at any given time, or in the same
parts of the hospital at different times, were reached. Strauss found
some of the sources of this fluidity.

(1) The fact that *within* any given group there is no firm consensus
as to the proper organisation of affairs. There are many different
schools of psychiatry and members of those different schools
will have quite different understandings about, for example, the
respective responsibilities, rights and obligations of therapists
and patients.

(2) The fact that *between* groups there is no consensus. Between
psychiatric and nursing staff there are often likely to be, for
example, different conceptions of the ways in which patients
should be nursed and their medical regime organised. The
psychiatric staff will have one set of views on how the nursing
staff should do their jobs and the nursing staff, though not
medically trained, will develop another set of views about the
propriety, effectiveness and practicability of various forms of
medical treatment.

(3) The fact that even 'the weak' have power. Although the
psychiatric staff may be thought of as being 'at the top' of the
hierarchy of authority within the hospital, nevertheless they are
not in a position to assert their expectations, preferences and
policies over other groupings. The 'weaker groups', such as
nursing staff or patients, are not completely without power
over their formal superiors. It is the nursing staff who have to
care for the day-to-day operation of the wards and administer to
patients the detailed regimes prescribed by the psychiatric staff.
If their co-operation with the psychiatric staff is reluctant they
can make life difficult indeed for their 'superiors'.

It is important to recognise that the concept of 'negotiation' must
be understood metaphorically. Strauss is not, by any means,
implying that people are all the time engaged in the explicit negotiation of their relative positions; they are not openly making deals or
writing out agreements. Sometimes they are, but more usually they
are involved in the kind of implicit, unspoken, mutual adjustment of

ing, attitude, interest and understanding which Strauss
e think of *as though* it were a process of negotiation and

ERVING GOFFMAN: THE SELF, SOCIETY AND SOCIAL INTERACTION

We recall that it was Mead's view that the self is a socialised entity,
something created in and through social interaction. The individual
was not merely *aware* of the 'generalised other'. Rather, he
'internalised' the attitudes and values current within his social milieu;
he learned attitudes and values and incorporated them into his
psychic make-up in such a manner that he could spontaneously strike
socially appropriate attitudes, experience socially appropriate feelings
and produce socially appropriate actions. Later developments in
Symbolic Interactionism have continued Mead's interest in, and
shared his conception of, the self and its nature, development and
transformation over time. One of the most central tenets of the
approach is that the member of the society is a *self*-conscious creature
who employs his intelligence in the organisation of his action. This
recognition that the individual does have a sense of self requires,
however, a consideration of its origins and development. How does
the self become defined? How is its pattern of definition modified
over time?

The examination of social life in its day-to-day settings, when
combined with an orientation to formal analysis, can lead to the
realisation that the organisation of social interaction has its own
distinctive character which can be analysed in its own right without
any necessary concern for the way in which the face-to-face
encounter fits into any wider social structures of which it may be a
part. Regardless of the kind of activity going on, there will be consequences for the organisation of action which arise from the fact of
people being physically present together in the same place, within
range of each other's observation and communication. Almost the
entirety of Erving Goffman's work can be seen as an ingenious and
persistent attempt to examine the implications of the fact of physical
co-presence.

It is regrettably common for categorisations of the kind used to
organise this book to be treated as though they were definitive and
rigid, rather than the educationally convenient devices that they are,
as though the people allocated to our different boxes had nothing at
all in common with one another.

Thinkers are seldom unswerving respecters of lines of demarcation and though we may have counted Durkheim as a 'structuralist' and Goffman as an 'interactionist', it should not be thought that they are opposed to each other on *all* important bases of comparison. Goffman's work does in fact exhibit the application of some central Durkheimian themes, connecting them up with those which are central to an 'interactionist' way of thinking. By linking things up in this way, Goffman is able to offer a distinctive view of social inter-action as a ritual process.

To see how he does so we need to take account of Durkheim's theories about religion.

Durkheim thought that the essence of religion was not found in beliefs about supernatural beings or forces, but in the making of a distinction between the sacred and the profane. The sacred is that which is set apart, regarded as special and treated with great respect and awe. It is only polluted by contact with the ordinary and every-day, that is, the profane. For example, Durkheim's conception of the sacred can be applied to Christian traditions. Religious symbols – crosses, altars and churches – are set apart physically and in places which are not available to entry by just anyone. They are made to look striking and impressive: church architecture is often intended to induce a sense of awe, and churches are decorated with beautiful and valuable artefacts. Those who approach religious places and symbols do so with gestures of humility, they cover their heads, get down on their knees, lower their voices. It is perhaps less obvious that this notion applies to things which are not conventionally regarded as religious. Thus, Durkheim might regard the Royal Family as an instance of the sacred. Members of this family are treated as very special people, being entitled to live a very different kind of life from the rest of us. They are cut off from our ordinary lives behind the walls and fences of castles, palaces and large estates, kept apart from the rest of us by a barrier of guards. Royal persons are treated as though they must be kept above and apart from the mundane con-cerns which occupy their subjects; and for them to be brought into contact with things that seem otherwise quite ordinary and harmless would be wrong and disrespectful. Thus, royal visitors to places are not even allowed to set eyes on such things as ordinary toilets which are concealed from their view and special facilities for their own exclusive use provided.

Durkheim, seeing that conventional religion was becoming less important in the life of the modern Western world, formed the view that 'the individual' was becoming more and more centrally the sacred thing. We are tending to make a religion of our individuality, of our personal uniqueness, wanting to protect that above and beyond everything else. 'Human rights' and 'individual freedom', now deeply rooted in Western tradition and the focus of a powerful and deep emotional attachment, are treated with that respectfulness which is the essential ingredient of the sacred.

Durkheim thought that the relationship with the sacred is through ritual action which, for him, can best be seen as 'expressive', rather than 'instrumental', conduct.

An instrumental action is done in pursuit of some practical end, for example, wearing spectacles in order to improve one's sight. The ritual action, however, does not do something practical. For example, the communion consumption of wafer and wine is not a way of satisfying hunger, but is a symbolic gesture. Through the symbolism of flesh and blood associated with the wine and wafer, believers are enabled to make a kind of statement in actions about their relationship to the church, to God and to each other. The expressive act is one which is performed to say something, to communicate.

Of course, the distinction of instrumental from expressive acts, if pressed very far, begins to lose its power. It seems more useful therefore to think of 'instrumentality' and 'expressiveness' as aspects of activity, so that even the most instrumental action will have some expressive aspect.

Although this argument may seem quite remote from the study of interpersonal relations, Goffman shows in his treament of ordinary conduct that this distance is not as great as it seems. Taking up the idea that the individual is a sacred object and that the means of relating to the sacred is through ritual, he was able to view the relationships between individuals as a set of rituals. By so doing, he almost literally opened the eyes of many sociologists, for he enabled them to see in sociological terms things which had been under their very noses, staring them in the face, but which had not previously seemed to possess any particular sociological interest or recognisable order.

Goffman's treatment of face-to-face relations in ritual terms implies that they be seen as communicative and examined for their expressive *rather than* their instrumental character. This is not to deny that they have an instrumental aspect, but to bring out their previously neglected expressive dimension.

Above, we mentioned the wearing of spectacles as an instrumental matter: something to be explained in terms of their use in assisting vision. However, a moment's thought indicates there is more to the wearing of spectacles; that wearing them has *expressive* significance and is seen as saying something about the wearer. People who need to wear spectacles, in the sense that their eyesight is poor, can resist wearing them because of what other people think of them if they do. Elderly people will sometimes be loath to begin wearing spectacles because other people will think not only that their eyesight is failing, but that they are on the road to senility.

Goffman provides the means for looking at all aspects of social interaction – posture, clothing, ornamentation, physical distance, the deployment of limbs, the distribution of looks and numerous other matters – to see what part they play in regulating the face-to-face encounters and communications between participants. To organise the understanding, he employs a theatrical metaphor.

When we enter a social occasion, we want to present a self to others, we want to appear to them as a certain kind of person. Since human beings are not mind-readers in the telepathic sense, they cannot know what kind of person we think we are/want to be taken to be, unless we convey an impression of self to them. The *only* way to do so is through our conduct towards others. To inform them as to who we are/think we are, we have to put on a performance which, Goffman thinks, makes a useful analogy to the performance going on in the theatre, when players seek to convey a theatrical illusion to the audience.

On stage, the actor has the task of presenting himself to the audience as the relevant character in the play and to make the audience aware that he is intendedly, say, a policeman through the use of props, scenery and dialogue. He does not have to shoulder the work of projecting a character all by himself because he is aided not only by the other players on the stage, but also by those who work behind the scenes – the make-up staff, scene-changers, directors, and so forth. All of these parties are all involved in staging the play and projecting the identities of the character to the audience.

The presentation of a play involves 'teamwork': all these parties act as a team seeking to maintain the conviction of the audience that they are witness to a struggle for power in a medieval court rather than watching some ordinary people dressed up in anachronistic clothing, reciting lines written for them by someone long dead. Thus Goffman's metaphor invites us to see that the presentation of a *self* in the context of everyday settings involves teamwork. For example, the staff of a hospital can be looked upon as a team, seeking to sustain for patients and their relatives the conviction that competent and effective medical work is being done on their behalf. The metaphor, applied still further, encourages the attempt to see to what extent settings like a hospital can be seen as divided, like the theatre, into front- and backstage regions, and to examine the ways in which interaction between the two is essential to maintaining the projected impression. For example, in hospitals, patients and their relatives are excluded from many areas of activity in order that things can get done which may be important for keeping up the image of competent work. Such backstage happenings, if witnessed by patients and their families, might be disillusioning, undermining the image of dedicated concern that is required to reassure the family that everything possible is being done. Goffman points out that the behaviour of the operating room staff belies the television drama image of the operating theatre as a scene of constant tension and drama. The staff fool about, make jokes, and so on, something essential to their own idea of themselves as people who can take the demands of routine surgery in their stride and without the need for maximum concentration. If witnessed by relatives, however, they would look as though they were being less than responsible in their work.

Again, then, Goffman is exemplifying one of Durkheim's themes: the individual is a collective creation, the projection of a particular conception of self is something that requires collaborative activity and is done by a team. The impression that one is a competent surgeon, say, is not given solely through one's own conduct, but requires the supportive action of medical colleagues, subordinates, and so on.

Goffman, however, is frequently criticised for the kind of picture he is imagined to be painting of people and their social lives. He is alleged to be presenting a conception of people's presentation of self which shows them as essentially self-conscious, manipulative and shallow creatures, entirely caught up with the creation of an image in the minds of other people. We shall not deny that there are aspects of Goffman's work which are compatible with such an 'interruption', and we certainly do not want to claim that Goffman is wholly consistent in his attitudes and treatment. Nevertheless, we maintain that these criticisms are not really important.

It is important to recognise that Goffman's method is an indirect one. He draws heavily upon examples from the world of con men, studies of asylums and concentration camps and other less-than-everyday places. He does not suppose that these places are no different from the environments of our ordinary conduct, but chooses them precisely because they are *extreme situations*, Goffman wants to point our attention to what we take for granted in the normal course of our lives. He makes us notice them by focusing our attention upon settings within which the things we ordinarily rely upon and take for granted are absent and therefore cannot be depended upon. They are more noticeable in their absence than their presence. Asylums and concentration camps are not like everyday life, but study of them can be used to illuminate it.

Consider the case of confidence tricksters. They are engaged in the self-conscious manipulation of appearances for the purposes of deception. They seek to give their victim (the 'mark') the impression that they are people possessing a character quite different to their actual one, that they are upright citizens in possession of a money-making proposition in which the victim can share. Requiring to act in ways appropriate for an upright and trustworthy citizen with a sound money-making proposition, they have to be very careful of all aspects of their appearance, manner and conduct to ensure that nothing is done or happens to create an incongruous impression. Towards such ends they would, on occasion, engage in quite extensive deception so that, for example, as many as fifty people could be involved in creating a fake betting shop and playing the parts of staff and customers in a setting literally built for the deception.

Of course there are aspects in which we can all be compared to confidence tricksters, times at which we act in a given way merely to give the impression that we are a certain sort of person. For example, we may self-consciously aim to deceive others about the type of person we are by the use of the 'coffee table book' as a way of giving false impressions of our intellectual interests or powers. If, however, we want to extract a general conception of what people are like from Goffman's writings, there is as much evidence there for the view that we are more usually like marks than con men. The confidence trickster relies upon the fact that people will take a great deal on trust and will put a lot of faith in appearances. Simply setting himself up with a minimal number of props required to convey a certain impression (say, of himself as a prosperous businessman) is enough to gain him the confidence of his intended victim, enabling him to be taken as a most reliable associate. The confidence trickster abuses the disposition of people to give their trust rather easily and exploits their inclination to take appearances for granted. Goffman's work, then, can be read to suggest that we ordinary people are not so much sophisticated and manipulative, but rather we are credulous and naive.

However, there is as much reason to maintain that the most interesting thing about Goffman is not that he makes us seem more or less bright or dim than we usually take ourselves to be, but that he uses a range of metaphors to enable us to become more aware of things of which we normally only take the most unself-conscious notice. Through using those metaphors, he has done much to open up the possibility of giving the kind of close, detailed and systematic attention to the organisation of face-to-face behaviour which others have taken advantage of (as can be seen in the section on conversational analysis in the next chapter on ethnomethodology).

HOWARD BECKER: SOCIALISATION AS AN 'ACTIVE' PROCESS

The consideration of the individual's communication of his sense of self naturally enough raises questions about the origins of that sense of self. How do we come to think of ourself as doctor, patient or whatever? How are we socialised, how do we learn?

Symbolic Interactionists have been leading advocates of research into adult socialisation and have been highly critical of those conceptions of socialisation which see the basic traits of behaviour as being laid down in childhood and as being unamenable to subsequent modification. In their view, such an understanding of socialisation smacks rather strongly of the idea that

what is learned in the very early phases of childhood	automatically leads to	certain kinds of unmodifiable behaviour patterns shown in adulthood

and that, again, resembles the view that

a stimulus	automatically leads to	a fixed response.

It is, therefore, hardly surprising that the proponents of Symbolic Interactionism are generally unwilling to accept a model which postulates that patterns of adult behaviour are to be understood as manifestations of patterns of reaction laid down in childhood. Accordingly, they take the position that socialisation, the process of learning to behave, is a continuing one, that is, it begins in childhood but it *continues throughout* adulthood. They argue that there is a need to recognise the existence and ubiquity of adult socialisation and to recognise that some of the processes of adult socialisation may be so drastic that they can lead to quite basic changes in the individual's conception of self. For example, the kinds of experiences involved in admission to total institutions are often sufficient to challenge our very sense of even being an adult. Admission to prisons, concentration camps and mental hospitals may involve violation of those rights of privacy and control of access to our own body which we take to be central and integral to our adult status. Admission procedures may involve the kind of humiliations and unpleasant experiences that drastically undercut our sense of being ourself, that is, being an autonomous individual entitled to respect and polite treatment from others. In these ways, the most basic character traits *can* be modified in adulthood and, hence, a theory of socialisation which does not allow this possibility is not satisfactory.

Of course, most patterns of adult learning are by no means so drastic in their character as those involved in entry into total institutions. Even so, the development of the adult life-cycle can be understood as a continuous modification of behaviour through learning. For example, Becker's study of the professional socialisation of medical students, *Boys in White,* showed that the medical students were involved less in learning to be like doctors than in learning how to be students.

He found that a pattern of 'cynicism' emerged among the students. Although they had started off with an 'idealistic' view of what they would do in medical school and a determination to become first-rate physicians, after a while the students aimed only to 'get through' medical school. Their unfolding experience of medical school made it increasingly obvious that they could not possibly absorb all the information their teachers were bombarding them with; nor could they even meet all the work assignments being set for them. The students felt they had to work out among themselves ways of pooling information and resources, work and examination techniques, so that they could ensure enough work was covered at least to graduate.

Becker argued that the students were operating on different time perspectives. They set out with a 'long-term' perspective, a view of how – in the longer term – they wanted to develop into first-rate physicians. Such a long-term perspective, however, proved to be untenable in the face of the realities of life in medical school. The students abandoned it in favour of a relatively 'short-term' perspective, involving 'getting through' the examinations. They became 'cynical' in the sense that they were prepared to do whatever was necessary to ensure their own graduation, but they did not altogether abandon their ambition to excel at medicine. They had merely suspended it in favour of practically coping with pressing and immediate requirements. They were convinced that after graduation they could reinvoke their aspiration to join the highest ranks of their profession and could devote themselves, at this later stage in their career, to developing and improving their skills.

This use of the concept 'time perspectives' and, indeed, this general concern to stress the continuity of the adult learning process, emphasise again the significance which Symbolic Interactionists place upon the temporal character of activities. Social life inescapably takes place in time; it is a continuously unfolding experience. The sociological analyst needs to be attuned to the fact that the events he is observing are occurring at some point along the course of a career of events and may not be fully understood unless they are understood relative to events which precede and succeed them. The nature of the medical student's 'cynicism' will be misunderstood if it is grasped simply as a calculating and strategic attempt to 'get by' in the profession. Rather, it is a relatively localised phenomenon; it is a temporary attitude which is adopted at a particular time in particular circumstances.

Symbolic Interactionists do not see the relation of the individual and society as operating in some deterministic fashion. For them, the individual is a social creature who is *not* a mere puppet of society; he is not moulded once-and-for-all by the impact of external factors. Rather, the relation involves interplay; the individual learns from his society and, at the same time, modifies his society through the use of his mind. The individual can invent and originate, he can use these capacities to renegotiate the very social order in which he is situated.

CONCLUSION: SOME CRITICISMS

If Symbolic Interactionism is critical of those who 'impersonate' the natural scientist, then those same sociologists are reciprocally critical of the way in which Symbolic Interactionism is indifferent to problems of evidence, proof and systematic theory. Likewise, the Symbolic Interactionists' criticism of those who take an overly deterministic view of the relationship between individual and society meets with the reply that they, in turn, are inattentive to the importance of 'structural' constraints and underestimate the extent to which choices are effectively foreclosed by given social circumstances. For those who emphasise the macro-sociological strategy of structuralism, the Symbolic Interactionist approach fails because it does not attempt to take some overview of the total societal organisation. In so far as it *does* give an account of the overall organisation of society, then, for many sociologists, it overplays the significance of ethnic, religious and similar divisions at the expense of those arising from social stratification. On that argument, the Symbolic Inter-actionist approach is closely allied with the liberal-pluralist view of society; it neglects the extent to which society is a system – and a class-system at that. Even ethnomethodologists, who are often viewed as being closely affiliated with Symbolic Interactionists, are apt to criticise it, to accuse if of being yet another conventional sociology, because it relies upon common-sense understandings of society which are not subjected to scrutiny.

In closing this chapter, we should perhaps note that, as is commonly the way in sociology, the Symbolic Interactionist approach is criticised from other sociological perspectives for differing from them. Its critics typically find that it lacks precisely those virtues which – it just happens – appertain to the critics' own position. The most serious criticism for Symbolic Interactionism is not, however, these adverse views from other sociological per-spectives. Rather, Symbolic Interactionism appears to resemble the other perspectives in having lost its impetus. The materials which we have drawn upon in this chapter are those which have played a crucial part in shaping the framework of this way of thinking, but they are all now relatively old pieces of work. Though many more people are now influenced by, if not working directly within, the interactionist scheme, their work tends to amount to variations on the established themes rather than real developments on them.

FURTHER READING

Manis, J. G., and **Meltzer, B. N.** (eds), *Symbolic Interaction: A Reader in Social Psychology* (Allyn & Bacon, 1967). For Blumer's 'Sociological analysis and the variable'.

Rose, A. M. *Human Behaviour and Social Processes: An Interactionist Approach* (Routledge & Kegan Paul, 1962). For Blumer's 'Society as symbolic interaction'.

Worsley, P. (ed.), *Problems of Modern Society: Selected Readings* (Penguin, 1972). For Blumer's 'Sociological theory in industrial relations' which explores some implications of symbolic interactionism for the study of work. For Everett C. Hughes's 'Mistakes at work' showing how persons organise to deal with their own mistakes and the mistakes of others. For E. Goffman's 'The road to the mental hospital' and 'Inside the asylum'. For E. M. Lemert's 'Primary and secondary deviation' showing the role of society's reaction in creating deviance. For D. Sudnow's 'Normal crimes' which describes plea bargaining in the negotiation of criminal charges.

Worsley, P. (ed.), *Modern Sociology – Introductory Readings* (Penguin, 1970). For Goffman's 'Characteristics of total institutions'.

Rubington, E., and **Weinberg, M. S.** *Deviance: The Interactionist Perspective* (Collier Macmillan, 1968). For Howard S. Becker's 'On labelling outsiders'. For Goffman's 'The moral career of the mental patient'. For Lemert's 'Paranoia and the dynamics of exclusion'.

Denzin, N. (ed.), *Studies in Symbolic Interaction,* Vols I, II and III (JAI Press, 1978–80).

Rock, P., *The Making of Symbolic Interactionism* (Macmillan, 1979).

QUESTIONS

1 Why, in Mead's view, is it misleading to oppose 'mind' to 'nature'?

2 Why is 'variable analysis' an inadequate basis for understanding society?

3 What kind of methodology does Blumer think appropriate to the study of social life?

4 How can the idea of 'career' be applied in the study of those who would not normally be thought to have any career?

5 Why is the 'underdog' view so interesting to Symbolic Interactionism?

6 Are the mentally ill more rational than is popularly supposed?

7 Why does Symbolic Interactionism reject a 'mechanical' image of man?

8 How is the emphasis on 'formal' analysis used by Symbolic Interactionism to illuminate social life?

9 What view does Symbolic Interactionism take of 'the deviant'? Discuss with reference to mental illness.

10 Why are work and occupations important to a Symbolic Interactionist understanding of contemporary society?

11 How can Durkheim's study of religion be seen to relate to Goffman's analysis of face-to-face interaction?

12 To what extent is everyday life theatrical?

Chapter 5

Ethnomethodology as a Perspective

INTRODUCTION

Ethnomethodology is a recent development in sociology. Although many of the ideas upon which it is based have a long history in sociology, its existence as a publicly identified approach dates only from the publication of Harold Garfinkel's *Studies in Ethnomethodology* in 1967. Today ethnomethodologists are still relatively few in number and the amount of work they have published is quite small. Nevertheless, ethnomethodology has attracted considerable attention and criticism within sociology. The impact of ethnomethodology has stemmed from what is seen as the radical nature of its ideas. On the surface, the concerns of ethnomethodologists are, in a general sense, similar to those of the Symbolic Interactionists described in the last chapter. Both Symbolic Interactionists and ethnomethodologists are principally concerned with studying interpersonal social interaction. Both regard social interaction as consisting of meaningful communicative activity between persons, involving mutual interpretive work. Beyond this superficial similarity, however, there are marked differences in ethnomethodology as an approach. They derive from different assumptions about the nature of man and his social world – originally presented in philosphical form by Edmund Husserl (1859–1938) and given a more sociological orientation by Alfred Schutz (1899–1959).

ALFRED SCHUTZ: PHENOMENOLOGY AND THE ORIGINS OF ETHNOMETHODOLOGY

Schutz aimed to lay the foundation of a new conception of the study of social life by drawing on the phenomenological philosophy of

Husserl. For Husserl, 'phenomenology' referred to his attempt to describe the ultimate foundations of human experience by 'seeing beyond' the particulars of everyday experiences in order to describe the 'essences' which underpin them. He maintained that our experience of the world depends on our ability to grasp the 'essences' of the phenomena we perceive. The grasping of essences is the foundation of all experience because only in this way are we able to recognise and classify in a manner which makes it intelligible to us.

In order to grasp these essences we must 'suspend the natural attitude'. By this Husserl means that we have to detach ourselves from our usual ideas about the world by means of the method of 'epoché'. This method requires the thinker to 'put the world in brackets', thereby 'freeing himself' in order to examine the 'stream of consciousness', the stream of experiences – past, present and anticipated – which constitute man's existence and man's knowledge.

Husserl proposes that in perceiving phenomena in the world as objects or events of some kind or another, we necessarily assume these objects and events can be seen, heard, touched, and so on, by others. In short, we assume they are, in essential respects, the 'same' object or event *for others* that they are for ourselves. Thus the foundations of experience do not reside within the mind of an individual in isolation, but rather, are part of what Husserl called the 'world of lived experience'. This world is a *social* world known in common with others.

Schutz's work is largely an attempt to develop and apply these ideas to the scientific study, rather than the philosophical contemplation, of social life. He wanted to produce a 'phenomenology of social life' which, for him, meant producing the basis for a better sociology. It would be better because it would rest on 'sounder' assumptions about the nature of man and his social world than those of existing sociological approaches.

Schutz first presented his ideas in terms of a critique of the conception of 'interpretative sociology' of Max Weber. Schutz begins by agreeing with Max Weber that human beings ('actors' in Schutz's terminology) experience their everyday social world as a socially meaningful reality. When we see or hear another person saying or doing something, we *understand* the meaning of those movements or words. The everyday social world is an 'interpretative reality'.

For Schutz, however, Weber's ideas are only the starting-point for an analysis of social reality. He believes that Weber's analysis of social reality ended at the very point the real problems begin. He argues that Weber's concept of social action is limited. Weber defined 'action' as 'all human behaviour when and in so far as the acting individual attaches a subjective meaning to it', and defined '*social* action' as action which 'takes account of the behaviour of others and is thereby oriented in its course'. Social action, then, is subjectively meaningful behaviour which is influenced by or oriented towards the behaviour of others. In any investigation, the sociologist must try to 'understand' the subjective meanings of social actions for the actors he is studying. If he fails to understand correctly or adequately, his theories and explanations will be based upon a misrepresentation of social reality and will be scientifically of little value.

Schutz takes issue with this conception of social reality. First, Weber's use of 'subjective meaning' seems to imply that an action has a single meaning, and that this meaning stems from the actor who is performing the action. Schutz believes that this way of stating things raises insoluble problems. On the one hand, it creates a picture of the social world as something which is subjectively understood by each and every individual within it, while on the other it appears to assume that these subjective understandings will *somehow* turn out to be sufficiently alike for social relationships and social interactions to be conducted successfully. Weber seems to picture a world of isolated individuals each forming subjective understandings of the actions of himself and of others. He provides no clue about how these understandings mesh together sufficiently to produce the sort of orderly and common social world we live in.

In Schutz's view, Weber crucially fails to bring out the *inter*-subjective nature of the social world. By this, he means that though the everyday social world is experienced through each individual's own consciousness, it is not a 'private' world, personal to each individual. The social world is experienced by the actors as *common* and *shared*. Events in the everyday social world are not experienced as entirely personal, as having a meaning for 'me' which may or may not happen to be the meaning they have for 'you'. If this were so, then communication between individuals would be a matter of chance. It would be rather like two persons talking to one another in a language the other does not understand, so that each person has to guess what the other is saying. Rather, the common 'objective' nature of everyday life is something which is taken for granted by us all as social actors. Social actors view the everyday world in this way using what Schutz calls the 'common-sense knowledge' which all socialised human beings possess.

The concept of 'common-sense knowledge' refers to the knowledge of the everyday world which social actors possess by virtue of living in and being part of that world. The social world, says Schutz, is experienced by social actors as a 'given' world, that is, it is organised, orderly, 'out there'; it is independent of, and pre-exists, any particular individual. At the same time, however, this world *has to be interpreted* and *made sense of* by each of us through our particular experiences. We see the world as orderly and organised through the use of the common-sense knowledge we possess. Common-sense knowledge enables us to categorise and name the things we experience so that we see 'what kinds of things' they are. The concepts which comprise our common-sense knowledge are 'typifications'; they refer to what is typical or standard among a collection of objects, events, or actions. The process of typification enables us to see items as forming a collection, as being the 'same kind of thing', for example, a 'tree', a 'family quarrel', a 'teacher', a 'promise', and so on. As members of our society, we possess a stock of typifications which enable us to see the everyday world as familiar, ordinary and mundane. Furthermore, these typifications are not our own personal invention, but are embodied in the language we share with others. Through language they have been handed down to us; through language we acquire an immense stock of knowledge of things in the world. Only a tiny fraction of this stock derives from our direct observation of the world. We can learn about the world indirectly – by hearing and reading. Much of our knowledge of the world is publicly available knowledge and consists of what anyone can and *should* know.

Schutz continues:

> If we put a letter in the mailbox we assume that anonymous fellow-men, called postmen, will perform a series of manipulations, unknown and unobservable to us, with the effect that the addressee, possibly also unknown to us, will receive the message and react in a way which also escapes our sensory observation; and the result of this is that we receive the book we have ordered. (Schutz, 1967, p. 55)

This quotation brings out two fundamental points. First, it illustrates the intersubjective nature of the social world. Although each individual has a different personal biography and different experience and interests, he can still see the social world as 'factual reality', that is, objects, events and actions are the same for other actors as for himself. For example, it is fundamental that something which we recognise as a letter is similarly recognised by the postman; and that what we write as a request for a book can be seen as such by the publisher or bookshop to whom it is addressed.

Second, in showing that our understandings of the social world are not unique for each individual, Schutz stresses the fundamental importance of what he terms 'the reciprocity of perspectives'. By this concept, he means that unless there is some reason for believing otherwise, social actors commonly assume that events and actions in the social world are understandable to others in the way that they are understandable to themselves. Schutz's analysis of social life is concerned, then, with the structure of the social world as it is experienced by individuals within it; and with how that experience is itself socially constructed and organised.

Schutz goes on to introduce the concept of 'multiple realities' by contrasting the structure and organisation of knowledge in the 'world' or 'reality' of everyday life with 'other realities', such as the 'world' of dreams and the 'world' of fantasies. Of particular relevance here is his comparison between the 'world' of everyday life and the 'world' of scientific theorising.

For Schutz, common-sense knowledge is essentially *practical*. It is acquired and used by social actors in the process of practical living, in coping with all the everyday situations and circumstances which they encounter. The goal of the common-sense actor, unlike that of the scientist, is not the pursuit of truth as assessed by some set of standardised objective criteria. Rather, his goal in any situation is to accomplish what Schutz calls his 'projects'. An actor's projects are the states of affairs he wishes to bring about by his actions. These projects are contingent upon several kinds of factors. First, there is what Schutz calls his 'biographically determined situation', that is, the features of his individual biography. Second, there are the specific features of any particular social occasion, most obviously the actions of other persons in a situation. Third, there is the actor's common-sense knowledge, his stock of typifications of the social world. An actor's projects may be as immediate as getting on to a bus or as long term as career ambitions, but in either case they constitute the meaning which his actions have for him and can have for others. These others, however, are also practical actors; they have their own practical interests, motivations and circumstances; they are not concerned to understand in all their ramifications the meanings that some actions have for the actor who performs them. Rather, they understand his actions in those respects which are relevant for their own practical purposes.

The scientist, however, is not a practical actor in this sense of being primarily interested in knowledge which relates to the particulars of a 'here and now' situation. Instead, he seeks knowledge which relates to his scientific project. The realisation of such a project is not dependent on everyday knowledge and standards, but on some 'objectivised' notion of proper scientific procedure. Consequently, the social scientist may introduce a disturbing and alien 'reality' into the everyday world unless his methods and procedures are suitably modified by grasping the nature of 'multiple realities'; by grasping that scientific reasoning is rather different from everyday practical reasoning. For example, the common-sense actor might find it sufficient for practical purposes to know that 'politicians cannot be trusted', without necessarily being concerned to know precisely *which* politicians and *to what extent*. The social scientist, however, in monitoring the world from his special frame of reference, pursues concerns with, for example, precision, accuracy and generalisation for its own sake. These concerns may have little or no relevance for actors in the 'world of everyday life'.

Schutz believes that these differences between the 'realities' of everyday life and scientific theorising raise particular problems for social science. Unlike the natural sciences, social science, particularly sociology, has to employ 'constructs of the second degree', that is, it has to use constructs, produced for scientific purposes, of phenomena and of human actions which already have meanings in common-sense terms. Schutz claims that the concepts of sociology must relate to the concepts by which actors understand social actions, that is, concepts of the 'first' or basic 'degree', if they are to reproduce in a scientifically useful way (that is, a way which enables precision, generalisability, and so on) the common-sense understanding of actors.

Finally, although Schutz can be seen to have laid the groundwork for a 'phenomenology of social life', he did little himself to operationalise it by producing research to demonstrate how his ideas can be applied to the empirical study of the social world. Later sociologists have tried to take his ideas further, as can be seen particularly in the development of ethnomethodology.

HAROLD GARFINKEL: A CONCEPTUAL FRAMEWORK FOR ETHNOMETHODOLOGY

In his PhD thesis 'The perception of the other' (1952), Harold Garfinkel closely analysed and tried to develop Schutz's ideas. Over time, these ideas were refined and first came to wide public attention in Garfinkel's *Studies in Ethnomethodology* (1967), which effectively founded ethnomethodology. Many sociologists regard this book as one of the most difficult books in sociology ever written. The reasons for this difficulty are twofold. First, Garfinkel's ideas are complex and differ radically from those found in other sociological approaches. Secondly, the language required to express these ideas is itself complex and at times unfamiliar. Therefore it is extremely hard to 'sum up' the book in a few simple points. One way to begin to understand the ideas it contains, however, is to appreciate the aim and character of the book as a whole.

It is first and foremost, as the title says, a book of *studies*. It describes a series of investigations into the organisation of social activities conducted by Garfinkel over several years. The aim of the book is to recommend such studies. It is important to realise that while *Studies in Ethnomethodology* contains a large number of original theoretical ideas, it is not intended to be a book of 'theory'. Garfinkel's aim is not to elaborate a new sociological theory, but to propose a programme of research on a new topic – the organisation of the activities of daily life. He wishes to 'open up' these activities to rigorous and detailed investigation and thereby to learn about them as phenomena in their own right. Consequently, the theoretical notions Garfinkel presents are best thought of as resources. They provide ways of looking at and conceiving of activities of everyday life so as to expose their detailed orderliness. The importance of a theoretical notion lies in its 'pay-off' in empirical investigations. In his studies, then, Garfinkel seeks to show how theoretical notions derived from the work of Schutz can open up the world of everyday life to sociological investigation. We will try to spell out the basic notions as simply as we can.

THE ORGANISATION OF ACTIVITIES 'FROM WITHIN'

The central idea of ethnomethodology is captured in the recommendation 'treat social facts as interactional accomplishments'. Garfinkel suggests that sociologists should seek the orderly features of social activities in the way they are produced by those who participate in them. For Garfinkel every activity, from the most mundane actions of daily life to the most arcane practices of science or religion, can be conceived as having a 'self-organising' character. That is, activities are not performed mechanically by participants according to some preset rules or requirements. Rather, participants ('members' in Garfinkel's terminology) produce the orderliness of their activities 'locally', that is, in the course of the activity itself. This conception of social order clearly differs from most sociological approaches, which conceive of the orderliness of social activities as the product of some 'external' causes or conditions. These external factors are typically referred to as 'the social structure' or 'culture'. Typically also the understandings that members have of the orderliness of their activities are seen as incomplete or distorted reflections of these 'real' external factors. In contrast, Garfinkel begins by asking what orderliness is available to and recognisable by the participants in an activity. He proposes that *this and only this orderliness* be treated as the sociological orderliness that the activity possesses. He proposes further that this orderliness be conceived as produced by members 'within' the activity itself.

For example, everyday activities can have such features as intelligibility, routineness, predictability, typicality and effectiveness to those who participate in them. They can also have unexpectedness, uniqueness, unintelligibility, ineffectiveness and danger. No matter, for whatever the features of an activity, the important methodological point is that they are seen as 'locally produced'. An activity possesses such features by virtue of the ways in which participants produce and recognise that activity for what it is. Activities are managed and organised in the course of their production. For Garfinkel, therefore, social situations, settings and events are not 'out there' and independent of the actions of members at any given moment. Rather they are ongoing accomplishments of the interactional 'work' in which the members of a setting or event are continuously engaged. The observable, 'factual' features of a setting or event are interactionally produced.

By conceiving of interactional activities as 'work', Garfinkel views the orderliness of activities as both the product and process of members' actions. He is proposing that members have to accomplish or achieve their social world. This accomplishment is 'practical'. By this term Garfinkel is drawing attention to the fact that members, in a variety of ways, perceive and treat their social world as a 'constraining' world. Often members do not regard themselves as free to perform their activities in ways they ideally might wish. They may perceive that they have little control over circumstances which can affect the outcomes of an activity. They may believe that they lack sufficient knowledge to decide properly how to act, but that their circumstances necessitate that a decision is taken nevertheless. They may find that an action for which they had anticipated one sort of consequence turns out to have quite another outcome due to circumstances 'beyond their control' and which they could not have foreseen. For Garfinkel the issue is not, and cannot be, whether members are 'right' or 'wrong' in these notions. Rather the question is how members achieve such perceptions of their circumstances and how these perceptions inform their actions. How do members 'assemble' a sense of an occurrence or setting? How do they 'recognise' unanticipated problems and emergent difficulties? How do they distinguish between features of a situation that are real, relevant and unavoidable and those which are irrelevant, imaginary and can safely be ignored? Garfinkel recommends that the ethnomethodologist treats the features of social settings as identical with the ways in which members perceive and recognise such features. This recommendation is expressed in his concept of 'reflexivity', which we shall explain more fully in the section on members' methods. Here it is sufficient to note that Garfinkel emphasises the contingent nature of everyday life. By contingent, he means to stress life as it is experienced, and not as theorists tell us it should look like, that is, the everyday world is continuously unfolding, emergent, requiring *ad hoc* and active involvement. In producing their activities, members have to recognise and handle contingent events somehow. They must cope with problems and difficulties as they arise to the best of their ability. Yet this contingent nature of social life does not necessarily generate anxiety for members, who usually can deal with events as and when they happen. The fact that they do not have 'perfect' or 'ideal' knowledge is not experienced as an all-pervading problem. If members are puzzled or confused by events they may simply wait to see what happens next to see if matters will be clarified. Garfinkel emphasises that in everyday activities members typically seek only to attain sufficient sense of an occasion to enable them to act in ways that are appropriate or adequate for all practical purposes.

MEMBERS' METHODS

Garfinkel proposes that the self-production and self-organisation of activities is a *methodical* accomplishment on the part of members. The events in our daily lives make sense to us as members of our society because of the ways in which we simultaneously produce and perceive them. We produce our activities in such ways as to make available to others the nature of these activities. In producing social activities such as, for example, 'a complaint', 'a lecture', or 'a joke', we achieve them by methods which make them unproblematically available to others. In recognising 'a question', 'a lie', or even 'a turn to speak', we are reproducing our social world as a factual world, which is known in common with others. What is happening is 'obvious' for all concerned. This routine, unproblematic and familiar character of everyday events is, however, the product of sense-making *work* on our part. Through members' methods for doing this sense-making work, we accomplish a common social world.

Of course, Garfinkel is not suggesting that misunderstandings, disagreements and failures to understand do not occur in the every-day social world. Through the selfsame sense-making work, that is, by using the same members' methods, we can show that some 'problems' or 'troubles' are present. We can make it clear to others that we do not know what they are talking about, or do not agree with what they are saying, or do not approve of what they have done. It is through mutual sense-making work that members bring to light such problems and attempt to resolve them. In short, Garfinkel is proposing that members have to accomplish or achieve their social world. They do so by members' methods, which are used in taken-for-granted, implicit and unanalysed ways. The task for ethnomethodology is to describe what these members' methods look like. In *Studies in Ethnomethodology* Garfinkel offers characterisations of a number of them, including the 'documentary method of interpretation', the practice of 'et cetera' and the 'retrospective–prospective sense of occurrence'. At this point we illustrate the notion of members' methods by examining the documentary method of interpretation.

The documentary method of interpretation allows members to make a definite sense of activities in the face of the 'indexicality' of speech and actions. By the concept, indexicality, Garfinkel is drawing attention to the *occasioned* nature of everyday social situations. His stress is on the particular character of each and every social happening, occasion and event. He proposes that members' actions and utterances are features of the socially organised settings of their use. Their sense therefore is 'indexical' to the settings in which they are produced and recognised. For example, words do not have unchanging meanings at all times, on all occasions of their use. What they mean here-and-now, in *this* particular utterance, is some-thing that members make sense of in and through an analysis of the occasion. Such analysis can involve who or what the speaker is, what the relevant relationships are between the speaker and those to whom his talk is addressed, what the proper reason or purpose of his talk is, and how his talk 'follows' previous talk by other participants.

Thus members have to 'repair' the indexicality of talk and actions. To make sense of what is being done they produce a 'gloss' or description of the occasion, such as 'a meeting', 'a dispute', 'an investigation', or 'an arrest'. In this way, they boil down all the possible ways of describing the many circumstances and details of any social encounter. They boil these down into a 'limited' description which provides a definite sense of 'what is happening'. The documentary method of investigation is the name Garfinkel gives to the method by which this selection or boiling down is done. Members select some items to 'document' what is of significance, as they see it, and describe what is happening in this 'shorthand' manner.

In this way members are able to impose a pattern upon the details of an occasion. Garfinkel goes on to suggest that not only members but also sociologists operate in this manner. It is in this way that members, engaged in their everyday activities, *and* sociologists, engaged in their 'scientific' ones, can derive 'objective', that is, general, factual statements about the social world. In *this* respect at least, sociology is no different from any other practical activity. This point also holds true for the ethnomethodologist. Like everyone else, he too must use the documentary method of interpretation to make sense of the activities and situations he studies. The difference between ethnomethodology and other practical investigations of social life, in everyday life and in sociology, lies in its *topic*. Members, including sociologists, use sense-making methods like the documentary method of interpretation in taken-for-granted, unexamined ways. For members, the social world is 'out there', 'given' and 'objective'. It is not viewed as a product, an accomplishment of the use of standardly available members' methods. In contrast, the ethnomethodologist seeks to examine and describe the methods of sense-making work which all members, including sociologists and ethnomethodologists, must employ to produce the unproblematic orderliness of everyday social life.

MEMBERSHIP AND THE OCCASIONED USE OF COMMON-SENSE KNOWLEDGE

So far in our outline of Garfinkel's ideas, we have made many references to the concept of 'member'. Garfinkel's use of 'member' instead of 'actor', the term Schutz uses, is intentional. For Garfinkel, this term refers to membership of a collectivity, which implies possession of a shared stock of knowledge about the world.

Following Schutz's lead, Garfinkel maintains that members accomplish their activities in and through the use of common-sense knowledge. He further proposes that in any encounter, members treat one another *as* members, that is, they allocate collectivity memberships to themselves and others (for example, 'customer', 'policemen', 'stranger', 'guest'), and they treat some items of knowledge as things that they 'know' others share. This universal membershipping activity is central to members' experience of the social world as an objective, factual reality which is seen and experienced the same way by everyone. For in any encounter it is possible for members to treat themselves and others as 'the same' in some respects. In treating others as 'the same' as themselves, members constitute their social world as a 'real' world which is 'there fore anyone to see'.

The concept of 'membership' invokes the traditional sociological concept of 'culture' in that it refers to a set of concepts and beliefs which constitute what 'anyone' in a given collectivity should know about their social world. But the concept of culture is used to refer to a decontextualised body of knowledge attributed to the members of a collectivity by sociologists in order to account for the activities of persons. Garfinkel wishes to examine how persons themselves treat their own and others' knowledge as socially organised. He seeks to study how *they* attribute knowledge to account for activities. To refer to 'members', then, is to direct attention to the ways in which persons treat themselves and others as 'members of a socially organised world'.

For example, if someone appears not to see the world as he 'should', members do not immediately doubt their own sense of the social world. Rather, they may seek to revise their understanding of the collectivity membership of that person. They may scrutinise him for what is 'wrong' with him or look for reasons why he cannot see what should be 'plainly there' for 'anyone like him' to see. In seeking a membership categorisation to account for the person's 'odd' behaviour, members might find that he is 'a foreigner', 'a newcomer', or 'someone with a lot on his mind at the moment'. Of course, these categories will not *always* adequately account for odd behaviour. Rather, these explanations are constructed *ad hoc*, there and then, to meet the requirements of a particular occasion. Thus common-sense knowledge is used in occasioned ways. Therefore Garfinkel's concept of common-sense knowledge goes beyond the concept of 'culture' in that it emphasises that knowledge is *used* by persons in ways others can see to be appropriate on a particular occasion. Once again, it is the *methods* of use that Garfinkel wishes to describe.

GARFINKEL: EMPIRICAL DEMONSTRATIONS

We now examine some of Garfinkel's empirical demonstrations which are intended to reveal the nature of the everyday social world and members' methods for constituting it.

DISRUPTING SOCIAL ORDER

In order to demonstrate the 'seen but unnoticed' order of everyday life is an accomplishment, Garfinkel asked some of his students to experiment with disrupting its taken-for-granted routine and familiar nature.

The students were asked to see themselves as 'strangers' in their own society, and thereby to suspend their taken-for-granted common-sense understandings. Here are two examples reported by Garfinkel in *Studies in Ethnomethodology* (pp. 42–4).

1 (S) Hi, Ray, How is your girl friend feeling?
  (E) What do you mean, 'How is she feeling?' Do you mean physical or mental?
  (S) I mean how is she feeling? What's the matter with you? (He looked peeved.)
  (E) Nothing. Just explain a little clearer what do you mean?
  (S) Skip it. How are your Med School applications coming?
  (E) What do you mean, 'How are they?'
  (S) You know what I mean.

2 The victim waved his hand cheerily.
  (S) How are you?
  (E) How am I in regard to what? My health, my finances, my school work, my peace of mind, my . . . ?
  (S) (Red in the face and suddenly out of control) Look! I was just trying to be polite. Frankly, I don't give a damn how you are.

In another case some students were asked to spend fifteen minutes to an hour in their own homes 'pretending' they were boarders. They were told to act as boarders might; to be polite, to avoid getting personal, to use formal address, and so on. Some refused, others just could not do it. For the rest, the consequences of the experiments or demonstrations were very noticeable. Generally, family members were stupefied, bewildered, anxious, embarrassed, or angry. The student was often charged with being mean, inconsiderate, nasty, impolite, or was assumed to be ill.

Garfinkel suggests that these 'experiments' demonstrate that in their everyday lives members expect others to know what they are really talking about, expect them to recognise the occasional use of expressions and behaviour, to understand the specific vagueness of references, to make a retrospective–prospective sense of a present occurrence, and so on. Members routinely furnish the seen but unnoticed features of interaction in recognising what is 'obviously going on'. Competent membership is continuously displayed in recognising and making the world what everyone knows it to be.

Further, these demonstrations also show the moral nature of the familiar social world. Upsetting the order, not displaying one's competence, can bring moral sanctions from other members who have been 'troubled'. The orderliness of social life is founded on a mutual trust members have and display to each other. Producing trouble for 'no good reason' breaks that trust and usually results in anger and reprimand. When the students, for example, explained to their victims what they were doing, why they were behaving so oddly, a 'good reason' was thereby supplied and trust could be restored. Future disruptions could be explained by reference to 'silly sociological experiments'. Even so, in some cases this explanation was not accepted as adequately accounting for the turmoil produced by disrupting normal appearances.

AGNES: SEX IDENTITY AS A MANAGED ACCOMPLISHMENT

Garfinkel's interest in how the normal appearances of daily life are produced and sustained in and through methodical sense-making work is further illustrated in his study of 'Agnes'.

To all appearances, Agnes was a normal girl living a normal kind of life. She was 19, shared a flat with a girlfriend and worked as a typist. She had a steady boyfriend called 'Bill', with whom she did normal things like going swimming at the beach, going dancing, necking and petting. These appearances notwithstanding, Agnes possessed physical and biographical characteristics which, should they become known, she knew would lead to her being denied the right to regard herself as a female, and her right to be treated as such by others. Not only did she have male genitals to go with her female breasts, but she had been brought up as a boy and had only switched to living as a girl at the age of 17. Agnes knew, therefore, that in terms of accepted conceptions of sexual identity she would be regarded as a 'freak'. Furthermore, if her physical and biographical details were to become known, she would be found to have violated the 'trust' of others by not 'really' being what she 'appeared' to be.

Despite her 'abnormality', Agnes shared the common-sense view that there are only two sexes, male and female, and that outward appearance should correspond to biological 'reality'. She explained her physical condition as a 'mistake of nature'. She claimed that she was 'really a woman' because she had always 'felt like a female', even when living as a boy. Therefore she wished to have an operation to remove her male genitals and have these replaced by female ones.

What interested Garfinkel was the fact that for Agnes sexual identity was obviously a continual and all-pervading problem. In contrast with other people Agnes could not simply take her sexual identity for granted. She had self-consciously to learn how to appear a 'normal, natural female'. She had to continually review her own actions and the actions of others to ensure that 'normal appearances' were sustained. She had to manage her relationships with friends and acquaintances, especially with her boyfriend, Bill, so as to avoid their discovering her non-female characteristics. She had to plan and organise her life so as to maintain its 'normal' character while at the same time avoiding suspicion and disclosure. In short, her practical task in everyday life involved 'passing' as a female.

CORONERS AT WORK

Coroners and suicide investigators, working for a Suicide Prevention Centre (SPC), face practical problems similar to those of the juror. For, at the conclusion of their investigations, they must produce a decision on the legal status of the death they have investigated. This decision is open to assessment and evaluation by others as to whether it is 'justifiable' or 'reasonable' in the 'circumstances'. Therefore the coroner, if he wishes to remain in office, must endeavour to be seen to produce the most appropriate decision in each particular case he examines.

The coroner's central problem is formulated by Garfinkel: presented with the body of the deceased, the physical location and arrangement of the body, the objects found in the vicinity of the body, the information about the deceased collected from relatives, friends, acquaintances, neighbours and, sometimes, strangers – in other words, presented with all those things which might be 'evidence' – the coroner must try to construct a recognisably rational account of the course of events which produced the body of the deceased as its end result. The only way that any one account of the evidence can be substantiated against alternative accounts, or against claims that the coroner's account is 'inadequate' or 'biased', is simply to appeal to 'what anyone can see', to what is 'obvious' and 'enough' and 'reasonable' and 'unbiased'. The only answer the coroner can provide to the claim that 'more' could possibly be discovered, which might place the present evidence in a different light, is simply to say that any amount of inquiry would still leave the problem of 'more'. All he can do is to appeal to the practical circumstances of his coroner's task. These practical circumstances are constraints which require that decisions be made on the basis of 'what any reasonable man would deduce' from the available evidence. Consequently coroners, like jurors, make decisions 'for all practical purposes'. In Garfinkel's own words:

> The coroner (and S.P.C's) ask this with respect to each particular case, and thereby their work of achieving practical decidability seems almost unavoidably to display the following prevailing and important characteristic. S.P.C's must accomplish that decidability with respect to the 'this's': they have to start with *this* much; *this* sight; *this* note; *this* collection of whatever is at hand. And *whatever* is there is good enough in the sense that *whatever* is there not only *will* do, but *does*. One makes whatever is there *do*. I do not mean by 'making do' that an S.P.C. investigator is too easily content, or that he does not look for more when he should. Instead, I mean: that *whatever* it is that he has to deal with, that is what will have been used to have found out, to have made decidable, the way in which the society operated to have produced *that* picture, to have come to *that* scene as its end result. In this way the remains on the slab serve not only as a precedent but as a goal of S.P.C. enquiries. (Garfinkel, p. 18)

GARFINKEL: SUMMARY

Clearly, many of Garfinkel's ideas stem from the work of Schutz, that is, the intersubjective character of the social world, the nature of common-sense knowledge and the practical orientation of social actors. Garfinkel does not merely restate these ideas; he has gone on to produce a theoretical conception of the nature of the subject matter of sociology which provides a basis from which empirical research can be done. Garfinkel maintains that a major subject for empirical study should be the methods by which members produce and recognise the contingent, occasioned events of social life so that those events can be seen in the ways they are – as familiar, obvious, exhibiting a standard appearance. Garfinkel's recommendation to sociologists who wish to study the everyday world is: Look around you and everywhere you will find ordinary persons going about their everyday business performing familiar, unremarkable activities. This mundane fact is the very crux of the social world. The ability of members successfully to perform practical activities in collaboration with others is what makes the social world possible. Therefore, take these practical actions and examine them for how they are accomplished. You will find that the methods involved are complex and sophisticated, yet they are possessed (and required to be possessed) by pretty well everyone.

AARON CICOUREL: ETHNOMETHODOLOGY AND 'CONVENTIONAL' SOCIOLOGY

In 1964 Cicourel published a book, *Method and Measurement in Sociology,* which attempted to evaluate existing forms of sociological research on the basis of ideas influenced by the works of Schutz and the then largely unpublished Garfinkel. Its particular relevance is not to spell out an ethnomethodological programme. Indeed, at this time Cicourel was somewhat hazy about what such a programme might look like in detail. Rather, it offers a radical critique of existing sociological methods from what was then an emerging ethnomethodological standpoint.

He argues that all forms of sociological research involve the process of imposing an order on observations or 'data'. At the most simple level, this ordering consists of classifying events or persons into 'types' on the basis of common characteristics. On more sophisticated levels, sociologists wish to measure these characteristics in terms of some standard unit so that they can compare how much of a certain property different events or persons possess (for example, the construction of measurement scales for 'authoritarianism' or 'racial prejudice'). In fact most sociological research involves measurement of some kind. Even 'straightforward' classifications, whereby we differentiate one 'set' of things from another, for example, 'students' from 'teachers', require us to use criteria of sameness and difference. These criteria have to be used in all measurement systems; measurement systems differ in their sophistication, basically in terms of including more complex and additional criteria. We have no need, therefore, to probe into stronger and more complex systems of measurement – systems which enable us to perform complex statistical operations on data – to see the problems involved in 'measuring' the social world. For simply classifying objects and events involves us in problems of measurement.

In Cicourel's view, in using any level of measurement system, sociologists inevitably draw on their common-sense knowledge. They perceive events and persons in the social world as 'this' or 'that', in exactly the same way as ordinary members of society. In this respect, sociologists operate just like ordinary members by using their common-sense knowledge in *unexamined* ways. Like any one else, they take it for granted that the characteristics of the social world are 'out there for anyone to see'. Sociological researchers are, first and foremost, members of their society, with the same kinds of interactional skills and common-sense knowledge which any member of the society possesses. Crucially, this membership of society involves mastery of everyday language. It is through language, says Cicourel, that experiences are identified and rendered meaningful. It is through the situated interactional use of language (that is, through what Garfinkel calls the 'repair of indexicality') that common understandings are achieved. The researcher, like any other member, relies upon his competence as a member to perceive the everyday sense of social phenomena. It is only in this way that he is able to classify events, persons and relationships, recasting them in terms of sociological concepts. Hence the frequent complaints from non-sociologists that much sociological research consists of 'things we already knew expressed in technical jargon'. Inevitably, argues Cicourel, such 'sociological' explanations of human behaviour will be compatible with common-sense knowledge because, as Schutz stressed, common-sense knowledge of everyday life is the 'paramount reality' in terms of which the social world is experienced. Further, the sociologist produces 'plausible' findings because he has used his common-sense knowledge to decide about the practical matters involved in any piece of research. He uses his common-sense knowledge to resolve such problems as: what sorts of circumstances can lead persons to behave in certain ways; what sorts of topics are 'sensitive' and require careful questioning; what topics are 'safe' and can be dealt with quickly; what sorts of 'test factors' might explain a correlation between two variables; what are the best ways of ensuring that the sociologist's presence in a situation does not affect participants' behaviour too much; what kinds of official information are likely to provide the most accurate and unbiased data. All of these problems, and many more, are the sorts of problems which are dealt with in sociological research in ways which, in the last analysis, turn upon what the sociologist (and 'anyone' else) 'knows' from common sense to be true.

Cicourel pursues this theme by examining each of the major forms of sociological research in turn (Participant Observation, Interviewing, Questionnaire Methods, Experimentation, and Content Analysis of written documents). He maintains that in all of these methods, common-sense reasoning and interactional skills are unexamined resources by which the sociologist constructs an account of that aspect of social life which is being studied. Sociological accounts, *in this respect*, are therefore no different from other members' accounts of these same topics. Instead of taking a substantive approach to research – where the researcher chooses some aspect of society, or some particular social group or category, as his topic for research so as to produce a sociological version of the orderliness of that aspect – the sociologist should research into the methods and process by which members of society (including sociologists) produce order and structure in their world. Thus Cicourel is suggesting that we should make a *topic* (that is, a problem) out of what sociologists usually take for granted as a *resource* in their work. We should study the taken-for-granted and unexamined methods which members (including sociologists) use to produce the shared meanings and collective behaviour which both characterise and constitute social life.

We note, however, that this summary of the nature of Cicourel's objections to 'traditional' sociology represents only one dimension of his critique. Another, and probably contradictory, dimension is his attempt to refurbish and improve 'traditional' methods by techniques which take account of the everyday interactional methods and processes of social life. Thus, confusingly at times, he seems to argue that, given an adequate knowledge of social processes, we can repair the deficiencies of current methods; at other times, he denies the utility of imposed systems of measurement because they distort the 'essential' nature of social processes. On this latter argument, to try to improve research methods as conventionally used would not be very useful. Instead, the sociologist must realise that even the establishment and use of classifications or categories in everyday life is a *member's* accomplishment, using members' taken-for-granted methods which the *sociologist himself must use* to devise them and to make sense of them. Here, Cicourel is clearly formulating the basic viewpoint of an ethnomethodological approach.

Cicourel gives some empirical expression to these concerns in his later book, *The Social Organisation of Juvenile Justice*. This book is a study of the phenomenon of juvenile delinquency as it is conceived, identified and processed in two Californian cities. In particular, it examines the methods by which police and probation officials carry out their everyday tasks of dealing with persons who are possibly or officially 'juvenile delinquents'.

Cicourel's critique of orthodox sociological methods is developed around the issue of the difference between his conception of 'juvenile delinquency' as a phenomenon for sociological research and the conception with which sociologists have traditionally operated. In Cicourel's view, juvenile delinquency cannot be divorced, as a sociological phenomenon, from the methods by which it is identified by members. Delinquency is whatever and wherever members constitute it through the processes by which they impose the title 'delinquent' on some actions and on some actors. Consequently, Cicourel's research concentrates upon persons who are officially charged with the task of identifying and controlling juvenile delinquency and whose everyday activities involve dealing with the 'problem'.

He suggests that the usual sociological conception of delinquency is to see it as a 'social fact', a general and recurrent form of behaviour which has common characteristics and, possibly, common 'causes'. For Cicourel, this view precisely mirrors the view which members have of delinquency. That is to say, both members and conventional sociological researchers view delinquency as an objective phenomenon, as something which is 'out there' in the social world, rather than as something which is constituted by the methods by which it is identified. For example, it is common-sense knowledge among policemen, probation officers, judges and sociological researchers that there are such things as 'unreported' acts of juvenile delinquency, as juveniles who are 'known to be delinquents' but who have 'managed to avoid conviction so far', and so on. From such knowledge, members can talk about a 'real rate' of delinquency which is greater than the rate of convictions for delinquency. These kinds of ideas underpin the activities of law-enforcement officials. With detailed materials, Cicourel tries to show that cases of delinquency which study the outcomes of law-enforcement processes (for example, statistics from official records), comparing these with the social characteristics of offenders, find the relationships they do largely because they are employing broadly the same kinds of common-sense reasoning as those involved. The alternative to this approach is to turn common-sense knowledge and the methods by which it is employed from an unexamined resource to the *central topic* of sociological research.

On the surface, Cicourel's approach to the study of juvenile delinquency may appear to be similar to the general approach to deviance of the labelling theorists. As we have seen in Chapter 4, theorists such as Becker tend to view 'deviance' as a label which is imposed on certain actions perceived by others to be violating some rule. In their analyses, however, they tend not to go much further than identifying particular social rules and locating them in various interest groups in society. Cicourel, on the other hand, is concerned to describe the *methods* of practical reasoning and decision-making by which both labels and occasion are mutually constituted.

CONVERSATIONAL ANALYSIS: MEMBERS' METHODS FOR ACCOMPLISHING SOCIAL ACTIVITIES THROUGH TALK

Garfinkel's ideas have influenced many researchers in different ways, and the research which has been generated from the ethnomethodological approach varies considerably in its topics, methods and findings. However, it falls broadly into two kinds. One consists of studies of 'practical reasoning' in organised social activities. We shall examine an example of this kind of work, Lynch's study of a scientific laboratory, later in the chapter. The other stream of work investigates the organisation of talk, particularly conversation. This field of inquiry is known as Conversational Analysis and, in the opinion of many, it is where the most elegant and rigorous work inspired by an ethnomethodological conception of social behaviour is to be found. The leading figure in this work was Harvey Sacks (1936–75).

HARVEY SACKS: THE ACHIEVEMENT OF DESCRIPTIONS

Sacks's earliest research on the social organisation of talk was concerned with the phenomenon of description. In their talk, members are continually describing their social world to one another. Whenever there is talk there are descriptions of such things as events, actions, feelings and states of mind. We are bombarded with descriptions in our everyday lives, not just in face-to-face interactions, but also from the television, from newspapers, from books, and so on. The ability to conduct our everyday affairs consists in large measure in being able to produce descriptions that others can understand. We in turn have to understand descriptions that others produce for us. Description, then, is a basic constituent of all of our everyday activities.

The aim of Sacks's research on description was to describe the cultural 'machinery' by which members produce and recognise descriptions. Members do not simply talk. In their interactions they talk *about* this, that, or the other. All talk has a topical character. Yet, as Garfinkel shows with his concept of indexicality, words can be seen to have potentially many meanings whereas only one meaning is selected there and then on a given occasion. So how do members accomoplish or assemble a sense of what some stretch of talk is referring to? Sacks proposes that there are some general methods members use and some general structures of common-sense knowledge they rely on.

In his investigations of description, Sacks proposes 'identity' or 'membership category' as the basic concept. He notes that for any person, there is a huge number of categories for 'correctly' describing him. For example, the reader may be describable as a 'student', a 'girl', a 'daughter', a 'motorist', a 'brunette', a 'pop-fan', a 'teenager', a 'sociologist', and so on. Thus one issue for analysis is how members can methodically select an appropriate category on a particular occasion. Here we note that in selecting a category, we might also be simultaneously (and reflectively) constituting the nature of the social occasion.

A second basic concept is the Membership Categorisation Device (MCD). Sacks suggests that members methodically select a *single* category (or identity) from a *group* or *cluster* of related categories. Such a cluster is an MCD. Thus an MCD is a *collection* of categories which 'go together', initially in the sense that when a category from a certain device is correctly applied to a person, it can be heard to exclude them from being identified with some other category from the same device. Categories within a single device are, therefore, in the first place hearable as mutually exclusive alternatives. The simplest example is the categories 'male' and 'female', which can be seen to constitute the membership categorisation device 'sex'. It is 'natural' for members to hear that a person who is identified as 'male' is not also 'female'. Members know that these two categories exhaust the possibilities of categorisation by sex, therefore it is also 'natural' for them to hear that if a person is not 'male' they 'must' be 'female'. By the notion of Membership Categorisation Device, Sacks is attempting to describe the organisation of membership categories into collections which are for members a taken-for-granted common-sense resource. As members, we know which commonly used categories belong together in which collections. For example, we all know what kinds of categories belong in the collection 'occupations', or the collections 'family', 'road-users', 'stage of life', or 'nationality'. Conversely, we all know in what sorts of collections such person-categories as 'architect', 'father', 'pedestrian', 'adolescent' and 'Briton' belong. This organisation of categories provides members with a basis upon which membership categoris-ations of persons can be heard as 'consistent' or 'inconsistent'. That is to say, MCDs provide a basis upon which, when one person has been identified by the use of a certain category, other categories can appropriately be selected for other persons. Furthermore, MCDs provide a basis on which the significance and relevance of contextual particulars for identification of persons can be judged. In this respect Sacks introduces the concept 'category-bound activities'. By this concept, he refers to the fact that many kinds of activities are by common sense 'tied' to certain membership categories. For example, if we hear of someone having been arrested, we hear that this activity has been done by the police; if someone identified as a husband com-plains of being nagged, we hear that the activity, nagging, is done by his wife.

Sacks's investigations into the organisation and use of membership categories are illustrated by his paper 'On the Analysability of Stories by Children', where he analyses a fragment from a story told by a 3-year-old child. The fragment is: 'The baby cried. The mommy picked it up.' Sacks begins by making a number of observations about the 'natural' way of hearing these two sentences. First, he notes that to hear 'the mommy' as the mother of the baby is the 'natural', that is, common-sense, initial hearing of these sentences. Secondly, it is 'natural' to hear that the mommy picked the baby up after it has cried and not before. In other words, the order of the actions described in the two sentences is heard as the same as the order of the sentences themselves. Thirdly, Sacks proposes that members also hear not just that the second occurrence happened after the first, but that it happened *because* of it, that is, the reason why the mommy picked up the baby was that the baby cried. These last two observations are related in that it is unlikely members would hear 'the baby cried' as the reason 'the mommy picked it up' if the sen-tences were in the reverse order. Sacks suggests that when members hear two consecutive sentences, both reporting events, they will hear that the events occurred in the order the sentences occur (*a*) if there is no information specifically to suggest the contrary and (*b*) if the order of the occurrences can be seen to constitute a normal and proper order in which such things happen.

Sacks observes that all these understandings can be made by any member without knowing any more about the baby or the mommy than is provided by the sentences themselves. In hearing the sentences as an understandable description of a social event, members do not need to know what particular baby or what particular mommy is being talked of, nor do they need to inspect the event to which they refer in order to see if they are a bona fide description. Whatever 'contextual' material members use to make the 'natural' hearing is contained in the sentences themselves. Yet the sentences do not speak for themselves; with just a little thought they can be given other possible hearings. Consequently, the natural initial hearing is obviously a cultural accomplishment.

Sacks proposes that the key to this accomplishment is the methodical use of MCDs. Members use MCDs in methodic ways which can involve an orientation to possible rules for applying them. One such rule is a 'consistency rule' which can be stated as follows:

> if some population of persons is being categorised, and if a category from some M.C.D.'s collection has been used to categorise a first member of the population, then that category or other categories of the same collection may be used to categorise further members of the population. (Sacks, 1974, p. 219)

Sacks then explains how the 'baby' and the 'mommy' are heard as members of the same family, that is, the baby is this particular mommy's baby and not someone else's. He proposes that this hearing derives from the structure of the MCD 'family'. The 'family' collection of categories has the structure of being a 'team' or, in Sacks's terminology, it is 'duplicatively organised', that is, the set of categories in the collection form an identifiable 'social unit'. Consequently, there is a proper number of incumbents (that is, occupiers) of some of the categories within such a unit. In other words, families can be regarded as 'teams' which have a minimum membership of one father, one mother and one child (and, of course, in the father and mother categories, one person is also a maximum proper number for each unit, whereas there can be more than one).

Sacks proposes that for MCDs which have this 'team-like' ('duplicatively-organised') structure, there is a 'hearing rule' to which members orient. This rule is:

where a speaker uses categories from a duplicatively organised collection to identify a number of persons, and these persons can be heard as members of the same *social unit*, then the hearer should hear it that way.

This hearing rule provides for how it is that we hear the 'mommy' as the mommy of the 'baby', and thus how 'baby' is heard in its family sense. The two categories 'mommy' and 'baby' are 'mutually constitutive', that is, we simultaneously derive our understanding of each from the use of the other.

Similarly, Sacks proposes that our hearing of 'baby' in its other sense, as a 'stage of life' category, is tied to the activity–descriptor 'cried'. As we have said, Sacks maintains that certain activities are 'category-bound', that is, they are taken by members to be 'properly' or 'normally' performed by certain categories of person. These common-sense relationships between activities and membership categories are utilised in all sorts of ways by members. For example, these relationships can form the basis for moral assessments of praise or blame. Sacks proposes that 'crying' is a category-bound activity which is bound (at least) to the category 'baby'. We can judge the nature of this connectedness, he says, by considering the activity of 'crying' in relation to the other categories in the stage of life collection, such as 'adolescent' and 'adult'. The stage of life collection has a kind of hierarchical construction, in that persons pass through its categories consecutively; one is first a 'baby', then a 'child', then an 'adolescent', then an 'adult'. As there are different activities which are bound to each of these categories, and as members regard the movement through these categories as a 'progression', the stage of life collection provides members with a machinery for making positive or negative moral judgements. How this machinery is used will depend on the particular circumstances. Most often the tendency is for persons who perform actions associated with categories further 'up' the scale to receive positive judgements, while those whose activities are associated with 'lower' categories receive negative ones. Thus someone who is a 'child' can be praised for 'acting like a big boy' or 'being grown up', whereas for someone who is an 'adult' 'acting like a baby' or 'being childish' is a form of disapproval. On occasion, however, a child can be censured for being 'too mature for his years', and an adult commended for 'youthful vitality'.

If this analysis is correct, it provides for how we hear 'baby' as a stage of life identification in this data. Once again the two contextual features (or 'indexical particulars'), the person-category 'baby' and the activity descriptor 'cried', are mutually constitutive in that we hear 'baby' in this sense because of 'cried', while we hear 'cried' in the way we do (rather than as, for example, a synonym for shouted) because of the presence of 'baby'. Finally, we hear 'baby' as referring to a young infant who is the child of the 'mommy' because our analysis of the contextual features provides us with two senses of 'baby' which are combinable in terms of our common-sense know-ledge. It is not a problematic matter for us that a person can be a 'baby' in both the 'family' and 'stage of life' senses. We know that such a combination is a routine feature of our society. By contrast, a combination of 'father' in its 'family' and its 'religious' sense might appear, in some situations, strange and requiring further explanation.

We have outlined Sacks's article at some length in order to demon-strate what kinds of cultural 'machinery' ethnomethodologists have proposed to describe members' sense-assembly or sense-making pro-cedures. This 'machinery' enables analysts to describe how members make perfectly ordinary, mundane understandings of the social world. Members appear not to reflect on how they do these things; they take the methods and abilities involved for granted. Even in those situations in which some persons fail to accomplish the 'correct' understanding of some set of indexical particulars, members are not led to question and examine the methods and abilities involved in making these understadings. Rather, they look for reasons to explain the 'failure' of persons to see or hear what is there for 'anyone' to see or hear.

EMMANUEL SCHEGLOFF: THE SEQUENTIAL ORGANISATON OF CONVERSATION

The study of identities was an important focus of early work in the field of Conversational Analysis. In recent years, however, it has taken second place to the study of the sequential organisation and structure of conversation. Conversation is a 'turn-taking' activity: participants take turns as speakers and hearers. Conversation analysts have examined the sequential mechanisms by which turn-taking is accomplished and the sequential structures through which particular conversational activities are performed. We can illustrate this work by describing two articles by an associate of Sacks's, Emmanuel Schegloff.

The first is an early article of Schegloff's entitled 'Sequencing in Conversational Openings'. In this article Schegloff examines 'the ways in which co-ordinated entry by two parties into an orderly sequence of conversational turns is managed'. His data consists of the first five seconds of some 500 telephone calls to and from a police station in the United States. He finds that he can describe the allocation of turns to talk between the parties to the call by means of a 'distribution rule' which simply states: 'answerer speaks first'. A subsidiary rule is: 'caller provides the first topic'.

He also finds, however, that he has a 'deviant' case in which a *caller* speaks first. Instead of treating this exception to his rule as a deviant case, he tries to locate a more general rule which can include all of his cases. He argues that he is not trying to 'fault' the everyday world or trying to knock it into a more convenient shape for the analyst, but rather, he is trying to describe it 'as it comes'. He wants to produce explanatory rules which are general enough to avoid excluding data which does not 'fit'. Thus Schegloff reconsiders his analysis and suggests that the answerer's initial utterance or turn in his telephone calls can be seen to be the 'answer' in a 'summons–answer sequence'. The 'summons' is provided by the ringing of the telephone. These S–A (summons–answer) sequences are very commonly used in everyday life; the telephone calls are simply one kind. They are made up of a 'first', which is an 'attention getting device', for example, the telephone bell, shouting someone's name, banging a gavel. The recipient(s) should then, as a 'second', 'answer' in some appropriate manner.

S–A sequences have several formal properties. First, they are 'non-terminal', that is, something should follow from them, they are not interactionally complete in themselves. Secondly, they are 'conditionally relevant', that is, the interactions that follow S–A sequences are dependent or conditional on the completion of the S–A sequence. Schegloff illustrates these properties by showing how persons actually apologise if they mistake a greeting for a summons ('I was only saying hello . . .'); and how, if a summons is not answered, it may be repeated – but it may *not* be repeated once an answer is obtained. Instead, something else must happen. In this way, he can meaningfully talk of the two parts of the S–A sequence making up a 'unit of talk'. For, given the 'first', a 'second' is expected; if the 'second' is not forthcoming, it is 'officially' absent, that is it is absent in an interactionally meaningful sense. Thus, from its absence we, as members, can make strong inferences about the would-be answerer, for example, he is 'ignoring' the summoner; or he is 'not in', 'not available'.

Schegloff therefore explains his 'deviant' case by suggesting that the sequence of actions is: (1) Summons (phone rings); (2) No answer (recipient says nothing); (3) Another summons (caller speaks, says 'hello'); (4) Answer (recipient answers, says 'hello'). In all of his other cases, an answer was received in slot (2).

He concludes by suggesting that S–A sequences are a powerful way of generating conversational interaction. The recipient of a summons feels impelled to answer. (We note that in Northern Ireland persons still answer the door and get shot – despite their knowledge that such things happen.) Moreover, the recipient usually answers by means of a question. This question generates further interaction, enabling the summoner to provide a first topic for discussion. The answer has also provided for the availability of the answerer to talk. For, Schegloff notes, the mere copresence of parties does not constitute interaction; they must have some means of coordinating their entry into interaction. The S–A sequence, with its built-in implications for further action, provides such a means.

In a more recent article, 'Identification and recognition in telephone conversation openings', Schegloff develops his analysis of the sequential organisation of conversational openings. He focuses upon the 'problem' of identification and recognition in telephone conversation. Schegloff proposes that in telephone conversations, as in other forms of interaction between persons, identification and recognition is a prerequisite of the production of appropriate behaviour. He further notes that the problem of identification and recognition has a special character in telephone conversations by virtue of the absence of visual accessibility, which can enable participants in face-to-face interaction to 'solve' the problem before they begin to speak. In telephone conversations the problem of identification and recognition can only be solved in and through the talk. Schegloff's aim is to describe the different forms that identification and recognition work can take in telephone conversation openings and to expose the interactional principles that govern the use of these forms. He begins by classifying openings into types in terms of what is done by the caller in the 'second turn' of the call, that is, the caller's first turn to speak following the answerer's initial 'Hello'. There are four 'second turn types' we will mention here. The first involves second turns in which no explicit identification of caller or answerer is contained and no 'identification sequence' is projected. Typical cases are where the caller uses his first turn to do a greeting, an apology, or a question:

Type 1

1 (A) Hello . . .
   (C) Good morning.

2 (A) Hello
   (C) Did I waken you dear?

3 (A) Hello
   (C) Hi. C'n you talk?

A second type involves the caller producing a definite identification of the answerer, in an assertive or 'terminal' voice intonation:

Type 2

4 (A) Hello
   (C) Phil!

5 (A) Hello
   (C) Hello Charles.

A third type involves the production by the caller of a second turn which projects an identification/recognition sequence. Typical cases here are (*a*) the use of answerer's (presumed) name in an interrogative voice intonation (which Schegloff calls the 'interrogative name' type), and the (*b*) request for self-identification by the answerer:

Type 3

(*a*) 6 (A) Hello
      (C) Miz Parsons?

(*b*) 7 (A) Yhello
      (C) H'llo who's this?

Finally, a fourth type involves the caller producing a self-identification:

Type 4

8 (A) H'llo?
   (C) Hi Bonnie. This is Dave.

9 (A) Hello?
   (C) Hi. This is David Williamson.

Schegloff first shows how identification/recognition can be seen to be at issue in the first and second categories of opening types. For although these types of utterances do not appear to treat identification/recognition as a 'problem' and are not designed to initiate a sequence of utterances concerned with solving that problem, in practice they do often result in such a sequence. They do so by virtue of their recognition status. Thus a greeting, for example, constitutes a claim of recognition by the caller of the answerer. And since greetings (like summons–answer sequences) properly occur as 'adjacency pairs', it also constitutes a claim that the caller should be recognisable to the answerer on the basis of the 'voice sample' provided by the greeting. Therefore a return greeting by the answerer can be heard as constituting reciprocal recognition. Schegloff notes that often this recognition is made overt:

(A) Hel*lo:::*
(C) *Hi:::*
(A) Oh: hi: 'ow are you Agnes?

It follows that answerers may 'withhold' a return greeting when they cannot identify the caller on the basis of his voice. A 'silence' following a caller's greeting can serve to redistribute the turns between the parties. A caller may analyse such a silence as the 'absence' of a return greeting and as indicating a 'recognition problem' on the answerer's part. The caller may seek to 'repair' the problem by providing additional recognition materials or a self-identification. In the absence of repair work by the caller, the answer may explicitly request it:

(A) Hello?
(C) Hello
    (1.5 seconds)
(A) Who's this?

Schegloff proposes that since overt identification/recognition is done in such cases as these only if there is a 'problem', participants can be seen to 'prefer' to do identification and recognition 'en passant' in the course of utterences performing other opening activities. Schegloff suggests that this preference follows from the general principle of 'recipient design' which informs conversational interaction. This principle requires a conversationalist to construct his talk in ways which display his attentiveness to the proper relationship which obtains with *this* co-conversationalist. In one form, this principle can be stated as the rule: 'Don't tell the recipient what you ought to suppose he already knows, use it'. This rule, together with a principle of 'economy', *generates* the preferences for identification 'en passant'. For it implies that a caller should supply an answerer with the minimum recognitional resources sufficient to enable that answerer to make a correct and proper identification. Thus where a caller has adequate reason to suppose that the answerer can and should be able to recognise him from his voice alone, an opportunity for such recognition should be provided.

Schegloff then turns to openings in which an identification/recognition sequence is specifically projected by the caller in the second turn slot. He shows how the principles of recipient design and economy account for the structures of these types also. For example, he notes that the significance of the 'interrogative name' type utterance is not simply that it proffers an identification of answerer for him to confirm or correct. It also provides the answerer with materials for identification of the caller. In this type the materials are not just a voice sample but also an indication of the relationship in which the caller believes himself to stand to the answerer. Since different names and address terms have different relational implications, the name or address term the caller uses can be analysed by the answerer to identify the caller. By the use of an 'interrogative name', the caller provides the answerer with an opportunity to identify him, without the caller having to produce a self-identification. Schegloff is thus able to propose that telephone conversational openings exhibit a *structure* of preferential organisation. If identification/recognition 'en passant' is the 'first preference', then identification-by-the-other is the 'second preference'. Only when these two are specifically excluded by the nature of the relationship between caller and answerer, or when an attempt to realise them fails, do speakers resort to self-identification. When self-identification is necessary, speakers seek to do it in the most 'economical' way that is consistent with recipient design.

LYNCH: NATURAL SCIENCE AS 'PRACTICAL INQUIRY' –THE ACCOMPLISHMENT OF SCIENTIFIC FACTS

A second line of development in ethnomethodology has been the study of 'practical inquiries'. As we saw with Garfinkel on coroners' work, ethnomethodologists have focused upon social settings in which they have tried to explore how such things as judgements of fact, making inferences, drawing conclusions, for example, are *done* as interactional activities by members. For ethnomethodologists, knowledge is socially organised in and through the ways it is treated as 'accountable knowledge' by members in their activities. Therefore what the ethnomethodologist wants to find out is not simply what are the standards or criteria that 'govern' members' inquiries, but what are the ways in which they actually conduct their inquiries so that those inquiries can be seen to conform to general ideas of 'proper inquiry' and 'adequate knowledge'. Examples of such studies of practical inquiries include the social organisation of judgements of mental illness, the ways in which judgements of children's reading abilities are made in schools, the interactional management of court-room proceedings, and how doctor–patient consultations are conducted.

Here, we will look at Michael Lynch's study of laboratory research in a psycho-biological laboratory engaged in experimental research on animal brain functions. Lynch wished to examine how the researchers' activities were conducted as scientific activities, that is, how 'discoveries' were made, how experiments were adjudged as 'successes' or as 'failures', how 'results' were achieved and how these were 'checked' against other results, and how the 'objects' that the research was directed towards were recognised and identified. Lynch points out that descriptions of science by sociologists, historians and philosophers typically are reconstructions and idealisations rather than descriptions of what scientists actually do. These idealised des-criptions usually characterise the *kind* of thing science is as a social activity or form of knowledge, rather than describing in detail the actual work involved in being a scientist. In contrast, Lynch aims to describe the actual, practical work of science.

Much of the work of the laboratory consisted in the construction and examination of 'specimens' of brain tissue, usually from rats. For example, slides of wafer-thin sections of brain tissue were prepared and examined under optical and electron microscopes. In this way, theories of brain structure and brain processes were developed and tested. In examining such specimens, research workers would occasionally discover 'artefacts'. An artefact is a visible feature of a specimen, or of a representation of a specimen (for example, a micro-photograph from an electron microscope), that 'ought not to be there'. An artefact does not represent the 'actual' phenomena that the researcher 'should' be able to see. It is not a 'real' feature of the specimen, but a product of some error or failure in laboratory technique. For example, an artefact may be identified as a 'staining error', deriving from careless use of staining fluid in the preparation of the slide. Or it may be 'knife marks', streaks on the photograph

aused by the microtome scratching the specimen during the cutting
process. Therefore, artefacts are 'troubles'. They get in the way of
the research and cause much frustration to the researchers.

Lynch found that artefacts are the objects of much interactional
activity in the laboratory. Newcomers are instructed in the 'typical
causes' of artefacts and the need for care at all stages of the work to
minimise them. When they are discovered, decisions have to be
taken about their 'seriousness', for example, do they make a
specimen unusable for research purposes? Lynch notes that these
decisions were taken in the light of specific practical circumstances.
Whether or not an 'imperfect' slide or photograph was used
depended not upon some universal absolute criteria, but upon the
circumstances of the occasion. For example, the researchers might
ask if they have time to prepare some more, or whether there were
other specimens that were 'OK' so that these flawed ones can just be
for 'corroboration', or whether a 'perfect' example was needed for
publication in a research journal. Lynch emphasises that from an
ethnomethodological point of view, the factual character of artefacts
as 'real problems' with which the laboratory researchers had to cope
can be seen to be constituted by the very activities of 'noticing',
'assessing' and 'explaining' them. Researchers were able to see that
something on a slide 'must be an artefact' because they 'knew' what
to look for and knew what they 'should' be able to see. For example,
researchers could find that, through no one's 'fault', laboratory
instruments could on occasion 'distort' the phenomena that they
made observable. In making such findings, researchers did not treat
as a logical problem the questions of how natural phenomena could
be found to have been 'distorted' by means of the very same technical procedures that made them visible in the first place. Rather,
they assumed that when some 'strange' feature was noticed, its status
as a 'distortion' or as some hitherto undiscovered 'real feature' of the
brain tissue under examination was a problem for which a definite
answer was both possible and necessary. Such occurrences were the
occasion of 'consultations' among members of the research team.
Opinions would be solicited and interpretations profferred, resulting
in a decision about whether the feature should be 'followed up' or
'ignored'. Over the course of further work, researchers would treat
subsequent specimens as further indicating what the previously
noticed feature 'must have been'.

Lynch's study, then, shows how the 'facts' of science are socially
constituted in the everyday activities of a research laboratory. Like
other ethnomethodologists, Lynch's purpose is not to criticise these

activities in terms of some version of how science should ideally b
done. Rather he seeks to show how laboratory researchers produc
'scientific knowledge' as a routine outcome of situated judgement:
work in the daily round of their experimental activities.

CONCLUSION

In this chapter we have described the major ideas and kinds of wor.
which comprise ethnomethodology. All the writers we have referre
to are committed to a conception of the social organisation of every
day life as an interactional accomplishment of sense-makin{
work by the members of society. We stress, however, that th
studies we have described do not form a tightly knit and uniforn
body of work. There are considerable divergencies of interest an
approach between ethnomethodologists, especially, as we have seen
between conversational analysts and what might be called 'situationa
analysts', that is, those concerned to study the nature of practica
reasoning in everyday situations. A major reason for this divergenc
derives from the different evaluation of *formality* as an important ain
for sociological analysis.

Conversational analysts treat the pursuit of formal descriptions o
interactional structures as their primary aim. Therefore they are concerned to study forms of talk which are enormously general an
found everywhere in social life. Their analysis is relatively
independent of 'contextual' features such as the identities of th
speakers, the nature of the occasion, or the specific topic of the talk
On the other hand, 'situational analysts', regard as their first priorit
the description of the socially organised basis of the naturalisti
character of everyday experience. The pursuit of generality an
formality is regarded as secondary to the aim of describing how th
'naturalness' of everyday settings, activities and events is accompl-
lished in and through situated practical reasoning. Not surprisingly
the nature and form of the findings of these two approaches withir
ethnomethodology are somewhat different.

Meanwhile, arguments over the status and merits of ethnomethodology as a sociological approach continue. Although any
sociological approach has its critics, ethnomethodology has com
under more fire than any other. We therefore briefly review some o
the most common criticisms.

First, in comparison with research topics generated in other socia
approaches, ethnomethodology is seen to be no more than a study o

microscopic social processes, usually resulting in a consideration of 'trivial' matters. Ethnomethodologists reply that such criticisms merely reflect 'perspectival bias'. Moreover, phenomena like 'power', 'socialisation' and 'stratification' are, they argue, produced in and through everyday interactional situations. These phenomena do not exist 'externally', independent of what members of society actually do in face-to-face interaction. Ethnomethodologists, therefore, are interested in describing how members can accomplish situations displaying such phenomena.

Secondly, and conversely, ethnomethodologists are seen to be critical of 'traditional' sociology and its methods and techniques, while failing to provide useful suggestions for improvement. Ethnomethodologists reply that these criticisms miss the whole point of what they are doing. For they wish to describe the methods which must be employed by members, including sociologists, to achieve their practical projects. For sociologists, it happens to be the case that these projects include the production of sociological accounts of the world.

Thirdly, a more fundamental criticism concerns the means by which ethnomethodologists study members' methods and yet, on their own arguments, they simultaneously employ these methods. Ethnomethodologists reply that there are dangers in producing a set of generalised methodological directives for application to any particular empirical setting. Instead, they ask for their work to be judged on the basis of their detailed arguments in actual empirical research studies.

Finally, critics point out that ethnomethodology is itself an organised social activity, an ongoing practical accomplishment. Thus 'it would be possible to take an attitude of "ethnomethodological indifference" towards members-doing-ethnomethodology; and to take an attitude of "ethnomethodological indifference" to *these* members-doing-ethnomethodology; and to take an attitude of "ethnomethodological indifference" . . . Yonder lies the abyss!' (Giddens, p. 41).

Here, Giddens is posing the problem of 'radical reflexivity', that is, the study of the study of the study . . . etc. Ethnomethodologists reply that this infinite regress is, of course, a logical possibility. They point out, however, that this problem is a problem for philosophers rather than sociologists interested in analysing the everyday world. Ethnomethodologists are concerned to describe how members can be seen to be achieving their everyday world; a world both they and anyone else can recognise. Of course, they accept that an ethnomethodological study can be made of ethnomethodological studies; and that a further ethnomethodological study can be made of the ethnomethodological study of ethnomethodological studies, and so on. They merely point out that it is not their particular interest to continue indefinitely along this chain. Moreover, the production of any account anywhere along this chain requires it to be accomplished by the use of members' common-sense methods of practical reasoning. Their interest is in these methods.

FURTHER READING

Lynch, M., *Art and Artefact in Laboratory Science* (Routledge and Kegan Paul, 1983).

Schutz, A., *On Phenomenology and Social Relations: Selected Writings of Alfred Schutz* (University of Chicago Press, 1970).

Grathoff, R. (ed.), *The Theory of Social Action: The Correspondence of Alfred Schutz and Talcott Parsons* (Indiana University Press, 1978). For Schutz's review of Parsons's *The Structure of Social Action* and the correspondence which ensued between them on the nature of social action and sociological theory.

Thompson, K., and **Tunstall, J.,** *Sociological Perspectives: Selected Readings* (Penguin, 1971). For Schutz's 'Concept and theory formation in the social sciences' which contrasts a 'phenomenological' approach with the standard 'behaviourist/positivist' approach of Nagel (which is the previous reading in the book).

Turner, R., *Ethnomethodology* (Penguin, 1974). For Sack's 'On the analysability of stories by children'. For Sudnow's 'Counting deaths' showing members' practices for counting and describing deaths in a hospital. For Weider's 'Telling the code' showing the practical nature of rules in everyday life. For Cicourel's 'Police practices and official records' showing the practical reasoning of police officers in typifying juvenile offenders.

Douglas, J. (ed.), *Understanding Everyday Life* (Routledge & Kegan Paul, 1974). For Zimmerman and Pollner's 'The everyday world as a phenomenon' which contrasts ethnomethodology with 'traditional sociology'.

Sudnow, D. (ed.), *Studies in Social Interaction* (Free Press, 1972). For Schegloff's 'Notes on a conversational practice: formulating place'. Also in an abbreviated form in P. P. Giglioli (ed.), *Language and Social Control* (Penguin, 1972). For Garfinkel's 'Studies in the routine grounds of everyday activities', which reports on distuptive 'experiments' in everyday life in order to display its routine, taken-for-granted features.

Psathas, G. (ed.), *Everyday Language: Studies in Ethnomethodology* (Irvington Publishers, 1979). For Schegloff's 'Identification and recognition in telephone conversation openings'. Also for Sacks's 'Hotrodder: a revolutionary category' on the use of membership categories to create a distinctive collective identity, and for Sacks and Schegloff's 'Two preferences in the organisation of reference to persons in conversation and their interaction'.

Schenkein, J. (ed.), *Studies in the Organisation of Conversational Interaction* (Academic Press, 1978). For Sacks, Schegloff and Jefferson's 'A simplest systematics for the organisation of turn-taking in conversation'.

Laver, J., and **Hutcheson, S.** (eds), *Communication in Face-to-Face Interaction* (Penguin, 1973). For Schegloff's 'Sequencing in conversational openings'.

QUESTIONS

1 What does Schutz mean when he calls the social world an 'intersubjective' world? What part does the 'assumption of the reciprocity of perspectives' play in intersubjectivity?

2 What is meant by Garfinkel's suggestion that social activities are 'self-organising'? What empirical pay-off does this suggestion have?

3 How does Garfinkel demonstrate the existence of 'seen-but-unnoticed background expectancies' in everyday life? Invent for yourself and describe some 'experiments' which might demonstrate them.

4 In what ways does Garfinkel seek to show via the case of 'Agnes' that the normal appearances of sex identity are the product of ongoing interactional 'work'?

5 How does Lynch propose that the facts of science can be seen as practical accomplishments?

6 What does Sacks mean by the 'consistency' and 'economy' rules in the use of membership categories in talk? How are they essential to understanding talk? Try to hold or invent a conversation in which these rules are systematically violated.

7 What is the problem of 'co-ordinated entry' in conversation? How do would-be conversationalists use the 'summons–answer' structure to deal with this problem?

8 What is the problem of 'identification and recognition' in telephone conversations? How are speakers' solutions to this problem governed by the requirement of 'recipient design'?

9 Consider the following data. What observations can you make on its sequential organisation?

(telephone rings)

(A)   Sociology
(B)   Who is it?
(A)   *Pardon?*
(B)   Huhh hhh um – is that Mr Doakes?

(A)   Yes, speaking.
(B)   O-h-h it's Elaine.

10   Consider the following extract from a telephone call to a Suicide Prevention Centre. What membership categorisations are used and what socially organised characteristics does their use display?

(S)   Let me ask you another thing. We're very interested here. We get calls from people who often are very reluctant to give their names or just don't. Why is that? What prevents you or what makes you hesitate?

(C)   Well. One feels like such a goddam fool you know?

(S)   Why?

(C)   I'm well over 21, and I should – you know – if I had a sister or a brother or a husband or somebody to talk to I'd talk to that person. But I feel like such an idiot when you have to call up a stranger and say will you please let me talk to you.

11   Newspaper headlines are a useful source of data containing membership categorisations and activity descriptors. Consider these examples:

FORMER M16 MAN GETS 3 YEARS IN DRUGS RING CASE
TOP BOSS SLAMS GAS SELL OFF
BLIND TODDLER REFUSED CASH FOR NURSERY

How have the particular categories and descriptors in these headlines been selected? What common-sense understandings are made possible by constructing the headlines in these particular ways? How do these headlines suggest to the reader the news-worthiness of the stories they head?

Chapter 6

Sociological Perspectives and Research Strategies

INTRODUCTION

In the sociological literature there are many accounts of 'the scientific method and sociology', and numerous guides to sociologists for collecting data. In this chapter we are not concerned with surveying the large number of data-gathering techniques and discussing their advantages and disadvantages; nor are we concerned with attempting to provide a lengthy description of the nature of 'the scientific method' in order to provide some sort of yardstick against which we could judge the worth of sociological research studies. Our aims here are altogether much less ambitious, yet the issues at stake seem to be curiously neglected in introductory textbooks to sociology.

Consequently, in this chapter we renew our more general consideration of the nature of sociological perspectives by considering the relationships that exist between research strategies and the other components of a perspective. In earlier chapters, we have explored some differences and links between sociological perspectives and, in so doing, have focused on the relationships between theoretical assumptions, conceptual frameworks and the questions asked about the social world. What also may have emerged from these chapters is the idea that research strategies, that is, commitments to certain ways of providing worthwhile knowledge and tendencies to opt for this or that sort of technique for collecting data, are very closely related to the other perspectival components. In fact, we suggest it makes good sense to regard these research strategies as an integral part of a sociological perspective. It makes good sense because it is increasingly becoming clear to sociologists that theoretical and methodological issues are well-nigh inseparable. While we recognise this integral relationship, we separate out, for analytical purposes, research strategies and other perspectival components.

In this chapter we will mainly be concerned with methodological issues, that is to say, issues about general research strategies involving, for example, decisions to study 'causes' rather than 'functions', to 'describe' the world rather than 'explain' it, and to explore 'the social construction of meanings' rather than use 'variable analysis'. Of course, as we shall see, such research strategies can influence the choice of particular research techniques (interviewing, questionnaires, observation, and so on).

SCIENTIFIC METHOD AND SOCIOLOGY

Sociologists have differing conceptions of the 'scientific method' based on their various assumptions of what is involved in being scientific, and what is worthwhile, warrantable, scientific knowledge. At different historical periods, different accounts of what the scientific method is, or should be, have been developed. This is an interesting point in itself, because it immediately makes clear that what is, or is not, seen to be a scientific approach is very much a matter of agreement at any particular time. At the present time, one portrayal, often termed the 'hypothetico-deductive' method, seems to be predominant. As outlined in the work of Karl Popper, it suggests that scientists, in any discipline, are basically testing hypotheses. Scientists start with ideas which may come from numerous sources – from reading past literature, from prior theory, from a dream, and so on. In fact, the source of the ideas does not matter very much because the scientific method is only concerned with how to go about supporting, justifying, warranting, the specific hypotheses we deduce from these ideas. The most important feature of any hypothesis is that it should be testable. In other words, we must, in principle at least, be able to refute the hypothesis by empirical test. According to Popper's account, we never prove our hypotheses, but we support them to the extent that they survive our attempts to knock them on the head by confronting them with empirical reality. More specifically, Popper argues that there is a basic unity of method covering the natural and social sciences: 'the methods always consist in offering deductive causal explanations and in testing them (by way of predictions)' (Popper, p. 131).

By contrast, we suggest, following Kaplan in *The Conduct of Inquiry*, that an account of 'the scientific method', such as Popper's, is a reconstructed, idealised picture of scientific practice. Kaplan makes the useful distinction between 'reconstructed logics', such as

Popper's, and 'Logics-in-use'. 'Logics-in-use' refer to the *actual* nature of scientists' practices in ongoing research. An account of 'logics-in-use' seldom reaches the surface in published form because, when it comes to writing up and presenting scientific research, the sociologist is involved in the business of demonstrating to others the scientific nature of his work. He is more concerned with showing how the work done meets the canons of scientific research, that is, the prevailing reconstructed logic, than with describing the detailed and specific circumstances of practical research work.

There are some interesting accounts of scientists at work which illustrate the nature of 'logics-in-use'. In the natural sciences there is Watson's *The Double Helix*, and in sociology Hammond's *Sociologists at Work* and Bell and Newby's *Doing Sociological Research*. In both areas we find that what scientists actually do can seem very distant from the finished picture as presented in their research findings. The discussion in Chapter 5 of Lynch's work also illustrates this point.

A problem inherent in the use of any single reconstructed logic is that it may exercise such a hold as to become a straitjacket for research practices. Any work which does not match its demands may be too hastily dismissed. For some may take the reconstructed logic to be a complete account of what good scientists do, and may thus not only never find out much about the variety of actual scientific practices, but also may attempt exclusively to model their work on such an account, thereby failing to see the possibility of alternative models for doing good scientific work.

Kuhn provides another line of criticism to Popper's portrayal of scientific work. He rejects Popper's characterisation of the open-minded and uncommitted scientist, testing his hypotheses. Instead, Kuhn suggests that scientists, by virtue of their training and apprenticeship in an established scientific discipline, become committed to particular ways of viewing their subject matter and to various ways of arriving at explanations in their discipline. In short, scientists are socialised into particular academic cultures; they develop their own 'scientific communities'. Kuhn reminds us that scientists are human beings, with beliefs and values like anyone else. They develop their own scientific communities which incorporate various beliefs, values and practices. Thus we can find, for example, some sociologists criticising others for aping the methodological approaches of the natural sciences, or for invoking reconstructed logics which are felt to be inappropriate to the study of the social world. On the other hand we find those criticised dismissing as unscientific the work of their critics.

Despite these possible variations, criticisms and counter-criticisms we suggest that there is broad agreement on the basic and fundamental characteristics of the scientific enterprise. We suggest that any work which claims to be 'scientific' involves at least commitment to an ongoing explicit relationship between ideas and empirical observation. The problem which any scientific researcher faces is to convince his professional colleagues that his findings, descriptions, or explanations are supported (warranted) by his reference to the empirical world. In other words, any scientist has, as his distinctive focus, the job of grounding his interpretations in empirical data and showing explicitly to others, especially to fellow members of his scientific community, how he went about it. This characterisation of what is involved in doing science is sufficiently general to allow for a considerable variety of positions within it. One particular position, however, dominates much of the discussion and argument about sociology and science – the extent to which sociologists can or should model their research strategies on the procedures used in the natural sciences (sometimes referred to as the 'more mature' sciences). We now turn to a consideration of this position.

POSITIVISM

'Positivism' is a word which sociologists seem to be increasingly fond of using. In particular, those sociologists who might regard themselves as interactionists and ethnomethodologists appear to use it as a catch-all way of characterising the research strategies most commonly used by structuralist sociologists. On the other hand, it is clear that certian sociologists are quite happy to characterise themselves as positivists. In fact, the term is used in many different ways, but for our purposes here, we suggest that a positivist approach in sociology involves the two following propositions:

(1) The kinds of explanations sociology should produce about the social world should be the same as those produced in the natural sciences, that is, law-like statements which have the form 'A causes B'; or, more concretely, 'Suicide varies inversely with the degree of integration of society' (an example we will be looking at in more detail in a moment).

(2) Sociology should as far as possible make use of the same sorts of methods as are used in the natural sciences for constructing and testing these explanations. An essential implication is that

sociologists need to model their approach on the logic of that exemplary tool of the natural sciences – the experimental method.

Positivists believe, then, that to make progress in sociology we must make use of, and strive to follow, the methodological paths already established as successful by physicists, chemists and biologists. We must, in short, treat the social world as if it were the natural world.

DURKHEIM AND POSITIVISM

Considering the achievements of the more mature sciences, it is hardly surprising that many contemporary sociologists adopt in large measure a positivist approach. There are excellent authorities for the worth of such an approach in the work of the great pioneering sociologists Comte and Durkheim. 'Treat social facts as if they were things' suggested Durkheim in *Rules of Sociological Method*. Durkheim set out a programme for defining what phenomena sociologists should study and what research strategies should be used. His work serves to spotlight the close relationship between how a topic for research is defined and the sorts of methodological strategies appropriate for its study. He suggests that sociologists are concerned with social facts, which he distinguishes from facts about individuals. Social facts are properties of collectivities; they emerge, like a chemical reaction, out of the interaction of individuals and come to exercise control over the action of individuals. In large part, Durkheim wanted to establish that social facts were different from psychological facts (that is, facts to do solely with individuals); they have their source in society itself and therefore are the distinctive phenomena for analysis by sociologists.

By arguing that social facts can be viewed as societal forces which shape individual behaviour, Durkheim indicates the extent to which they seem to have the characteristics of external objects, that is, they have a 'thing-like' quality. Consequently, there is little difficulty in applying to these 'objects' procedures of objective classification, analysis and explanation similar to those used by natural scientists in their study of plants and rocks and so on. Durkheim's rule, 'treat social facts as if they were things', could thus be amplified by adding, 'treat social facts this way . . . *because they are thing-like*'. This amendment is a little unfair to Durkheim because he does argue that there are peculiar difficulties standing in the way of sociologists who want to be as objective in their approach as natural scientists. Nevertheless, he does argue that by getting rid of our common-sense biases and thoretical preconceptions, we can establish the relationships between social facts. We can therefore obtain the social laws, which are 'out there', waiting to be discovered. Furthermore, since social facts are at a different level of reality from psychological facts and states of consciousness of particular individuals, we can ignore whatever individuals may say about the way they see the world. Instead, we should look for observable manifestations of, or measures of, the properties of collectivities, that is, social facts.

Durkheim's work produces a heritage for later sociologists. In particular, strucural sociologists, with their emphasis on discovering 'structural' properties and on showing how structural properties shape the behaviour of individuals, display Durkheim's approach to social facts. They tend to preserve his stress on how 'social facts' can be treated as 'things' which constrain individuals. We can see how Durkheim put these methodological assumptions into practice in his study, *Suicide*.

DURKHEIM ON SUICIDE

A brief extract from a recent article about Durkheim's study of suicide illustrates the prevalent contemporary view of its worth:

> Sixty-eight years after it first appeared in print, Emile Durkheim's *Suicide* is still a model of social research . . . few, if any, later works can match the clarity and power with which Durkheim marshalled his facts to test and refine his theory . . . Durkheim recognised and solved many of the problems that beset present-day research. (Selvin, p. 113)

The author goes on to say:

> the empirical analysis in *Suicide* is as vital today as it was in 1897– perhaps more so, since the quantitative approach which Durkheim pioneered has since become widely accepted among sociologists. (Selvin, p. 136)

The 'quantitative approach' to which Selvin refers is a major characteristic of positivism. It derives its importance from the significance of the experimental method as used in the natural sciences. In the ideal experiment, the scientist can control all important variables except one, and then see what happens when that one is varied. For example, if we wish to study the effects of a certain chemical on the growth of runner beans, or if we wish to test a specific hypothesis to the effect that the presence of this chemical and plant growth have a stated relationship, then 'all' other factors, for example, sunlight, water, seed, soil, must be the same for all the sample plots. Then, the varying amounts of the chemical on different test plots can be held responsible for the different growth rates observed of the runner beans. By controlling the conditions, that is, 'other factors', we have a method for observing and comparing which allows us to infer specific causal relationships.

We can take this example a little further. The statement that the chemical improves plant growth may be true, but it is hardly precise and, therefore, is perhaps not a very useful finding. If, however, the experimenter weighs how much chemical is applied to each sample plot and also measures differences in plant growth, he might hope eventually to develop certain equations which show specific quantitative relationships between the variables. He might then be able to predict and test exactly how much growth should follow upon the addition of how much of the chemical. His tests, therefore, become that much more rigorous.

To positivists, the successful achievements of the natural sciences in predicting, explaining and controlling the natural world are intimately bound up with this ability to *quantify* (to count and measure) their objects of study. Durkheim's study of suicide is regarded by many as being not only the first, but also one of the greatest attempts to show how sociologists could match the rigour of the laboratory experiment. In his preface to this study, Durkheim makes clear his ambition to discover definite laws, social laws, about how society works. He argues that his book demonstrates that such laws have been discovered and that it shows sociology can deal with 'realities as definite and substantial as those of the psychologist or the biologist'. Next he argues that, just like botanists or zoologists, we must start with an objective definition of our phenomena for study, and definites what a suicide 'really is': 'Suicide is applied to all cases of death resulting directly or indirectly from a positive or negative act of the victim himself, which he knows will produce this result' (Durkheim, 1952, p. 44).

In the first half of the book Durkheim examines several influential contemporary theories on *non-social* causes of suicide rates. He finds them inadequate, partly by argument alone, but, more importantly, also by scrutiny of the relationships between statistics on the rate of suicide and statistics on the suggested non-social causes. For example, he finds that the rate of mental illness does not seem to vary with the rate of suicide, so how could one be the cause of the other? He then proceeds to use statistics of the number of suicides each year in various countries to demonstrate that each society seems to have its own distinctive and remarkably stable suicide rate. So he arrives at the initial conclusion–cum–hypothesis that suicide, that is, suicide *rates*, must vary with the specific character or structure of each society. He says: 'Each society is predisposed to contribute a definite quota of voluntary deaths', thereby claiming to establish the right of the sociologist to regard the suicide rate as a collective property amenable to sociological explanation. For him, suicide rates are clearly social facts, in so far as they reflect the way a society functions to produce almost exactly the same number of individuals committing suicide year after year after year.

In his use of statistics we can see Durkheim's attempt to cope with the unavailability to sociologists of laboratory experiments for developing and testing hypotheses of this nature. The method he pioneered, although he did not invent it, is now commonly known, in its more sophisticated form, as 'multivariate analysis' or 'variable analysis'; as originally outlined by J. S. Mill it was termed 'The Method of Concomitant Variations'. Durkheim deals with this method at some length in *Rules of Sociological Method* and claims that it is the only way in which sociologists can effectively establish causal propositions. We can follow the logic of this method in Durkheim's attempts to show that suicide has social causes.

Durkheim starts by studying the publicly available information, the official statistics, on the rate of suicide for various countries in Europe. He notes that suicide is much more common in Protestant countries than in Catholic countries. In trying to establish the extent religious persuasion is linked with suicidal tendencies, Durkheim's problem resembles that of the researcher in the laboratory: how to control the conditions. In the above example, it could be that being Protestant is causally linked to a tendency to commit suicide, but it could also be that being German is the real determining agent. What Durkheim does is to hold nationality constant. He controls for the influence of the variable 'nationality' by comparing the influence of the two religions within a single society. For example, he finds that Bavaria has the fewest suicides of all the states of Germany, and it also has the most Catholics. He goes on to strengthen the empirical support for the link by showing that if we compare the provinces within Bavaria, we find that suicides are in direct proportion to the number of Protestants and in inverse proportion to the number of Catholics. In other words, where there are more Catholics there is less suicide, and where there are more Protestants there is more suicide.

Durkheim has by no means proved that being Protestant and the tendency to commit suicide are definitely causally linked. The more times he demonstrates, however, that these two variables 'go together' in different situations, and the more he eliminates third variables (for example, 'nationality' (German), 'region' (Bavaria)), the more empirical support he provides for inferring a causal link.

For Durkheim, the link between Protestant and suicide is explained via the argument that Protestant communities are less integrated than Catholic communities: Protestantism encourages individualism, whereas members of Catholic communities are much more closely tied to the community as a whole. It is not very clear exactly what Durkheim means by integration. He may mean certain shared meanings, or the amount of physical interaction with others, or the nature of the social bonds created by commonly held ideas. What is clear, however, is that integration is a collective property, a social fact. Durkheim believed he had arrived at part of a socio-logical, law-like explanation of suicide, namely, 'suicide varies inversely with the degree of integration of religious society'.

To test further the relationship between suicide and integration, he goes on to examine 'domestic society' and finds that his predictions hold true: the suicide rate is higher for single than married people; is higher for married people without children than for married people with children; is higher for married people with only a few children than for married people with a lot of children. In each of these examples, and in many more, Durkheim manipulated the statistical data he had available in order to refine the analysis. In this way, he strengthened his hypothesis about the relationship between social integration and suicide and arrived eventually at the conclusion that the cause of one type of suicide was insufficient societal integration.

Durkheim then demonstrates that there are at least two other types of suicide, which are stimulated by two other societal conditions. For our purposes, however, we can leave Durkheim's study of suicide and briefly examine a much more recent attempt to build on his approach. We will then have enough material to examine how structuralist assumptions and conceptual frameworks are related to a strongly positivist position.

GIBBS AND MARTIN ON SUICIDE

Gibbs and Martin aim to 'generate specific empirical propositions as opposed to vague ideas that often pass as theory in Sociology' (Gibbs and Martin, p. 140). They suggest that although 'Durkheim proceeded to formulate what remains today the foremost sociological theory of variability in suicide rates' (p. 140), his concepts, such as 'integration', lack clarity and measurability. Accordingly, they in effect update Durkheim's work. First, they define clearly the object of study – suicide rates. Secondly, they formulate general hypotheses, for example, 'The suicide rate of a population varies inversely with the stability and durability of social relationships within that population' (p. 143). Thirdly, they deduce from the above an empirically testable hypothesis and operationalise the concepts, that is, they make them measurable. They use official statistics on the suicide rate as their measure of the 'real' suicide rate, and they derive a quantitative measure of status integration. Fourthly, they use statistical techniques, such as the correlation coefficient, which can be used to establish the extent to which two variables seem to be associated. They also apply tests of statistical significance, which under certain conditions bolster confidence in the findings, that is, these tests show that the statistical link between the variables is so great that it can only occur by chance in one out of a hundred cases. Finally, they analyse the findings, and produce law-like generalisations.

Gibbs and Martin's work provides a good illustration of the general steps seen as necessary if social scientists are to emulate the detached, objective and precise approach within the 'mature' sciences. It is worthwhile noting their conclusions: 'Judging from the results so far obtained, the tests of the theory demonstrate its predictive power' (p. 147). For the positivist, sociological theory often seems to be evaluated in terms of its 'predictive power'.

POSITIVISM AND THE STRUCTURALIST APPROACH: A SUMMARY

In earlier chapters we examined 'conflict' and 'consensus' as approaches within the structuralist perspective. Both approaches are concerned with studying societies as 'wholes', as 'social systems' or 'social structures'; both produce explanations of individual action, in terms of the way it is shaped, or determined, by societal forces. Just as Durkheim sees suicide as determined by the degree of integration of the system, so structural functionalists provide similar explanations in terms of functions fulfilled for the social system by the 'parts' of society. We should note that for Durkheim social facts required explanation both in terms of their causes *and* their functions.

In structuralist approaches the focus of attention is on the 'whole'. Individual action is explained by reference to how that whole is seen to work. Whether socialisation is viewed in part as the process by which individuals come to internalise the common basic values necessary to a society's existence, or, in part, as the process by which most of the members of a society are made falsely conscious of their true objective interests, in both cases the sociologist is approaching individual action in terms of its dependence on the consequences for the system as a whole.

One consequence of this position is that the social world is seen as accessible to understanding and explanation by the use of the research strategies of the natural sciences. The structuralist position implies that the action of individuals is a product of social forces of one kind or another and that sociologists can uncover the nature of social reality by this approach. Social reality is revealed, for example, by the location of the 'latent functions' of a religious rite; or by uncovering the ways in which certain groups are 'falsely conscious' of their 'real objective interests'. The sociologist, by adopting what he takes to be the objective, detached and rational, methodological strategy of the natural scientist, aims to cumulate a body of scientific knowledge, of well-supported theories and laws explaining the 'real workings' of the social world. Here is the heritage of Durkheim's definition of social facts, which produces data similar to the phenomena with which the natural scientist is believed to work. The sociologist, then, need have no doubts in principle about the appropriateness of applying a natural scientific vocabulary to the social world, since, analytically, the social world is the same as the natural world.

We suggest that some aspects of the positivist approach are also reflected in the work of Marx. For example, Marx attempted to apply certain general socio-historical laws to a specific set of historical circumstances — nineteenth-century industrial capitalism. In so doing, he arrived at certain predictions as to future development. In turn, Marx's work has been criticised by positivists for its lack of precision. They argue that his theoretical concepts were never translated into the language of research (operationalised) in a sufficiently rigorous manner to make them testable.

We mentioned earlier in this chapter that, unlike Durkheim, some other sociologists are doubtful about the use of a strongly positivist approach. One such sociologist was Max Weber.

WEBER AND POSITIVISM

If it were the purpose of this book conveniently to slot sociologists into pigeon-holes such as 'structuralist' or 'interactionist', and 'positivist' or 'anti-positivist', then Weber would pose very great problems as can be seen by our reference to him in several previous chapters. Here is a sociologist who was concerned with vast issues such as the emergence of Western capitalism; a sociologist who generalised extensively about the relationships between different institutions such as religion and the economy across a variety of societies. Yet here too is a sociologist who defined sociology as the study of 'all human behaviour when and in so far as the acting individual attaches a subjective meaning to it'; a sociologist whose prime concern was with human beings as 'cultural beings', who attach meaning to the world.

This latter concern led Weber to be very wary about approaching societies as 'wholes', and certainly provides a sharp contrast to Durkheim's definition of the subject matter for sociologists. It also led Weber to believe that to model sociology exclusively on the methodological strategies and ambitions of the natural sciences was a serious mistake. It was a mistake because explanations in sociology, if they are to be complete, can and should be built in part on our understanding of the ideas and goals which move men to do the things they do. For Weber sociology is 'a science which attempts the interpretative understanding of social action in order thereby to arrive at a causal explanation of its course, and effects' (Weber, 1964, p. 88).

He argued that the attempt to arrive at law-like statements, such as A varies with B, or A causes B, by means of the objectifying procedures of the natural sciences, was misplaced as far as sociology was concerned. This does not mean that Weber was unwilling to make use of any available quantitative data. He does, for example, make use of it in the early part of his study *The Protestant Ethic and the Spirit of Capitalism*, where he points to statistical relationships between religious affiliation and the amount and kind of economic activity: relationships which suggest a possible causal link. Again, in his extended comparative studies of Western Europe, China, Ancient

Judea and Islamic societies, he uses a form of experimental logic for inferring a possible causal link between the Protestant ethic and the emergence of capitalism. For example, he argues that in many ways both China and Britain had the material potential for the development of capitalism. This adds some further support to the hypothesis that the Protestant ethic was a crucial variable – present in the West, but not in China. To establish such objectively possible relationships by means of forms of variable analysis is only a necessary condition of a sociological explanation. We need to add the sufficient condition of knowing how the persons involved produced this relationship by their individual actions. In Weber's term, explanations must also be 'adequate at the level of meaning', that is, we must be able to comprehend, to understand, the ways in which our subjects make sense of the world. Such an understanding makes explanations of social behaviour subjectively plausible and convincing.

In many ways, Weber can be seen to have attempted to bridge the gap between those who believe that the social sciences should attempt to follow the path of the natural sciences, and those who argue that the study of man as a social being, as a being with a 'mind', is entirely distinct from other sciences. In the terminology of Bruyn, as we will see, Weber can be said to have adopted aspects of both an 'inner perspective' methodology and an 'outer perspective' methodology. Weber did not simply pose the problem as to how we can, as scientists, come to grips with the subjective meanings of human beings in particular historical contexts: he tried to solve it. He proposed a number of appropriate methodological devices, which could enable the sociologist to move beyond a descriptive account of this or that unique set of historical circumstances. By means of these devices the sociologist could generalise about the social world, that is, he could locate uniformities and similarities and differences in a systematic way. One such device is the ideal type.

Weber did not claim to have been the first to use ideal types. What he tried to do was to make as explicit as possible a procedure already used by those working in several disciplines, particularly historians. In short, the ideal type is developed by the researcher to help him anslyse a particular set of actual historical events. It consists of the researcher's own selection of evidence and observations from reality to create a tool for the specific problem he has set himself. Ideal types are sometimes referred to as 'pure types', and the researcher's selection and possible exaggeration of the evidence and observations is designed to provide an unambiguous, clear-cut and meaningful purity. It is not 'ideal' in any moral sense but rather is ideal in providing a standard. This standard helps us to locate similarities and differences in actual historical situations. We use it for the purpose of comparison and set it out clearly for all to see, criticise and possibly improve. In *The Protestant Ethic* Weber constructed ideal types of how individuals typically act under the influence of the 'Protestant ethic' and the 'spirit of capitalism'. Weber's argument is that there is an 'elective affinity' between the two: the implications for action of the Protestant *ethic* seem to have a remarkable correspondence to the requirements of the capitalist *spirit*. This analysis, rooted in the comparison of ideal types, does not in itself establish a causal relationship between the two. What it does, in a fairly rigorous and explicit manner, is make the affinity or congruence between the two sets of attitudes a credible one.

For Weber, the methodological practices of the sociologist *did* need to be different from those of the natural scientist in *certain* respects. He attempted to demonstrate how an interpretative understanding of social behaviour could be achieved in a consistently rigorous and explicit manner. He disagreed with those who suggested that sociologists should attempt to produce definitive sets of law-like propositions for predicting social behaviour. Such an ambition neglects the fact that members of society are cultural beings attaching meanings to events in particular situations. It also neglects the fact that the sociologist himself is a cultural being. In contrast to Durkheim, who seemed to believe in the existence of a set of social laws awaiting discovery by the objective scientific researcher, Weber argued that facts do not speak for themselves. As a 'cultural being' himself concerned with studying other 'cultural beings', the researcher poses different sorts of questions, and is in certain respects hoping to gain different sorts of knowledge from those characteristically associated with the natural sciences.

'INNER PERSPECTIVE' AND 'OUTER PERSPECTIVE'

Our discussion of Weber provides an appropriate opportunity to review and preview some of the methodological issues raised in this chapter. Whereas the major debates in British sociology during the 1950s and 1960s centred around the theoretical claims dividing consensus and conflict approaches, the later 1960s and 1970s brought methodological issues into sharper focus. This development was not by chance, but came hand-in-hand with the growth of so-called 'micro' or 'interpretative' perspectives, that is, Symbolic Interactionism, phenomenology, ethnomethodology. The central question for many sociologists became, as it was for Weber, what sort of science should sociology be? Although there are serious disagreements between interpretative sociologists as to how that question might be answered, all reacted strongly to aspects of structuralist perspectives and positivism.

Some shared features of this reaction were captured by Denzin. He contrasts models of 'sociological-scientific conduct, which stand in opposition to one another . . . The quantitative method calls for a more distanced, objective, standardized, classifiable mode of investigation . . . The naturalistic model of inquiry . . . reflect[s] a respect for the phenomena of the everyday worlds of natural interraction' (Denzin, p. 3). Bruyn sets up a similar contrast between the 'outer-persective' methodology corresponding clearly to positivism as we have outlined it, and the 'inner perspective' methodology. According to Bruyn, those working with 'inner perspective' are observing man concretely and subjectively as opposed to the abstract and objective approach of the traditional empiricist and theorist; they are observing him 'as a social being with freedom and purpose as opposed to observing him deterministically as the product of external forces' (Bruyn, p. 281).

For interpretative sociologists, a shared starting-point is a 'respect' for human beings as interpreters of the world. The term 'interpretative sociology' is doubly appropriate, however, for it also points to the concern amongst such sociologists that we recognise the sociologist to be operating also as a human being within society. One implication is that the social world is not to be treated as if the social scientist were independent of it, that data, for example, are better viewed as 'constructed' by the sociologist rather than 'collected' and that the process by which it is constructed should be monitored and explicated.

We now move into a more detailed consideration of some aspects of the theoretical positions which are closely associated with an 'inner perspective' methodology.

SYMBOLIC INTERACTIONISM AND POSITIVISM

Students of human society will have to face the question of whether their preoccupations with categories of structure and organisaton can be squared with the interpretative processes by means of which human beings, individually and collectively, act in human society. It is the discrepancy between the two which

plagues such students in their efforts to attain scientific propositions of the sort achieved in the physical and biological sciences.
(Blumer, p. 191)

In this short extract Blumer is pointing to some basic diferences in
the research strategies practised by structuralists and Symbolic Interactionists. There is, he argues, a difference in focus, a difference of
emphasis, concerning the topic of study which reflects different
methodological assumptions. This differential focus can be briefly
summarised as follows: structuralists tend to start with assumptions
about, and questions relating to, the structure and functioning of
collectivities, of societies, of 'wholes'; Symbolic Interactionists tend
to start with assumptions about, and questions relating to, what we
might think of as 'man as a social being'. In their focus on the nature
of man as a social being, interactionists have been severely critical of
certain structuralist approaches. They have reacted to the structuralist
perspective, by arguing that it tends to make man out as a passive
object, whose actions are determined by societal forces. Symbolic
Interactionists claim that structuralists, in neglecting to study man as
an active attacher of meanings to the world, end up by imposing
their own meanings on him. In adopting the viewpoint of the
detached, objective observer, in applying wholesale the methods of
the natural sciences, they ignore what social life is all about. In
attempting to arrive at law-like statements by accurate measurement
and by attempting to quantify features of social life, they make their
work seem scientifically respectable, but they prevent themselves
from ever studying what really counts.

In papers such as Blumer's, we find a strong critique of structuralist assumptions and prevalent research strategies. We also unfortunately find some ambiguity at times. For example, every now and
then Blumer refers to the 'social structure' as 'influencing', rather
than 'determining', individual action and then argues that structuralists have an unfortunate concern with 'categories of structure'. Yet
he himself is clearly working with a notion of an objective social
structure, external to indivuduals, but he is not sure what to do with
it, except to say that it has received too much attention. This ambiv-
alence at the theoretical level is reflected in his methodological position. Blumer is very unclear as to what sort of scientific propositions
Symbolic Interactionists should be trying to attain.

In practice, Symbolic Interactionists stress the need to get at
people's meanings, at their definitions of the situation and at changes
in these over time through the processes of Symbolic Interaction. It

is not surprising, then, that their studies are often studies of interaction in particular, small-scale settings: a study of one mental hospital; of one hospital ward; of one group of students progressing through college; of one classroom. We rarely find interactionists attempting to cover populations as extensive as those commonly studied in structuralist studies. The interests of interactionists lead them to focus on the details of action in particular contexts. Their major initial task is usually one of discovery: discovering how the people they are studying see themselves and their settings. We do not very often find interactionists setting up very explicit hypotheses before they move into the field. Their question is 'what is going on here?', rather than, 'what data are needed to test this hypothesis from this theory?'

It is not surprising that the ideas of Glaser and Strauss in *The Discovery of Grounded Theory* have had a continuing appeal for Symbolic Interactionists. Glaser and Strauss argue, with a somewhat missionary fervour, that there has been too much emphasis on the testing of preconceived theory, and that sociologists could fruitfully pay more attention to generating conceptual categories and hypotheses as the research process develops. Grounded theory emerges during the actual researching itself, that is, it derives from what appears to be theoreticaly relevant to the researcher at that point of time in the research process. Further comparisons are made, further data are selected, as the need arises. Hence they speak of 'theoretical sampling' which is to be contrasted with 'random sampling'. There is a continuous intermeshing of data collection and analysis. The methodological prescriptions of Glaser and Strauss, with their stress on theory as an emerging, ever-developing entity, corresponds nicely with the Symbolic Interactionist view of social life itself as emergent and fluid. Perhaps this correspondence should be expected: Glaser and Strauss are Symbolic Interactionists themselves and their book benefited from the comments of many well-known researchers of similar persuasion.

Symbolic Interactionists also react against attempts to gain precision by measuring the social world as one does natural phenomena; therefore it is not surprising to find in interactionist studies a relative paucity of tables of statistics, of complex measurement scales and of attempts to apply mathematical formulae to social life. Their research strategies tend to be qualitative rather than quantitative. Symbolic Interactionists are concerned not to lose the particular qualities of words and actions by trying to count and measure them. It is their concern with meanings in social settings which leads them to undertake qualitative studies of particular cases. This same concern has led them to make considerable use of such data-gathering techniques as participant observation and informal and open-ended interviewing. These techniques allow the researcher to give extensive quotes from his subjects for the reader to peruse in the published presentation of the research. Consequently, interactionist studies often contain many illustrative examples of conversation and descriptions of specific incidents. Our opportunity to read these, together with the researcher's presented interpretations of them, is in large part what provides the empirical warrant for the findings of such studies. One of Glaser and Strauss's points about judging credibility is of interest here. They note that 'if a reader becomes sufficiently caught up in the description so that he feels vicariously that he was also in the field, then he is more likely to be kindly disposed towards the researcher's theory than if the description seems flat or unconvincing' (Glaser and Strauss, p. 230).

Symbolic Interactionists, in their focus on man as a social being and in the light of their theoretical assumptions, are somewhat doubtful about the extent to which it is desirable to apply the methods of the natural sciences to the social world. They are particularly critical of certain structuralist research strategies and feel that the wholesale acceptance of a positivist position may attain only a pseudo-scientific respectability because it neglects the distinctively symbolic and interpretive nature of social process. At the same time, however, their own work can be seen to contain certain methodological aspects which are similar to those found in structuralist studies. Their reaction to positivism, therefore, is best viewed as only partial. To illustrate further the nature of the Symbolic Interactionist research strategies and their partial reaction to positivism we turn now to some examples of empirical studies.

DOUGLAS ON SUICIDE

Although his concerns seem to be primarily those of interactionism, the fact that Douglas can at times be seen to be working along ethnomethodological lines is another useful reminder that the notion of a sociological perspective is no more than an organising principle. Douglas feels that there is considerable ambiguity in Durkheim's study of suicide, arguing that Durkheim was not the objective analyst he claimed to be. Although Durkheim said that the researcher must get rid of all his common-sense notions and preconceptions, he was actually applying his own common-sense knowledge, but not explicitly, throughout his study of suicide.

More concretely, Douglas argues that Durkheim in fact works with an implicit theory of shared social meanings. These meanings are the real causal agents in Durkheim's findings. For example, in interpreting the statistical association between variables such as the suicide rate and religious affiliation and domestic status, Durkheim gives brief sketches of how a Protestant, or married man, sees the world. At another point, Durkheim interprets the lower suicide rate of women in terms which would make any female campaigner for women's liberation tear her hair out. Basically, Durkheim says that women are more easily satisfied than men; women are less complex beings who are happy in the company of a few pets. The question is: From what research does Durkheim derive these meanings? As Durkheim's own prescriptions in *The Rules of Sociological Method* prevent him from studying the meanings which individuals attach to the world, he is forced to supply them himself. In doing so, he contradicts his own rules.

Douglas argues that even in Durkheim's *Suicide*, a classic sociological study, the weaknesses of a positivist position are made apparent. Durkheim's views on the correct scientific approach, together with his strong structuralist position, prevented him from studying what he constantly invoked: social meanings. His implicit assumptions about, and use of, social meanings are brought out by examining Durkheim's use of official statistics.

Durkheim was interested in locating the social causes of a certain form of behaviour: suicide. Having given his own definition of suicide, he used the official statistics as the operational measure of the 'real' rate of suicide as he had defined it. Douglas argues that if we look at the workings of the official agencies, it will be seen that in each and every case of a death being investigated, officials are involved in interpreting the world, of deciding that this is, or is not, a suitable motive for suicide; that this cannot be a suicide because nobody would intentionally kill themselves in that way for that reason; that anybody who plays Russian roulette with five chambers loaded must have intended to commit suicide, and so on. What ends up in the official statistics as a suicide can be the outcome of a lengthy process of decision-making, involving in any one case the assignment of particular social meanings to various events. Durkheim assumed that a suicide was an easy thing to see and that the social meaning of suicide was unproblematic. For him, there are out in the world certain objects describable as suicides; for Douglas, this uncritical acceptance of the official statistics as unproblematic represents the positivist aproach at its crudest.

By contrast, Douglas suggests that we look at detailed case studies of death defined as suicide. By examining the construction of meanings in particular contexts, we will eventually be able to classify different patterns of suicidal meanings. The message is clear: suicide is a matter of social definition and these definitions vary; there is nothing 'out there' with the intrisic meaning 'suicide'. The way forward is to analyse the meanings our subjects attach to the world. To do so, we must look in depth at their words and actions in all their qualitative detail.

Douglas's ideas provided the basis for some research by Atkinson on the work coroners do when categorising a death as a suicide. Atkinson argues that the official statistics are still useful, but that our focus should be on the producers of these statistics, for example, coroners, and the sort of things they use as indicators of suicidal intent, which enable a death to be explained, and thus categorised as a suicide. Atkinson goes on to sketch out what he calls a 'dynamic model of the transmission of shared definitions of suicide through a social system', definitions of suicide, that is, which may be shared by coroners, researchers, journalists, and so on. In Atkinson's view, the model suggests that 'the shared definitions themselves have a marked effect on suicidal behaviour, as those who actually attempt and commit suicide are unlikely to be ignorant of the meanings commonly associated with suicide' (Atkinson, p. 188).

Both these studies illustrate the danger of exaggerating the interactionist reaction to positivism. It is not the case that structuralists measure, while interactionists do not. Interactionists merely tend to have a distaste for certain ways of measuring. For example, Douglas starts to classify patterns of meanings and to group cases, calling some 'revenge suicides'. We recall that simple classification into such categories as 'revenge suicide' or 'not revenge suicide' is a form of measurement. Although it is the 'weakest' form of measurement, it is measurement all the same. Atkinson's reference to those who 'actually attempt and commit suicide' in his dynamic model seems to presume the capacity to recognise 'a suicide' independently from the processes by which that recognition is produced. Yet these processes of meaning construction by coroners are his central interest.

Similar features characterize the Symbolic Interactionist study we consider next, where our concern is to illustrate the relationships which can exist between methodological commitments or general research strategies and specific research techniques.

PREFERRED RESEARCH TECHNIQUES
PARTICIPANT OBSERVATION AS AN EXAMPLE

In *Making the Grade*, Becker (with Geer and Hughes) studies student life in an American University from an explicitly Symbolic Interactionist orientation. In this study, the researchers rely heavily on the method or technique of participant observation to collect their data. Elsewhere Becker and Geer define participant observation as: 'that method in which the observer participates in the daily life of the people under study, either openly in the role of researcher or covertly in some disguised role, observing things that happen, listening to what is said, and questioning people over some length of time' (Becker and Geer, p. 102). The issue we consider here is the preference of Symbolic Interactionists for using participant observation.

In *Making the Grade*, Becker states explicitly that his interest is in learning about college life as it is subjectively experienced by students. He wants to discover how students define the situations they are in and how they construct their actions accordingly. He considers that the technique of participant observation is the best method for collecting these kinds of data. He argues that the participant observer, by taking the role of others (the students), can gain insight into the ways the students make sense of their situations. As Becker notes, the participant observer can himself absorb the particular language of those with whom he mixes. He sees statements in context, observing processes of definition and the construction of action as it happens. In short, he can 'catch social reality in flight'.

More generally, certain assumptions made by Symbolic Interactionists render questionnaires logically inappropriate for collecting 'worthwhile' data. For example, they make the assumption that the individual's personality and self-identity are not static, but can change over time as the individual interacts with others in other settings. They argue that questionnaires cannot cope with these dynamic aspects of social interaction. Questionnaires allow subjects only to recall, to remember and to reconstruct. The questionnaire can only therefore take still pictures of the social world, whereas participant observation can capture social processes in all their richness.

The use of participant observation can, however, give rise to problems in the presentation of research findings. The major problem is presenting the findings in a way which shows them to be warranted, to be grounded in the data. In dealing with this problem,

Becker again demonstrates that the reaction of Symbolic Interactionists to positivism is only partial. He develops the major hypothesis that college students in their approach to academic matters are only concerned with getting from staff adequate grades, that is, adequate assessments of their academic work. The students require adequate grades to free them for their more valued social and political activities in college. Becker argues that students have a dominant set of attitudes to their work which he terms the 'grade-point average perspective'. He tries to convince us, his readers, that this is the case by, in part, providing us with extensive illustrative pieces of conversation. He also argues that certain of his empirical observations can be seen as reflecting the presence of the perspective, for example, the sorts and number of books in a student's room (we have here a clear-cut example of his operationalisation procedures). He says elsewhere that a detailed history of the research – of the activities of the observers and how they presented themselves to their subjects – is also very useful, because the reader can follow and check through the researcher's activities and interpretations. Unfortunately, Becker does not help us in this way in *Making the Grade*. What he does provide, however, is a chapter on the evidence for the perspective. Here we see him adopting techniques which suggest that he wants his work to be seen as meeting several criteria which we might describe as positivistic. For he presents tables which classify and count the number of observed occurrences which support his hypothesis. The tables also show the number of negative cases. These tables appear curiously out of place when we consider some of the interactionist critiques of other sociologists. The tables, together with attempts by writers to establish the 'objective nature' of participant observation if 'properly conducted', suggest that in several respects Symbolic Interactionists can be using positivist research strategies.

Although we have focused only on participant observation, out of the large range of date-gathering techniques used by sociologists, we may have at least illustrated the relationship between research strategies and the tendency to opt for a particular kind of data-gathering technique. Of course, we are talking only in terms of tendencies. Certainly interactionists use questionnaires at times and structuralists use participant observation.

Finally, we briefly examine what we have so far only implied, namely, the sort of knowledge which interactionists are hoping to arrive at. Clearly, they would reject the suggestion that they are trying to produce sets of law-like propositions governing social behaviour – a rejection which corresponds in part to Weber's position. For Weber, Blumer, Becker, or Douglas, this rejection does not mean that the researcher's end product can only be a rich, qualitative, descriptive account of social behaviour in one particular setting. Interactionists do attempt to generalise about social life. Admittedly, the generalisations appear at times rather ambiguous and imprecise and different in kind when compared with the clear-cut productions of the rigorous positivist. For example, Becker says:

> In this volume, then, we will analyse the patterns of collective action students develop in their academic work . . . We will thus enable ourselves to understand what the academic side of college life looks like to students and to understand as well how the environment they operate in constrains them to see things as they do. Our analysis should lead both to a deeper understanding of similar relationships in other kinds of social settings and to a more adequate conceptualisation of some of the problems of college life conventionally studied by social scientists. (Becker *et al*., p. 12)

This excerpt is fairly typical of the sorts of comments found at the beginning or end of many interactionist studies, together with the rider that 'this study is only exploratory'. The suggestion is that qualitative studies of social action in particular social settings can lead to a 'deeper understanding' of the processes by which human beings attach particular meanings to the world in other settings. There is a *relative* absence in interactionist writings of terms such as 'cause', and even 'explanation'. Such terms are perhaps too strongly associated with positivist ambitions.

ETHNOMETHODOLOGY AND POSITIVISM

We have indicated that Durkheim and the structuralist approaches tend to view the social world as an objective reality. They make the assumption that there are in the world certain forms of behaviour, such as suicides, and certain societal forces which give rise to this behaviour. They also assume that by adopting the detached approach and objectifying procedures of the natural scientist, that is, 'positivism', the sociologist can cut through common-sense ideas and value judgements, and eventually reveal the workings of the social world by establishing its law-like character. In short, they tend to 'treat social facts as if they were things'.

By contrast, we have suggested that interactionists tend to view the social world and social reality as the product of the interpretations and meaningful constructions of individuals. For example, in their approaches to suicide, or to deviance more generally, interactionists argue that someone is deviant if he is socially defined as such, someone is a suicide only by virtue of a corpse being socially defined in this way. To some extent, ethnomethodologists take a similar view of social reality in their initial emphasis on man as a constructor of the social world. Ethnomethodologists depart from the interactionist position, however, in trying to go beyond the question of what the world looks like to people in order to locate and describe the methods which people use to make the world like that. For ethnomethodologists, social facts, social reality, are members' 'accomplishments'.

This assumption casts a different light on Durkheim's prescription and more generally invites a reconsideration of all attempts to refine and make more sophisticated for sociological purposes the equipment of the natural sciences. Ethnomethodologists agree that the world does in many ways seem to have an external and object-like character. Certainly members of society adopt this viewpoint; we all come across 'things' such as 'suicides' and 'criminals', 'good neighbourhoods' and 'bad neighbourhoods'. In fact if we, as members of society, do not work in our everyday lives with such assumptions, and if we did not take it for granted that others do the same, our social worlds would be very chaotic and very strange. Ethnomethodologists argue that Durkheim, in suggesting that social reality has an objective character, is taking for granted exactly what members of society take for granted; in attempting to disentangle themselves from common sense, via the use of the appropriate objectifying techniques, positivists end up by adopting unexplicated common sense themselves. Ethnomethodologists point out that by adopting a positivist approach and attempting to produce general propositions of a sort similar to those produced in the physical and biological sciences, sociologists are bound to ignore the context-bound nature of talk and conduct, that is, the indexical properties of interaction. For example, to arrive at the social causes of suicide, sociologists have to define and classify suicides in terms of their common features; and to warrant the conclusion that students use a particular perspective on their academic work, they have to classify student talk and conduct, showing how each observed item can be seen to be similar. In this way, the sociologist moves beyond the particular features of any setting. Here, ethnomethodologists point to the fact that in providing such generalising accounts, sociologists are employing the same sense-assembly practices of any member of society. In providing accounts of the world, in observing and reporting, all of us, scientists included, are constituting the world for what it is at any particular time and place, in the light of particular practical circumstances and practical concerns. Scientific productions are not 'objective' in the sense of being free of any particular context; they are grounded in the scientists' everyday practices in specific contexts. Scientists 'doing science' provide the ethnomethodologist with examples of practical reasoning; examples which are as open to investigation as practical reasoning in any other setting. Ethnomethodologists do not claim, however, that by virtue of the application of certain methodological procedures they can detach themselves from personal involvement and somehow take themselves out of society for the purposes of objectivity. They recognise that there is no higher plan of detached objectivity to which they could aspire. In other words, no one can escape his own membership in society, his own use of common-sense reasoning as an ongoing resource, whether he be layman or sociologist. They insist that they are not trying to compete with lay members by producing versions of the world which are more accurate, true, or objective. Instead, they take as their task the description of the common-sense practices through which human beings construct and sustain their social world; a world in which there may appear such things as 'suicides', 'truths' and the 'realities' of everyday life.

Ethnomethodologists have spent a lot of effort in making clear to themselves, and others, just what it is that they are interested in studying. They have also, as we have seen, very definitely ruled out of court certain methodological procedures and ambitions as inappropriate to their topic of study. Unfortunately, they have as yet had little to say explicitly as to how that topic should be approached. The tendency in this respect is to let their research studies speak for themselves.

One aspect of their research strategy is very clear: their preference for collecting data which represents interaction 'as it happens'. By using tape recorders, video-tapes and participant observation techniques, they can study people 'doing their everyday lives', for example, chatting on the telephone, walking along the pavement, taking part in conversations, and so on. In this way they attempt to capture the 'raw materials' of interaction.

The sort of findings or conclusions ethnomethodologists produce from such data have their own particular characteristics. Instead of trying to produce 'deductive causal explanations' (Popper) or sets of law-like propositions, they aim to produce *descriptions*. These descriptions concern the methods members use to accomplish the world for what it is. In the descriptions and analyses of these methods, ethnomethodologists, like other social scientists, are attempting to generalise about social life. In their case, these generalisations are about the sort of 'apparatus', the 'sense assembly equipment', that human beings use to construct and sustain their everyday social lives. In perceiving this ambition of ethnomethodologists, we might also see that they can have no real interest in, for example, locating members' practices in any broader historical context or social structural context. Any concern with the causal conditions of certain practices becomes irrelevant and misconceived in terms of their programme. It is hardly surprising, then, that for many sociologists ethnomethodology represents the ultimate retreat from social problems, from issues such as the distribution of power and social change. It is at points such as these that sociologists who have become committed to a perspective such as ethnomethodology often have vague worries about the extent to which their route towards a viable social science has led them away from earlier commitments to sociology as a way of understanding social problems and as, perhaps, an initial step towards changing the world. Finally, although ethnomethodologists have dropped both the vocabulary of the natural sciences and a 'positivistic' approach to studying social life, their work does seem to fit the characterisation of science which we provided at the beginning of this chapter. What the ethnomethodologist would claim he was bringing to his materials is a commitment to explicating as far as possible the relationships between his analyses and the empirical data with which he is working. This commitment involves making explicit the use that the researcher is making of his own common-sense resources in observing what he observes and hearing what he hears. We, as readers and assessors of the worth of an ethnomethodological study, are invited to comment and criticise with reference to the analyst's work on the materials he provides. A useful feature of much ethnomethodological research is that we do have to hand these 'raw materials'. We conclude our discussion of ethnomethodological research strategies by taking the ethnomethodologists at their word and observing their research strategies as they can be seen to operate in actual empirical study, namely, Sacks on suicide.

SACKS ON SUICIDE

In an early paper, 'Sociological Description', Sacks argued that 'in terms of the history of sociology nothing is more tragic than that Durkheim's *Suicide* should be conceived as a model investigation' (Sacks, 1963, p.3). He goes on to say that modern sociology has taken a direction which can in part be traced back to Durkheim's work: 'the crucial feature is acceptance of common-sense categories as sociological resources rather than as features of social life which sociology must treat as subject matter' (Sacks, 1963, p. 15). In his own study of materials on suicide, 'The Search for Help: No One to Turn to', Sacks demonstrates the research implications of accepting this view.

Sack's data consists mainly of verbatim transcripts of tape-recorded conversations between staff members of a Suicide Prevention Centre and callers who are either suicidal or calling in reference to someone who is suicidal. It should be noted that these transcripts are only *part* of his data. In approaching this data as an analyst, Sacks has additional 'data', namely, his own common-sense knowledge and members' methods which he must use to repair the sense of his materials. His aim is to explicate them as far as he can in his analysis. Sacks starts his article:

> I shall aim to construct a description of how the conclusion a suicidal person may reach (that he has no one to turn to) may be reproducibly provided for. The aim may be satisfied by (1) locating the collections of membership categories in terms of which the search for help is properly formulated; and by (2) describing the ways such collections are used to determine whether there are eligible persons available. (Sacks, 1967, p. 203)

Sacks noted that *both* parties described or accounted for the call as the 'suicidal' person having 'no one to turn to', even though, clearly, the person in the Centre was offering help and was, seemingly, being turned to. Sacks shows that this apparently paradoxical description by members of what was happening is due to the way that our common-sense knowledge is organised. Sacks proceeds to take the conclusion, no one to turn to, and consider what sort of practical reasoning could lead to it.

He shows how the parties to the call, even though they have no biographical knowledge of each other, can conduct, solely on the basis of a simple identification of the caller, a systematic 'search procedure' for an appropriate person to turn to. Knowing, for example, that the caller is a 'husband' can permit a discussion of the 'wife's' availability to help. On the basis of knowledge of such 'pair relationships', husband–wife, mother–son, and so on, a systematic search can be made for proper or appropriate persons to turn to. For members, it is not enough for 'anyone' to offer help; an offer must come from an appropriate person. Someone who can be identified as 'anyone' can, in suicidal cases, also be identified as 'no one'. It is an identification accepted as correct by all parties concerned – the caller, the called, Sacks and, perhaps, the reader.

Thus Sacks describes a 'sense assembly apparatus' which consists of the selection and use of standard identities for the proper conducting of a search for help. As we saw in Chapter 5, when Sacks refers to categories he is referring to common-sense categories which, upon inspection of the conversational materials, seem to be used by the persons participating in the talk. Also Sacks 'hears' them as being used and we, as readers of his analyses, have access to the same materials and have the opportunity to evaluate Sack's analyses by reference to the talk. The same points hold for Sack's use of the term 'collection': the term is only used to refer to some group of categories which people do group together, for example mother–father, wife–husband, stranger–stranger. Such collections, plus their rules of application to populations, provide part of the apparatus by which people do the business of observing and reporting on the world. By using such an apparatus, members can produce recognisably sensible descriptions of the world – recognisable to themselves, to others and to the analyst, for example, descriptions such as 'I have no one to turn to'.

In this analysis by Sacks, we can see a different research strategy in operation to those used by Durkheim, Douglas and Atkinson. The latter three are concerned with the phenomenon 'suicide'; they all, in different ways, wish to provide sociological explanations or understandings of suicide. Durkheim aimed to discover social laws, laws which determine the rates of suicide. Douglas argued that to understand suicide we must get at the social meanings which may be involved in particular cases. For Atkinson, building on Douglas, the study of definers of central reality, such as coroners in the suicidal process, may allow us to elucidate relationships between shared definitions of suicidal situations and actual behaviour. Sacks, on the other hand, is not really interested in explaining suicide at all; he is interested in the methods people use to produce recognisable descriptions of the world. He is attempting to generalise about the sort of apparatus that human beings use to find what they find in the world, and to have those findings received as understandable by others.

TOWARDS A SYNTHESIS: METHODOLOGICAL ISSUES

Several sociologists have attempted to interrelate aspects of inter-pretative and structuralist, particularly neo-Marxist, approaches. This ambition is captured by Apple when he argues that the focus should be on 'the ideological and cultural mediations which exist between material conditions of an unequal society and the formation of the consciousness of the individuals in that society' (Apple, p. 2). Recalling Bruyn's comments on the virtues of the 'inner perspective' as allowing for observations of man 'as a social being with freedom and purpose', it is the lack of recognition of, or capacity to handle, constraints on that freedom which troubles many sociologists. The lack of consideration for external constraints, Apple and others see as a crucial weakness in interpretative approaches. However, the methodological problems involved in such an attempted synthesis are apparent in studies such as Willis's *Learning to Labour* and Sharp and Green's *Education and Social Control*.

Both studies display a clear research interest in the interpretative sociologist's concern for how participants socially construct meanings, leading the researchers to use techniques such as partici-pant observation and open-ended interviewing. At the same time, however, we find the more central concern is to locate the conscious-ness of their subjects in a wider structural context, in both cases involving Marxist conceptual frameworks. Interpretative sociologists might regard such studies as beguiling for the detailed ethnography they contain in parts. In other parts, however, there is little in the way of Denzin's 'respect' for the 'everyday world of natural inter-action'. For example, Willis's study might be characterised as an attempt to subject 'micro' data to 'macro' interpretations. Similarly, Sharp and Green's study is designed, somewhat retrospectively, to point to the limitations of a purely phenomenological analysis, but provides little empirical reference concerning these limitations.

It is perhaps not surprising, however, that such studies, drawing as they do on differing traditions, should come under attack from rep-resentatives of these traditions. Many sociologists certainly see it as a major task to relate differing levels of analysis, drawing on the strengths of differing conceptual frameworks. The question remains as to how this end can be achieved in such a way as to avoid *imposing* synthesis. Rather, researchers must demonstrate an ongoing explicit relationship between ideas and empirical observation at both levels. Consequently, sociologists must find ways, as Weber attempted to do, of relating 'inner perspective' and 'outer perspective' methodologies.

TRIANGULATION: MIXING RESEARCH TECHNIQUES

Sociologists have in practice never been as reluctant to use a variety of research techniques as some may believe. This has been made more explicit in discussions of the virtues of a 'triangulation of methods' (see Denzin, p. 339), where differing research techniques in the same study are used to illuminate differing aspects of a problem. It has been suggested that differing research techniques can not only complement one another in a variety of ways, but can also add to the credibility of a study, providing an internal cross-checking or monitoring device during the research process.

A study by Delamont, 'Beyond Flanders' Fields: the relationship of subject matter and individuality to classroom style', suggests some ways in which data-gathering techniques associated with very different methodological traditions can be fruitfully combined. The study appears in a book of articles on classroom observation, many of which are highly critical of 'systematic observation schedules' such as Flanders' Interaction Analysis Categories (FIAC). FIAC is designed to produce quantitative profiles of the distribution of teacher and pupil talk according to a set of prespecified categories. The observer is encouraged to operate like an automaton, coding the talk every three seconds. Delamont applies FIAC to a sample of teachers, covering a range of school subjects, and then uses unstructured observation, plus formal and informal interviews, in an attempt to understand certain interesting anomalies in the quantitative patterns. For example, one focus is on why two of the science teachers are so different from all the other scientists according to various statistical measures applied to the FIAC data.

In her conclusion, Delamont notes that systematic observation schedules can be sensitive research tools, but are 'immeasurably strengthened' by the addition of unstructured types of observation which produce qualitative data. At one time, books on research techniques frequently suggested that techniques such as participant observation should be regarded as useful exploratory tools before moving on to quantitative data. Interestingly, Delamont reverses this order!

Delamont's study is, of course, only one of many which use both qualitative and quantitative data to illuminate each other. As we have argued throughout, however, it is important to attempt to make explicit the assumptions about the world built into these research techniques.

CONCLUSION

In this chapter we have been considering the relationships which can exist between research strategies and other perspectival components. In so doing, we have inevitably drawn some very broad distinctions and simplified the issues involved by compartmentalising socio-logical approaches. Our essential theme has been the interdependence of theoretical and research issues. This interdependence is genuine and should not be seen as 'one way traffic'. We have stressed the ways in which certain theoretical assumptions about the nature of the social world lead to certain research strategies and data-gathering techniques being adopted as especially appropriate. We note, how-ever, that these methods and techniques carry with them assump-tions which are usually implicit concerning the nature of social reality. In short, by making research decisions, the sociologist is also making theoretical assertions.

FURTHER READING

Magee, B., *Popper* (Fontana, 1973). Especially Chapter 2, 'Scientific method – the traditional view and Popper's view', showing the difficulties of producing a determinate view of 'the scientific method' and outlining the nature of the hypothetico-deductive model.

Barnes, B. (ed.), *Sociology of Science: Selected Readings* (Penguin, 1972). For Kuhn's 'Scientific paradigms' providing a critique of Popper's view of scientific work. Also relevant for argument is Chapter 7.

Wiseman, J. P., and **Aron, M. S.,** *Field Projects in Sociology* (Transworld Publishing, 1972). For Chapter 13, 'Explanatory survey and multivariate analysis', discussing major sociological methods for locating and testing causal relationships.

Hollinghead, A. B., and **Redlich, F. C.,** 'Social stratification and psychiatric disorders' (Bobbs Merrill Reprint S.120) illustrating structuralist/positivist approach using variable analysis to test explicit hypotheses.

Hammersley, M., and **Woods, P.** (eds), *The Process of Schooling* (Routledge & Kegan Paul, 1976). For Blumer's 'The methodological position of Symbolic Interactionism'. For G. C. F. Payne's 'Making a lesson happen: an ethnomethodological analysis'.

Manis, J. G., and **Meltzer, B. N.,** *Symbolic Interaction* (Allyn & Bacon, 1972). For H. Becker and B. Geer's 'Participant observation and interviewing: a comparison'. Also in W. G. Filstead (ed.), *Qualitative Methodology* (Markham, 1970).

Cohen, S. (ed.), *Images of Deviance* (Penguin, 1971). For J. M. Atkinson's 'Societal reactions to suicide: the role of coroners' definitions', illustrating Douglas's criticism of Durkheim and also some of the problems of 'uncritically' accepting 'official statistics'.

Shipman, M., *The Limitation of Social Research* 2nd edn (Longman, 1981). An extremely useful book overall, but especially for Chapter 9, 'Interpretative social science and ethnography'.

Woods, P. (ed.), *Teacher Strategies* (Croom Helm, 1980). For the Introduction, which overviews the articles in the book and in so doing discusses attempts to use the strengths of both interpretative and structuralist approaches.

Woods, P. (ed.), *Pupil Strategies* (Croom Helm, 1980). For M. Hammersley's 'On interactionist empiricism' which raises some methodological problems and possibilities involved in the attempt to relate differing levels of analysis, the 'micro' and the 'macro'.

Stubbs, M., and **Delamont, S.** (eds), *Explorations in Classroom Observation* (Wiley, 1976). For V. Furlong's 'Interaction sets in the classroom: towards a study of pupil knowledge' which is particularly explicit as to why certain data-gathering techniques such as questionnaires and sociometric devices were inappropriate for the largely Symbolic Interactionist study. The study is also published in M. Hammersley and P. Woods, op. cit.

QUESTIONS

1 Do you think it is (*a*) possible, (*b*) desirable to provide a detailed blueprint of 'the scientific method'?

2 What do you think Durkheim meant by 'treat social facts as if they were things'?

3 What do you understand by 'multivariate analysis'?

4 Why did Weber believe that to model sociology exclusively on the methodological strategies and ambitions of the natural sciences was a serious mistake?

5 Why do Symbolic Interactionists prefer to use qualitative rather than quantitative data?

6 'Ethnomethodologists aim to produce descriptions of the methods that members use.' What does this mean?

7 In what ways could ethnomethodological studies, such as the work of Sacks, be regarded as 'scientific'?

8 Choose any two research studies which in your view are rooted in different sociological perspectives and which make use of differing research strategies. Compare and contrast their research strategies with particular reference to the theoretical assumptions and conceptual frameworks which they employ.

9 What in your view are the major methodological problems involved in attempts to relate interpretative and structuralist approaches?

10 In what ways can very different research techniques contribute to the value of a research study? What problems might be involved in using a variety of research techniques in one study?

Chapter 7

Some Conclusions

At the beginning of this book, we suggested that sociology could be viewed as being made up of a number of distinctive though linked perspectives. We then identified and described the characteristics of the consensus and conflict perspectives as variations within one broad approach in sociology which we called the structuralist perspective. We continued by describing Symbolic Interactionism and ethnomethodology and showed how those approaches can be viewed as further sociological perspectives. We saw that within each perspective there was some diversity in the range of work and in the approaches used to study the social world. It has been our intention, in fact, to show how 'sociological perspective' is a convenient device which is useful for organising and systematising the work done in the field of sociology. It is a device which provides us with a meaningful way of presenting the field so that important differences and similarities between individual thinkers and groups of thinkers can be clearly described. It is meaningful because, as we have seen, the differences between the perspectives do reflect very real differences between researchers in the field of sociology. In short, the device 'sociological perspective' permits an accurate representation of many of the major theoretical and research issues which generate a great deal of discussion, controversy and interest within sociology.

We are suggesting, then, that to view sociology as comprising a number of distinctive though linked perspectives is convenient and useful, but not arbitrary. It is not arbitrary because this view enables us to display many of the real and persisting issues and controversies in the subject. We must point out, however, that there is considerable danger in this view of sociology if the device 'sociological perspective' is used too rigidly. To attempt to force all aspects of all work in sociology into one or other of the perspectives which we have identified is to adopt a blinkered and insensitive approach; an approach which can ultimately check and stultify further and deeper understanding. The notion of sociological perspective, as an organising device or concept, provides us with 'temporary scaffolding', by means of which we can construct a sound initial understanding of the nature of sociology. Deeper understanding can come from the careful and detailed study of particular empirical studies. A grasp of the nature of sociological perspectives should, however, facilitate such further detailed study, by enabling students to raise pertinent questions and to see the relationship of a particular study to the wider context of the field of sociology. In short, an orientation to sociological perspectives should enable students to know what sorts of things to look out for, what sorts of issues to consider, as they develop a deeper understanding of sociology by the careful study and analysis of empirical studies.

We are certainly not suggesting, however, that these further studies will result in a finding that sociology is, after all, a unified subject with a single approach or perspective. Though sociologists in all approaches are united in so far as they all endeavour to study in a scientific manner, that is, they all try to make statements about the social world which are clear enough to be tested empirically, they do differ, as we have seen, with respect to what kind of statements these should be, what sorts of phenomena should be studied and, finally, how these phenomena should be studied.

Why is it, then, that sociology is not a single unified approach? There are a number of possible answers to this question; in these concluding remarks, however, we shall focus on one deriving from the work of Thomas Kuhn, which we have already encountered in Chapter 6.

In his book *The Structure of Scientific Revolutions* Kuhn argues that an area of knowledge is most clearly scientific if it can be characterised as having a single 'paradigm' (or, as he later calls it, a 'disciplinary matrix'). A paradigm consists of the shared agreements of a community of scientists on what will be studied, how it will be studied and what is assumed to be fundamental knowledge (that is, basic assumptions and verified findings). The paradigm provides scientists with shared beliefs about the world, with criteria for judging and testing theories, with notions of what constitutes margins of permissible error and, importantly, with 'exemplars'.

Exemplars refer to the sorts of standard and concrete solutions of problems which we can find in scientific textbooks. In revealing methods, experiments, problems and solutions, exemplars accurately reflect the distinctive way of viewing the world of a scientific community. In short, a paradigm provides a group of scientists with a 'licensed way of seeing the world'. It is 'licensed' in that each member of the group supports other members in so far as they do their scientific work within the bounds set by the paradigm. When scientists are operating in this manner, Kuhn suggests that they are doing 'normal science'. Normal science is simply everyday, routine scientific activity which involves scientists in trying to solve the puzzles or problems generated by the paradigm within which the scientists are working.

Scientific revolutions occur when an existing paradigm is ousted by a new paradigm. Kuhn argues that in any paradigm there are anomalies which cannot be solved within the terms of reference of that paradigm. To solve them requires a fresh way of looking at the natural world: a way provided by the new paradigm. A new paradigm develops from the efforts of those scientists who are more troubled by the anomalies of the existing paradigm than they are satisfied with the solutions it can provide. Not surprisingly, supporters of a new paradigm tend to be young scientists who have less commitment to 'traditional' ways of scientific thinking and are energetic enough to sustain the controversy, arrguments and even bitterness that a 'battle of the paradigms' can entail.

Clearly, there are some interesting points of comparison between Kuhn's work on the history of the natural sciences and the nature of sociology as a field of knowledge.

We note that Kuhn's use of the concept 'paradigm' is virtually synonymous with our use of the concept 'perspective'. Thus we see why sociology could be described, in Kuhnian terms, as 'preparadigmatic'. By having a number of perspectives, by failing to display a single unifying paradigm, it would appear that sociology is not 'clearly scientific'. For it lacks consensus about what to study, how to study, and so on. Therefore 'normal science', with its routine problem-solving activities, cannot develop. On this line of thinking, breakthrough for sociology will occur when sociologists are converted to just one of the perspectives available to them. Only then can sociology abandon its preparadigmatic stage and begin to operate as normal science; only then will sociologists cease arguing about fundamentals and get on with the job of puzzle-solving within the bounds of a single paradigm.

Certainly, a number of sociologists would agree with the general notion that sociology is preparadigmatic or undeveloped or pre-scientific. For example, Robert Merton argues that sociology is still a new discipline and cannot in fairness be expected to match the results of older, more established sciences. As yet, sociology is a fledgling discipline; its results should properly be compared with the work not of twentieth-century, but of seventeenth-century natural scientists. Currently, sociology is failing to advance as fast as it could because its work lies either in the area of over-grandiose theory building or in the area of collecting lots of facts with little or no regard for their relevance to the development of sociological theories. Merton therefore advocates that sociologists should avoid the extremes of theoryless fact-grubbing or fact-less overgeneralised theory by pursuing the golden mean of what he calls 'middle-range theories'. Such theories would be firmly rooted in empirical observation and sensibly restricted in the range of their application. Their development can be assisted by striving for the greatest possible clarity of concepts, thereby avoiding intellectual and operational muddles. As we saw in Chapter 2, Merton illustrates these views by his attempt to make structural functionalism a more useful approach. His attempt sought to clarify some of its basic confusions and to suggest a clear and connected schema for a more general use of the approach.

In this way, Merton wishes to accelerate the development of sociology towards the breakthrough of a unification of the subject. For, presumably, he sees the sort of approach which he advocates, namely structural functionalism, as being *the* approach in sociology. We can thus regard him as endeavouring to persuade his fellow sociologists, his scientific community, to adopt appropriate ways of working and of thinking about the social world. Here, we note that the operative word is 'persuade', for his arguments are couched in terms of what can be done, not what has been done. Furthermore, though operating from the base of structural functionalism, which, as we have seen, can be regarded as only one of the several perspectives comprising sociology, Merton appears to write in the name of the whole of sociology.

In fact, adherents of a particular perspective tend to view their own approach as the only viable one for doing sociology. They operate within the framework of thinking provided by the perspective and tend to be less than sympathetic to alternative approaches available within other perspectives. To a great extent, each perspective offers a 'complete', a self-contained way of thinking about and studying the social world. In a very real sense, to see the promise of an alternative perspective is to go a long way to abandoning the presently held perspective. It is for this reason that a unified sociology cannot be brought about by simplistically 'adding together' the 'best bits' of each perspective.

Thus structuralists, like adherents of other perspectives, tend to view their own particular approach as *the* approach to sociology.

This view does not mean, however, that structuralists are fully agreed on the best means of improving their approach. For example, Lazarsfeld and Rosenberg, unlike Merton, do not talk about middle-range theory and schemata for functionalism. Instead, they stress the paramount need to improve on the operationalisation of concepts and the importance of accurate measurement if sociology is to advance. To these ends, they have done much work on the uses of indices and on the elaboration of multivariable analysis in sociology.

In contrast, interactionists do not accept structuralism as *the* approach; nor do they accept its recommendations for the speedier advance of sociology. As we have seen, thinkers like Blumer explicitly attack the whole structuralist position and advocate an alternative. Here we can see something like a 'battle of the paradigms' in so far as interactionists reject the study of social 'wholes' like total societies. They prefer to focus on face-to-face interactions and to use 'softer' research methods, arguing that rigorous systems of measurement tend to distort or even destroy the essential features of the phenomena they wish to study. Inter-actionists therefore feel that the way to sociological development lies in *their* approach. We have also seen, however, that like the structuralists, interactionists show some variety in their particular recommendations as to how such advance will best be facilitated. For example, they differ with respect to the range and scope of the sort of generalisations they wish to make and in the extent to which they do use measures of a quantitative kind.

We found a similar diversity of emphases within ethnomethod-ology when we examined it as constituting a further approach within sociology. We saw, however, that ethnomethodology could be treated as a single perspective in that its practitioners agree that their phenomenon, members' practices, is neglected by other approaches in sociology. Moreover, ethnomethodologists appear to wish to abandon the traditional concerns and controversies of other approaches. For example, they wish to 'describe' rather than to 'explain'; to reproduce the 'indexical particulars' of a given situation, rather than to construct theories. In short, ethnomethodologists wish to produce statements about the social world which, somehow, are at one and the same time highly context-specific, yet also very general. In these ways, we can see that they are offering an altern-ative way of thinking about and studying the social world.

From this brief overview of the various approaches or perspectives which can be seen to comprise sociology, it does not appear that a Kuhnian breakthrough to a single paradigm/perspective, to normal science and to a unified discipline is at all likely or imminent. While it is true that some sociologists do work at trying to bridge differences and to find underlying links between the perspectives, it appears that the vast majority of empirical work done in the subject can be justly characterised as falling within one or other of the perspectives. As we have already suggested, the description of sociology in terms of these perspectives does reasonably accurately reflect the general state of the discipline. We would emphasise that it has been our concern throughout this book to provide the reader with a description of sociology as it is currently practised. We feel that such an approach avoids the twin evils of (*a*) making false promises about the utility and practicality of the subject; and (*b*) providing too simplified an introduction, which has to be 'unlearned' at a later stage.

With this view of sociology clearly stated, we can now raise the question: What is the point of studying sociology? Certainly, if we rigidly adhere to the Kuhnian view of science, we can answer, 'very little at all'! For we might feel that it is somehow degrading or pointless to study a subject which claims to be scientific and yet is merely in a preparadigmatic stage of scientific development, with very little prospect of suddenly becoming 'normal science'. The Kuhnian view of science does, however, present a number of problems. For if science can only properly be practised by a community of scientists who all subscribe to a single paradigm or perspective, then how can we describe the activities of scientists who are working to develop an alternative paradigm? In what sense is their work 'preparadigmatic' or 'prescientific'? We suggest that Kuhn's definition of science does not provide for any discipline where we can find *several* communities of scholars at work. Just as we can find at least two such communities in Kuhn's own 'battle of the paradigms' in natural science, so too might we find a somewhat larger-scale battle between the various approaches in sociology, where we might discern a number of scientific communities at work. Furthermore, the view of knowledge and what it is to be 'scientific', which we have employed throughout this book, seem to help us to overcome what might be seen to be a purely semantic or definitional problem generated by Kuhn's terminology. For we have suggested that it is preferable to understand the nature of scientific activity by comparing scientific ways of understanding the world with non-scientific ways of understanding it, that is, mathematical, philosophical, literary, aesthetic and religious ways. These distinctions can be made in terms of the kinds of bedrock justifications which workers in each of these areas of knowledge can properly make of their work. While scientists, natural or social, ultimately have to base their work on such matters as its empirical reference, its testability and the clarity of its methodical procedures, the 'test of truth' for novelists/writers, philosophers and mathematicians has different bases, as we illustrated in Chapter 1. With this notion of science, we can therefore usefully differentiate major approaches to understanding within the whole field of knowledge and see what sociologists of whatever perspective should be doing if they are to be described as operating 'scientifically'. We need not disqualify sociologists from the corpus of science simply because they do not share a single paradigm: we must disqualify them if their work can be seen ultimately to rest on aesthetic or literary or mathematical or religious grounds, rather than on scientific ones.

We are suggesting, then, that the notion of science used throughout this book avoids the dilemma of arbitrarily disqualifying the quest for scientific knowledge simply because the workers in a field pursue knowledge by different routes. If we can accept that a field of knowledge can include a number of scientific communities, as Kuhn himself implicitly does (for how else can scientific revolutions occur?), then we might find that sociology being 'preparadigmatic' is not after all such a terrible thing.

Such an answer to the question 'What is the point of studying sociology?' might still be considered less than satisfactory. For, given the fact that sociology comprises a number of perspectives, who can say which perspective promises or gives the most 'truth'? To ask such a question, however, completely ignores the general point we have been making throughout this book. For we have tried to argue that it makes little sense to evaluate ways of thinking simply in terms of 'truth' or 'falsity'. Instead, sociological perspectives, as ways of thinking about and studying the social world, are better judged in terms of how useful they are in giving us some understanding of the social world. Of course, the empirical work done under the auspices of a particular perspective has to match up with the criteria or standards for sound work which are employed by its practitioners. It is of little use, however, to seek confirmation of the value of such work from the exponents of other sociological perspectives because, as we have shown, although all perspectives have in common the basic justification of treating the social world scientifically, they are operating with different basic assumptions, different research methods and strategies and, finally, they come up with different kinds of findings, explanations, or solutions. Sociologists themselves presumably prefer a particular perspective to others because they find that the sorts of questions posed, methods used and explanations achieved are more congenial and more intellectually satisfying to them. There is no *scientific* method, however, for *proving* the validity of a preference for a particular perspective. Here we agree with Kuhn, who argues that to switch from one paradigm (perspective) to another is much akin to a conversion process. Such a process depends as much on belief and conviction as on the nature of the findings which a way of thinking makes possible. It is only when the basic assumptions which underlie any perspective are accepted that particular researches done under the auspices or framework of the perspective can be evaluated scientifically in the terms set by the perspective.

Of course, if there existed somewhere a sure and certain method of gaining access to the 'ultimate truth', and if such ultimate knowledge could ever be possible, then all perspectives in sociology – and, indeed, all literary, philosophical, mathematical, religious and aesthetic ways of thinking about the world and gaining knowledge of it – could be merged into one omnipotent and magnificent approach. 'The truth' could be decisively and finally discovered and the quest for further knowledge could be abandoned because we 'know it all, or 'have it all'. As there is no such magical or mysterious way of gaining such knowledge or such access to knowledge, then our only guarantee of the worth of such knowledge that we do have is the extent to which we can persuade our fellow experts or specialists about our findings. Given that persuasion in the sciences should not depend on rhetoric and debating skills, but on the clarity of methods and hence the testability by others of our results, it is no light or facile matter to produce warranted findings which can pass such scrutiny. In short, we are utterly dependent on our fellow human beings in our scientific community for the quality and validity of our findings; we can appeal to no one or to nothing else. We might convince ourselves that our theory and our experiments 'work', but if they are to have any scientific purchase we must persuade our fellows in our scientific community that (*a*) they do work and (*b*) they mean something.

Thus scientific work is not simply the 'cookbook' application of a set of inviolable and desiccated rules. It involves questions of belief and persuasion as well as proof and experiment. Consequently, we may feel that Kuhn has presented us with an idealised and stylised picture of the workings of 'normal science'. Normal science might well be more controversial and less singly paradigmatic than he suggests. In fact, we gave some supporting examples of this point in Chapter 1.

Without doubt, sociology as a field displays plenty of perspectival controversies and conflicts. As we have said, there seems little likelihood that this state of affairs will alter in the near future. Instead of being alarmed by this prospect, however, we might find it intriguing and exciting for several reasons. One reason might be that conflict and controversy can stimulate thought and mobilise energy. Another might be derived from Kuhn's suggestion that in science one paradigm frequently ousts another. As we are aware that no single paradigm – or even a number of them – can produce ultimate truth, we might be more reassured rather than alarmed that sociology comprises a number of ways of approaching the social world. In short, a number of perspectives might represent more in the way of challenge and intellectual adventure than a single monolithic approach.

In fact, this view of the nature of sociological knowledge is very close to the position of one of the most renowned of all sociologists, Max Weber. Weber was always very reluctant to legislate dogmatically on proper ways of doing sociology. His intellectual humility derived from his awareness of the great complexity of the social world and of the even greater difficulty of studying it with the rigour and care required of any scientific approach. He recognised that over time the significances, values and problems of social scientists change. Moreover, at any one point in time the values and preferences of individual researchers mould the nature of sociological inquiry. In the light of these inescapable facts about sociologists and human beings, we should not be overambitious about the possibilities of a science of society. In his view, we can never produce single or final causes of phenomena, but only a number of possible causes; we cannot rigidly quantify phenomena, but only try to grasp aspects of their meaning by means of the limited tool of the ideal type. Moreover, by advocating the study of subjective meanings as well as social causes of events, Weber showed himself to be an example of a sociologist who attempted to bridge several perspectives. Finally, he talked about the sort of knowledge we can obtain from this limited though careful and rigorous approach to the study of society. The most we can ever achieve, even after the most careful and stringent studies, is to shed a little light on some aspect of social life. As time passes, and as our values and interests change, so will our vantage-point alter; further research will illuminate some other aspect of the phenomenon under study. No matter how intensively researchers study a phenomenon, we can never exhaust the possibility of inquiry into anything. We can only know a little more; be a little clearer.

This view of the sort of knowledge we can obtain from sociological inquiry can only be bitterly disappointing for anyone demanding *the* facts, *the* truth and the completion of an inquiry. Of course, researchers do end inquiries when their interest or time is exhausted. Inquiries must come to an end for particular researchers who satisfy their practical purposes at that point in time. From a more general view of science, however, the practical ending of an inquiry does not mean that a phenomenon is finished or 'used up'. It can always be reopened, studied from fresh vantage-points and something new can be learned. If, then, we accept this view of knowledge and of the nature of inquiry, we can see that the existence of a number of perspectives in sociology affords us a number of ways of approaching and shedding some light on a phenomenon of concern or interest. We may feel that more illumination derives from a number of approaches than from a single approach. Moreover, though we have argued that there is no way of proving that one perspective is 'truer' than any other, we may certainly feel that one is clearer, showing us more in relation to the sorts of concerns and interests we happen to have.

This view of knowledge must also be very disappointing for anyone who requires of sociology that it be a spearhead of social reform and revolutionary change of society. The subject gives us an opportunity to study and to examine social life in a careful, rigorous and systematic way. It may give us some greater understanding of some aspects of social life. It does not, however, provide us with short-cut solutions and recipes for reshaping the social world; it does not give us a licence for saying what a 'better society' would look like. For no scientific subject can prescribe what persons *ought* to do or where society *ought* to go. Such prescriptions would require us to enter the field of values. But scientific approaches do not afford us ways of grading, ranking and testing values. In modern societies, there are generally recognised social problems concerning old age, racialism, unemployment, and so on. Sociology can offer no ready-made solutions to such problems, telling us what we ought to do about them. Instead, it can offer the careful and systematic investigation of such problems with the possibility that we may understand them a little better. It may be the case that if we can increase our understanding of a social problem, then we put ourselves in a better position to do something about it. But in doing something about it, we are no longer operating *as sociologists*, as students of social life: we are operating as social reformers, as politicians, or as citizens. *As sociologists*, all we can do is to study social life as carefully and as competently as we can.

We have posed the question: Is sociology worth studying? Our answer so far has focused on the kind of knowledge we can obtain through sociological inquiry and we have suggested that it is best regarded as shedding a little light on some aspects of social life in which we are interested or concerned. Even this limited claim of shedding a little light might be considered to be pretentious or grandiose. If so, we can only refer to the actual empirical work done in sociology. In the last resort, only the student of sociology can say if such work does, in fact, produce for him a little more understanding of some aspect of social life; only he can know if such work helps him to see his own social world more sensitively or more penetratingly or more clearly. In short, only he can answer the question: Does empirical work in sociology in fact shed for him a little more light on some aspect of social life?

We have suggested that a satisfactory answer should properly depend on further study of particular empirical works in the field of sociology. A provisional answer, however, might be derived from the range of empirical studies touched on in this book. We recall that we have surveyed a number of such studies: approaches to the sociological study of mental illness; the Western Electric researches; studies in deviant behaviour in past and present societies; functionalist analyses of education and of political power; Marx's theories of class, power, religion and knowledge; studies of trainee doctors, perceptions of college students and occupants of mental institutions; studies of 'correct' jury decisions; studies of creating conditions for social disorder; studies of suicide; studies of conversational practices.

In this book, we have primarily focused on methodology: on the manner in which sociologists, from their various perspectival standpoints, endeavour to understand the social world. In the course of so doing, we have drawn on and outlined a wide range of varying researches, some of which we have just enumerated. We may therefore have provided sufficient materials to give at least a provisional answer to the question: Is sociology worth studying?

FURTHER READING

Becker, Howard S., 'Whose side are we on', in *Sociological work: Method and Substance* (Allen Lane, 1971). Treats in lively fashion the problem of values for the social scientist.

Gerth, H. A., and **Mills, C. W.** (eds), 'Science as a vocation', in *From Max Weber: Essays in Sociology* (Routledge & Kegan Paul, 1948). For Weber's classic statement of his views about the nature of science and what is involved in being a social scientist.

Worsley, P. (ed.), *Modern Sociology: Introductory Readings* (Penguin, 1970). Part I, 'Sociology as a Discipline', provides a varied selection of important readings which amply display the varied approaches, value positions and intellectual standpoints of different sociologists. See in particular the readings by C. W. Mills, H. Stuart Hughes, Thomas S. Kuhn and Norbert Elias.

Barnes, B., *T. S. Kuhn and Social Science* (Macmillan, 1982). Difficult, but shows the continuing importance and significance for sociology of the issues in this chapter and in this book.

QUESTIONS

1 What is Kuhn's view of the development of science? Do you agree that sociology appears to be in a 'preparadigmatic' stage?

2 Outline Weber's view of the nature of social science and contrast it with other views found in earlier chapters of this book.

3 Is sociology scientific?

4 'No matter how intensively researchers study a phenomenon, we can never exhaust the possibility of inquiry into anything.' Discuss.

5 What are the advantages and disadvantages of seeing sociology as a number of perspectives?

6 Which sociological approach contributes most to *your* understanding of the social world? Why?

7 Is sociology worth studying?

References and Selected Bibliography

CHAPTER 1

Bredemeier, H. C., and Stephenson, R. M., *The Analysis of Social Systems* (Holt, Rinehart & Winston, 1967).

Dunham, H. W., and Faris, R. E. C., *Mental Disorders in Urban Areas* (Phoenix Books, University of Chicago Press, 1967).

Hall, C. S., *A Primer of Freudian Psychology* (Mentor, 1954).

Hollingshead, A. B., and Redlich, F. C., *Social Class and Mental Illness* (Wiley, 1958).

Rosen, G., *Madness in Society* (Routledge & Kegan Paul, 1968).

Scheff, T. J., 'The societal reaction to deviance: ascriptive elements in the psychiatric screening of mental patients in a Midwestern state', *Social Problems*, vol. II (1964), pp. 401–13.

Stafford-Clark, D., *Psychiatry To-day* (Penguin, 1973).

Szasz, T. S., *The Manufacture of Madness* (Paladin, 1973).

Turner, R., 'Talk and troubles: contact problems of former mental patients', unpublished PhD dissertation, University of California, Berkeley, 1968.

CHAPTER 2

Bell, N. W., and Vogel, E. F., *A Modern Introduction to the Family*, rev. edn (Free Press, 1963).

Davis, K., and Moore, W., 'Some principles of stratification', *American Sociological Review*, vol. 10 (1945), pp. 242–9.

Dreeben, R., 'The contribution of schooling to the learning of norms', *Harvard Educational Review*, vol. 37 (1967), pp. 211–37.

Durkheim, E., *The Division of Labour in Society* (Free Press, 1964).

Durkheim, E., *The Rules of Sociological Method* (Free Press, 1964).

Durkheim, E., *The Elementary Forms of the Religious Life* (Allen & Unwin, 1968).

Erikson, K. T., *Wayward Puritans* (Wiley, 1966).

Farmer, M., *The Family* (Longman, 1979).

Fletcher, R., *The Making of Sociology*, Vols 1 and 2 (Nelsón, 1972).

Litwak, E., 'Extended kin relations in an industrial democratic society', in E. Shenas and G. F. Streibb, *Social Structure and the Family: Generational Relations* (Prentice-Hall, 1965).

Madge, J., 'Pioneers in industrial sociology', Chapter 6 in *The Origins of Scientific Sociology* (Tavistock, 1963).

Malinowksi, B., *A Scientific Theory of Culture* (Oxford University Press, 1960).

Merton, R. K., *On Theoretical Sociology* (Free Press, 1967).

Mitchell, W. C., *Sociological Analysis and Politics; the Theories of Talcott*

Parsons (Prentice-Hall, 1967).

Parsons T., *The Social System* (Routledge & Kegan Paul, 1951).

Parsons, T., 'The social structure of the family', in R. N. Anshen (ed.), *The Family: Its Function and Testing* (Harper, 1959).

Parsons T., *Societies: Evolutionary and Comparative Perspectives* (Prentice-Hall, 1966).

Parsons, T., *The System of Modern Societies* (Prentice-Hall, 1971)

Radcliffe-Brown, A. R., *Structure and Function in Primitive Society* (Cohen & West, 1952).

Radcliffe-Brown, A. R., *The Andaman Islanders* (Cambridge University Press, 1922).

Roethlisberger, F. J., and Dickson, W. J., *Management and the Worker* (Harvard University Press, 1939).

Rosser, C., and Harris, C., *The Family and Social Change: A Study of Family and Kinship in a South Wales Town* (Routledge & Kegan Paul, 1965).

Smelser, N. J., *Social Change in the Industrial Revolution* (Routledge & Kegan Paul, 1959).

Young, M., and Willmott, P., *The Family and Kinship in East London*, rev. edn (Penguin, 1962).

Young, M., and Willmott, P., *The Symmetrical Family* (Penguin, 1975).

CHAPTER 3

Avineri, S., *The Social and Political Thought of Karl Marx* (Cambridge University Press, 1969).

Beynon, H., *Working for Ford* (English Universities Press, 1975).

Bottomore, T. B., and Rubel, M., *Karl Marx: Selected Writings in Sociology and Social Philosophy* (Penguin, 1965).

Braverman, H., *Labour and Monopoly Capital: The Degradation of Work in the Twentieth Century* (Monthly Review Press, New York/London, 1974).

Dahrendorf, R., *Class and Class Conflict in Industrial Society* (Routledge & Kegan Paul, 1959).

Engels, F., 'Condition of the working classes in England', in *Marx-Engels on Britain* (Foreign Languages Publishing House, Moscow, first pub. 1845).

Gerth, H. H., and Mills, C. W. (eds), *From Max Weber: Essays in Sociology* (Routledge & Kegan Paul, 1967).

Goldthorpe, J. H., Lockwood, D., Bechhofer, F., and Platt, J., *The Affluent Worker: Industrial Attitudes and Behaviour* (Cambridge University Press, 1969).

Jordan, Z. A. (ed.), *Karl Marx: Economy, Class and Social Revolution* (Michael Joseph, 1971).

Lefebvre, H., *The Sociology of Marx* (Allen Lane, 1968).

Lockwood, D., *The Blackcoated Worker* (Unwin University Books, 1966).

Parkin, F., *Class Inequality and Political Order – Social Stratification in Capitalist and Communist Societies* (MacGibbon & Kee, 1971).

Weber, M., *The Protestant Ethic and the Spirit of Capitalism* (Unwin University Books, 1965).

Westergaard, J. H., 'The withering away of class, a contemporary myth', in P. Anderson *et al.*, *Towards Socialism* (Fontana, 1965).

Westergaard, J. H., and Resler, Henrietta, *Class in a Capitalist Society: A Study of Contemporary Britain* (Penguin, 1976).

CHAPTER 4

Becker, H. S., *Outsiders; Studies in the Sociology of Deviance* (Free Press, 1963).
Becker, H. S., Geer, Blanche, Hughes, E. C., and Strauss, A. L., *Boys in White; Student Culture in Medical School* (University of Chicago Press, 1961).
Blumer, H., *Symbolic Interactionism; Perspective and Method* (Prentice-Hall, 1969).
Denzin, N. (ed.), *Studies in Symbolic Interaction,* Vols I, II and III (JAI Press, 1978–80).
Goffman, E., *Asylums; Essays on the Social Situations of Mental Patients and Other Inmates* (Anchor, 1961).
Goffman, E., *Encounters: Two Studies in the Sociology of Interaction* (Bobbs-Merrill, 1961).
Goffman, E., *The Presentation of Self in Everyday Life* (Penguin, 1971).
Goldthorpe, J. H., 'Social stratification in industrial society', in Paul Halmos (ed.), *The Development of Industrial Society,* Sociological Review Monographs no. 8 (1964).
Goldthorpe, J. H., 'Attitudes and behaviour of car assembly workers: a deviant case and a critique', *British Journal of Sociology,* vol. 17 (1966), pp. 227–44.
Hughes, E. C., *The Sociological Eye: Seclected Papers* (Aldine, 1971).
Jarvie, I. C., *The Revolution in Anthropology* (Routledge & Kegan Paul, 1964).
Kerr, C., Dunlop, J. T., Harbison, F. T., and Myers, C. A., *Industrialisation and Industrial Man* (Heinemann, 1962).
Lemert, E. M., 'Paranoia and the dynamics of exclusion', *Sociometry,* vol. 25 (March 1962), pp. 2–25.
Louch, A. R., *Explanation and Human Action* (Cambridge University Press, 1966).
MacIntyre, A., *Against the Self-Images of the Age* (Schocken, 1971).
Mead, G. H., *On Social Psychology: Selected Papers,* ed. A. Strauss (University of Chicago Press, 1964).
Parsons, T., *The Structure of Social Action* (Free Press, 1949).
Parsons, T., and Shils, E. A. (eds), *Toward a General Theory of Action* (Harper Torchbooks, 1962).
Popper, K., *The Poverty of Historicism* (Routledge & Kegan Paul, 1960).
Popper, K., *The Open Society and its Enemies,* 2 vols (Routledge & Kegan Paul, 1962).
Rex, J., *Key Problems of Sociological Theory* (Routledge & Kegan Paul, 1961).
Rock, P., *The Making of Symbolic Interactionism* (Macmillan, 1979).
Simmel, G., *Conflict and the Web of Group Affiliations* (Free Press, 1964).
Strauss, A. L., and Becker, H. S., 'Careers, personality, and adult socialisation', *American Journal of Sociology,* vol. LXVII (November 1956), pp. 253–63.
Strauss, A. L., Schatzman, L., Bucher, R., Erlich, D., and Sabshin, K., *Psychiatric Ideologies and Institutions* (Free Press, 1964).
Thomas, W. I., *On Social Organisation and Social Personality,* ed. M. Janowitz (University of Chicago Press, 1966).

Weber, M., *The Theory of Social and Economic Organisation,* ed. Talcott Parsons (Free Press, 1964).
Winch, P., *The Idea of a Social Science and Its Relation to Philosophy* (Routledge & Kegan Paul, 1958).
Wolff, K. H., *The Sociology of Georg Simmel* (Free Press, 1950).
Woodward, Joan, *Management and Technology* (HMSO, 1958).

CHAPTER 5

Berger, P., and Luckmann, T., *The Social Construction of Reality* (Penguin, 1971).
Blum, A., 'The sociology of mental illness', in J. Douglas (ed.), *Deviance and Respectability; the Social Construction of Moral Meanings* (Basic Books, 1970).
Cicourel, A., *Method and Measurement in Sociology* (Free Press, 1964).
Cicourel, A., *The Social Organisation of Juvenile Justice* (Heinemann, 1976).
Garfinkel, H., 'The perception of the other: a study in social order', unpublished PhD thesis, University of Harvard, 1952.
Garfinkel, H., *Studies in Ethnomethodology* (Prentice-Hall, 1967).
Giddens, A., *New Rules of Sociological Method* (Hutchinson, 1976).
Sacks, H., 'On the analysability of stories by children', in R. Turner (ed.), *Ethnomethodology* (Penguin, 1974).
Schegloff, E., 'Identification and recognition in telephone conversation openings', in G. Psathas (ed.), *Everyday Language* (Academic Press, 1979).
Schegloff, E., 'Sequencing in conversational openings', *American Anthropologist,* vol. 70 (1968), pp. 1075–95.
Schegloff, E., 'Notes on a conversational practice: formulating place', in D., Sudnow (ed.), *Studies in Social Interaction* (Free Press, 1972).
Schegloff, E., and Sacks, H., 'Opening up closings', in R. Turner (ed.), *Ethnomethodology* (Penguin, 1974).
Schutz, A., *Collected Papers,* Vol. I: *The Problem of Social Reality* (Martinus Nijhoff, The Hague, 1967).
Schutz, A., *The Phenomenology of the Social World* (Heinemann, 1972).
Weider, D. L. 'Telling the code', in R. Turner (ed.), *Ethnomethodology* (Penguin, 1974).

CHAPTER 6

Apple, M. W., *Ideology and Curriculum* (Routledge & Kegan Paul, 1979).
Atkinson, J. M., 'Societal reaction to suicide: the role of coroner's definitions', in S. Cohen (ed.), *Images of Deviance* (Penguin, 1971).
Becker, H., and Geer, Blanche, 'Participant observation and interviewing: a comparison', in J. A. Manis and B. M. Meltzer (eds), *Symbolic Interaction* (Allyn & Bacon, 1972).
Becker, H., Geer, Blanche, and Hughes, E., *Making the Grade* (Wiley, 1968).
Bell, C., and Newby, H. (eds), *Doing Sociological Research* (Allen & Unwin, 1977).
Blumer, H., 'Society as symbolic interaction', in A. M. Rose (ed.), *Human Behaviour and Social Processes* (Routledge & Kegan Paul, 1971).
Bruyn, S. T., 'The new empiricists: the participant observer and phenomenologist', in W. J. Filstead (ed.), *Qualitative Methodology* (Markham Publishing, 1970).

Delamont, S., 'Beyond Flanders' Fields: the relationship of subject matter and individuality to classroom style', in M. Stubbs and S. Delamont (eds), *Explorations in Classroom Observation* (Wiley, 1976).

Denzin, N. H., *Sociological Methods*, 2nd edn (McGraw-Hill, 1978).

Douglas, J. D., *The Social Meanings of Suicide* (Princeton University Press, 1967).

Durkheim, E., *Suicide* (Routledge & Kegan Paul, 1952).

Durkheim, E., *The Rules of Sociological Method* (Free Press, 1964).

Filstead, W. J. (ed.), *Qualitative Methodology* (Markham Publishing, 1970).

Furlong, V., 'Interaction sets in the classroom: towards a study of pupil knowledge', in M. Stubbs and S. Delamont (eds), *Explorations in Classroom Observation* (Wiley, 1976).

Gibbs, J. P., and Martin, W. T., 'A theory of status integration and the relationship to suicide', *American Sociological Review*, vol. 23 (1958), pp. 140–7.

Glaser, B. G., and Strauss, A. L., *The Discovery of Grounded Theory* (Weidenfeld & Nicolson, 1968).

Hammond, P. E. (ed.), *Sociologists at Work* (Basic Books, 1964).

Kaplan, A., *The Conduct of Inquiry* (Chandler Publishing, 1964).

Kuhn, T. S., *The Structure of Scientific Revolutions* (University of Chicago Press, 1970).

Kuhn, T. S., 'The function of dogma in scientific research', in A. C. Crombie (ed.), *Scientific Change* (Heinemann, 1963).

Lazarsfeld, P. F., Pasanella, A. K., and Rosenberg, M. (eds), *Continuities in the Language of Social Research* (Free Press, 1972).

Popper, K., *The Poverty of Historicism* (Routledge & Kegan Paul, 1960).

Sacks, H., 'Sociological description', *Berkeley Journal of Sociology*, vol. 8 (1963), pp. 1–16.

Sacks, H., 'The search for help: no one to turn to', in E. S. Schneidman (ed.), *Essays in Self-Destruction* (Science House, 1967).

Selvin, H. C., 'Durkheim's *Suicide*: further thoughts on a methodological classic', in R. A. Nisbet, *Emile Durkheim* (Prentice-Hall, 1965).

Sharp, R., and Green, A., *Education and Social Control* (Routledge & Kegan Paul, 1975).

Watson, J. D., *The Double Helix* (Weidenfeld & Nicolson, 1968).

Weber, M., *The Protestant Ethic and the Spirit of Capitalism* (Allen & Unwin, 1965).

Weber, M., *The Theory of Social and Economic Organisation* (Free Press, 1964).

Willis, P., *Learning to Labour* (Saxon House, 1977).

CHAPTER 7

Gerth, H. H., and Mills, C. W. (eds), *From Max Weber: Essays in Sociology* (Routledge & Kegan Paul, 1948).

Kuhn, T. S., *The Structure of Scientific Revolutions* (University of Chicago, 1970).

Lazarsfeld, P., and Rosenberg, M. (eds), *The Language of Social Research* (Free Press, 1955).

Merton, R. K., *Social Theory and Social Structure* (Free Press, 1957).

Ritzer, G., *Sociology: A Multiple Paradigm Science* (Allyn & Bacon, 1975).

Ritzer, G., *Towards an Integrated Sociological Paradigm. The Search for an Examplar and an Image of the Subject Matter* (Allyn & Bacon, 1981).

Weber, M., *The Methodology of the Social Sciences* (Free Press, 1949).

Author Index

Subject Index

241